ILLEGALITY IN MARINE INSURANCE LAW

CONTEMPORARY COMMERCIAL LAW

Causation in Insurance Contract Law
by
Meixian Song
(2014)

Insurance Law in China
by
Johanna Hjalmarsson and Dingjing Huang
(2015)

Maritime Law in China
by
Johanna Hjalmarsson and Jingbo Zhang
(2016)

ILLEGALITY IN MARINE INSURANCE LAW

BY
FENG WANG

informa law
from Routledge

First edition published 2017
by Informa Law from Routledge
2 Park Square, Milton Park, Abingdon, Oxon OX14 4RN

and by Informa Law from Routledge
711 Third Avenue, New York, NY 10017

Routledge is an imprint of the Taylor & Francis Group, an informa business

© 2017 Feng Wang

The right of Feng Wang to be identified as author of this work has been asserted by him in accordance with sections 77 and 78 of the Copyright, Designs and Patents Act 1988.

All rights reserved. No part of this book may be reprinted or reproduced or utilised in any form or by any electronic, mechanical, or other means, now known or hereafter invented, including photocopying and recording, or in any information storage or retrieval system, without permission in writing from the publishers.

Trademark notice: Product or corporate names may be trademarks or registered trademarks, and are used only for identification and explanation without intent to infringe.

British Library Cataloguing in Publication Data
A catalogue record for this book is available from the British Library

Library of Congress Cataloging in Publication Data
Names: Wang, Feng (writer on maritime law).
Title: Illegality in marine insurance law / by Feng Wang.
Description: Abingdon ; New York, NY : Informa Law from Routledge, 2017. |
  Based on author's thesis (doctoral—Exter University, 2015) issued under title:
  Warranty of legality and public policy.
Identifiers: LCCN 2016016347| ISBN 9781138655638 (hbk) |
  ISBN 9781315622392 (ebk)
Subjects: LCSH: Marine insurance—Law and legislation—Great Britain. |
  Illegal contracts—Great Britain. | Marine insurance—Law and legislation. |
  Illegal contracts.
Classification: LCC KD1845 .W36 2017 | DDC 346.41/0862—dc23
LC record available at https://lccn.loc.gov/2016016347

ISBN: 978-1-138-65563-8 hbk
eISBN: 978-1-315-62239-2 ebk

Typeset in Plantin
by Apex CoVantage, LLC

CONTENTS

Foreword   ix
Preface   xi
Table of cases   xiii
Table of statutes   xvii

INTRODUCTION   1

Part 1   The warranty of legality in marine insurance law

CHAPTER 1   MARINE INSURANCE LAW OF WARRANTY IN GENERAL   9

1.1 Warranties in contract law   9
1.2 Origin and development of warranties in insurance law and marine insurance law   10
1.3 Construction of warranties   16
1.4 Classifications of warranty   19
1.5 Implied warranties other than warranty of legality   20
1.6 The effect of breach of warranty: The law before 12 August 2016   24
1.7 Waiver of warranty   25

CHAPTER 2   ILLEGAL PERFORMANCE OF MARINE INSURANCE CONTRACTS   29

2.1 Introduction to the warranty of legality in marine insurance law   29
2.2 Origin and formation of the warranty of legal adventure in marine insurance law   30
    2.2.1 The origin of the warranty of legal adventure   30
    2.2.2 Explaination of the word "lawful"   32
    2.2.3 Formation of illegal adventure   34
2.3 Origin and scope of the warranty of legal performance in marine insurance law   36
    2.3.1 Origin of the warranty of legal performance in marine insurance law   37
    2.3.2 Species and formation of illegal performance   38
    2.3.3 Scope of "so far as the assured can control the matter"   40

2.4	The insufficiencies of section 41 of the 1906 Marine Insurance Act	42
	2.4.1 Should the warranty of legality be regulated as an implied warranty in section 41?	47
2.5	Conclusion on nature of section 41	51

Part 2 Background to common law illegality

CHAPTER 3 THE ILLEGALITY DEFENCE IN TORT LAW AND THE *EX TURPI CAUSA* DEFENCE IN INSURANCE — 55

3.1	The illegality defence in tort law	55
	3.1.1 The origin of the illegality defence in tort law	55
	3.1.2 Which kinds of claimant's illegality may trigger the illegality defence?	56
	3.1.3 The principle based on which the claimant's claim is barred because of illegality	60
3.2	The application of the tort illegality defence to insurance law	74
	3.2.1 Why the *ex turpi causa* defence is important in insurance	75
	3.2.2 General principles under insurance law which relate to the illegality defence in tort	77
3.3	Conclusion	89

CHAPTER 4 THE ILLEGALITY DEFENCE IN CONTRACT LAW AND ITS APPLICATION IN INSURANCE CONTRACTS — 91

4.1	Introduction	91
4.2	Contracts rendered illegal by statute	91
4.3	Contracts rendered illegal by common law	96
	4.3.1 The origin and development of contract illegality in common law and public policy	96
	4.3.2 General principles of illegality under common law	97
	4.3.3 The rationales behind the public policy which renders the contract illegal	107
4.4	The difference between statutory illegality and common law illegality under both tort law and contract law	113
4.5	The application of contract law illegality principles in insurance	115
	4.5.1 Statutory illegality rules in insurance	116
	4.5.2 Insurance illegality under common law	121
4.6	The difference between tort illegality and contract illegality	126
	4.6.1 The differences between contract law and tort law when dealing with the illegality defence	126
	4.6.2 The reason for these differences	127
4.7	Conclusion	128

Part 3   Common law rules in marine insurance: A necessary reform or a supplementary instrument?

CHAPTER 5   THE DIFFERENCES BETWEEN THE ILLEGALITY DEFENCE IN COMMON LAW AND THE WARRANTY OF LEGALITY IN MARINE INSURANCE AND THE REASONS FOR THE DIFFERENCES   131

5.1   The nature of section 41   131
   5.1.1   Is violation of section 41 a statutory illegality?   132
   5.1.2   Section 41 – a pre-contractual or a post-contractual requirement?   133
5.2   The differences between the common law illegality defence and the warranty of legality in marine insurance   134
   5.2.1   The nature of these two defences is different   134
   5.2.2   The consequences of a breach of the law are different   135
   5.2.3   The rationales underlying the common law illegality defence are more persuasive   136
   5.2.4   Factors and exceptions are different   137
   5.2.5   The specificity of section 41 in marine insurance law   138
   5.2.6   Conclusion   139
5.3   Why the courts adopt another method when dealing with illegality in marine insurance cases   139
5.4   Conclusion   141

CHAPTER 6   FOREIGN LAW ILLEGALITY IN MARINE INSURANCE LAW   143

6.1   The English legal position on foreign law illegality in common law   143
6.2   The English legal position on foreign law illegality in marine insurance   148
6.3   A criticism of current marine insurance law with regards to foreign law illegality   149
6.4   Possible methods for dealing with foreign law illegality in marine insurance   150
6.5   Conclusion   151

CHAPTER 7   THE MARINE INSURANCE LEGALITY ISSUE IN AUSTRALIA AND OTHER COMMON LAW JURISDICTIONS   153

7.1   The Australian legal approach to the illegality issue   153
7.2   The warranty of legality issue in New Zealand and Canada   158
7.3   Conclusion   160

CHAPTER 8 WARRANTY OF LEGALITY FROM THE PERSPECTIVE OF THE INSURANCE ACT 2015 — 161

- 8.1 Reform recommendations of the Law Commission — 161
- 8.2 Warranties in the Insurance Act 2015 — 164
- 8.3 Causal link and section 11 — 166
- 8.4 The application of the 2015 Act on warranty of legality — 168
- 8.5 The market's reaction to the new Act — 173
- 8.6 Conclusion — 175

CHAPTER 9 A PROPOSAL FOR THE REFORM OF SECTION 41 — 177

- 9.1 The need for reform — 177
- 9.2 Reform proposals — 177
- 9.3 Conclusion — 183

Bibliography — 185
Index — 187

FOREWORD

The law of illegality in contract and tort is fiendishly complex and elusive. On one view the courts should adhere to strict principles which are to be applied unvaryingly and without judicial discretion, and should refuse to enforce a contract if its making or performance is tainted by illegality. The opposing view is that illegality may arise for a variety of reasons and the courts should be able match the outcome to the seriousness of the offence and its causal relationship to the claim made by the illegal performer. The courts have moved from one view to the other, the English Law Commission has decided not to intervene and the most recent authorities show a complete division of opinion on the matter. Marine insurance is, at least in theory, outside this debate. The warranty of legality, set out in section 41 of the UK's Marine Insurance Act 1906 and replicated in the marine legislation of much of the English-speaking world, operates independently of the general law. The warranty is, as Wang Feng shows, the result of a series of eighteenth and nineteenth century cases largely concerned with trading with the enemy and with other infringements of Government decrees affecting commerce, and was elevated into a general principle by Chalmers' drafting. Since then it has been applied in a variety of circumstances. The novelty of this excellent book, apart from being the first detailed study of illegality of marine insurance contracts, is that it compares the common law with the statutory implied warranty, and shows that there has been a gradual erosion - at least in England - of the strictness of the warranty. It is now arguable that the two disparate lines of authority are moving into alignment. Wang Feng has shed a great deal of light onto one of the darker corners of marine insurance law. The analysis is clear and incisive. This work is a substantial addition to the literature on the law of marine insurance and the author is to be congratulated on his efforts. It goes without saying that *Illegality in Marine Insurance* should be on the bookshelf of every insurance practitioner, as well as being compulsory reading for all students of marine insurance.

Professor Rob Merkin QC

PREFACE

It has been pointed out by numerous authorities that the issue of legality is one of the most complex and difficult areas in English law. Countless rules and principles have been created by former authorities, on one hand, principles which have been created by common law give guidance to the English courts when dealing with this issue, on the other hand, however, these judgments make this area far from clear and stable.

However, compared with one more specialist area, the legality issue in marine insurance law, the instability of rules in English common law makes itself a useful instrument. Section 41 of the Marine Insurance Act 1906, which is known as warranty of legality, requires that the adventure is lawful and so far as the assured can control the matter, the adventure shall be carried out in a lawful manner. However, this piece of law has imposed a rigid and unfair system on the assured. According to former authorities, it can be seen that the illegality rules in marine insurance law are far more complex than section 41; and moreover, English common law also provides useful instruments for marine insurance law.

With the exception of section 41, the general rule of warranty in marine and non-marine insurance law came under criticism for many years. In light of these backgrounds and the upcoming Insurance Act 2015 this book begins with the general introduction of marine insurance warranty and the defects of current principle, analysis of section 41 in marine insurance law and tries to explore the true scope of section 41 in marine insurance. The principles of the legality issue in English common law will be discussed in detail. Furthermore, because of the common grounds Australia and New Zealand and the UK share, the pattern to resolve legality issue in these two countries will be introduced as well. Based on the introduction of the reforms which have been made by Australia and New Zealand, this book will try to explore the positive methods which can also be absorbed by English law.

In addition, the new reform of English law on the warranty issue in insurance and marine insurance law, which has been confirmed by the Insurance Act 2015, will be analysed, as well as its impact on the illegality issue in marine insurance cases. Finally, based on former analysis, this book will propose a practical method to reform this issue in English law, applying the common law rules in marine insurance law.

TABLE OF CASES

Alexander v Rayson [1936] 1 K.B. 169 .... 101, 102
Allison Pty Ltd Tans Pibara Marine Port Service v Lumley General
    Insurance Ltd [2006] WASC 104 156
Archbolds Ltd v S Spanglett Ltd [1961] 1 Q.B. 374 .... 92, 95, 108, 114
Ashton v Turner and Another [1981] Q.B. 137 .... 57, 63
Ashmore, Benson, Pease & Co. Ltd. v A. V. Dawson Ltd [1973] 1 W.L.R. 828 ..... 95, 106
Atkinson v Abbott (1809) 11 East 135 .... 39, 44
Australian Aviation Underwriting Pty Limited v Henry (1988) 12 NSW LR 121 122
Awwad v Geraghty [2001] Q.B. 570 .... 107, 108
AXN v John Worboys and Inceptum Insurance Co Ltd [2012] EWHC 1730 (QB)....88, 89
Baring and others v The Royal Exchange Assurance Company (1804) 5 East 99 39
Bell, and other v Carstairs (1811) 14 East 374 .... 39, 151
Bedford Insurance Co v Instituto de Resseguros do Brasil [1985] Q.B. 966 117
Beresford v Royal Insurance Company [1938] A.C.586 .... 75, 110, 121
Bennett v. Bennett, 208 U.S. 505 (1908) 97
Bird v Appleton 102 E.R. 45 120
Birkett v Acorn Business Machines Ltd [1999] 2 All ER (Comm) 429 112
Bowmakers Ltd v Barnet Instruments Ltd [1945] K.B. 65 65
Burrows v Rhodes [1899] QB 816 .... 69, 70, 71
Busk v The Royal Exchange Assurance Company (1818) 2 B &Ald 73 41
Carstairs and Others, Executors of Lyon v Allnutt (1813) 3 Camp 497 .... 41, 42
Cakebread v Hopping Brothers [1947] K.B. 641 74
Chalmers and Another v Bell (1804) 3 B & P 604 50
Charlton v Fisher [2002] Q.B. 578 .... 85, 88, 124, 125
Clifford v Hunter (1827) M & M 103 36
Clunis v Camden and Islington HA [1998] Q.B. 978 .... 56, 59
Cleaver v Mutual Reserve Fund Life Association [1892] 1 Q.B. 147 80
Clugas v Penaluna 100 E.R 1122 144
Cohen v Hinckley (1808) 1 Taunt 249 .... 35, 43
Cope v Rowlands 150 E.R. 707 .... 93, 107
Coral Leisure Group Ltd. v Barnett [1981] I.C.R. 503 104
Courage Ltd v Crehan [2002] Q.B. 507 108
Colen and Another v Cebrian (UK) Ltd [2004] I.C.R. 568 .... 105, 106
Cross v Kirkby 2000 WL 530 .... 58, 66, 69, 73
Cunard and Others v Hyde (1858) EB & E 670.. 35
Davies, Turner & Co. Ld. v Brodie [1954] 1 W.L.R. 1364 95
Denison v Modigliani (1794) 5 TR 582 45

TABLE OF CASES

Delaney v Pickett [2011] EWCA Civ 1532 67
Director of Public Prosecutions v Bhagwan [1972] A.C. 60 .... 93, 94
Dixon v. Sadler (1841) 8 M & W 895 .... 22, 29, 31
Doak v Weekes (1986) 82 FLR 334 154
Dunbar v Plant [1998] Ch. 412 .... 78, 79
Eden v. Parkinson (1781) 2 Doug KB 732 29
Egerton v Earl Brownlow (1853) 4 H.l.Cas.1 149 114
Elafonissos Fishing and Shipping Company v Aigaion Insurance Company
 SA [2012] EWHC 1512 (Comm) 182
Euro-Diam Ltd v Bathurst [1988] 2 All ER 23 48
Euro-Diam Ltd v Bathurst [1990] 1 Q.B. 1 .... 121, 147, 148
Farmer v Legg (1797) 7 TR 186 .... 30, 31, 33
Federal Business Development Bank v Reinsurance and Excess Managers Ltd.
 (1979) 13 BCLR 376 160
Fitzgerald v F J Leonhardt Pty Ltd C.L.R.215 105
Fielding & Platt Ltd. v SelimNajjar [1969] 1 W.L.R. 357 100
Foster v. Driscoll [1929] 1 K.B. 470 .... 100, 144
Furtado v Rogers (1802) 3 B & P 191 37
Gardner v Moore [1984] A.C. 548 80
Gary Close v Colin Wilson [2011] EWCA Civ 5 94
Gedge and others v Royal Exchange Assurance Corporation [1900] 2 QB 214 49
Godbolt v. Fittock (1963) 63 S.R. (N.S.W.) 617 63
Gray and Another v Lloyd (1811) 4 Taunt 136 35
Gray v Thames Trains Ltd [2009] 1 A.C. 1339 .... 56, 67, 68, 71
Gray and Another v Barr [1971] 2 Q.B. 554 .... 60, 78, 79, 83, 85, 124
Hagedorn v Bazett (1813) 2 M & S 100 .... 35, 43, 49, 50
Hardy v Motor Insurers' Bureau [1964] 2 Q.B. 745 .... 77, 84, 87
Hall v Hebert [1993] 2 SCR 159 .... 61, 68, 109
Harbour Inn Seafoods v Switzerland General Insurance Ltd (1991)
 6 ANZIns 61,048 159
Harry Cross v William Dickinson Kirkby 2000 WL 530 .... 58, 66, 69, 73
Heyman and others v Parish (1809) 2 Cowp 149 41
Hentig and Another v Staniforth (1816) 5 M & S 124 42
Hewison v Meridian Shipping Ltd [2002] EWCA Civ 1821 .... 56, 73
Hinckley v Walton (1810) 3 Taunt 131 31
Hobbs v Hannam (1811) 3 Camp 93 41
Holman v Johnson (1775) 1 Cowp 341 .... 29, 48, 53, 55
Horsell International Pty Ltd v Divetwo Pty Ltd [2013] NSWCA 368 123
Hounga v Allen [2014] 1 WLR 2889 .... 61, 62, 71
Ingham and others v Agnew (1812) 15 East 522 44
Jackson v Harrison (1977–1978) 138 CLR 438 63
James Yachts Ltd. v Thames and Mersey Marine Insurance Co Lloyd's
 Rep [1977] Vol. 1 at 206 160
Johnson v Moreton [1980] A.C. 37 .... 94, 95
Joyce v Obrien [2013] EWCA Civ 546 .... 64, 67, 68, 74
Kensington v Inglis and Another (1807) 8 East 273 34
Keir v Andrade (1816) 6 Taunt 504 .... 43, 50
Kiriri cotton co ltd v Dewani [1960] A.C. 192 114
Lane v Holloway [1968] 1 Q.B. 379 58
Law v Hollingsworth (1797) 7 TR 160 .... 31, 33

TABLE OF CASES

Les LaboratoiresServier v ApotexInc [2011] EWHC 730 70
Les LaboratoiresServier v ApotexInc [2013] Bus LR 80 70
Les LaboratoiresServier& Anor v ApotexInc&Ors [2014] 3 WLR 1257 .... 56, 71, 72, 74
Lilly v 8PM [2009] EWHC 1905 69
Lowe v Peers (1768) 4 Burrow 2225 96
Lubbock and Another v Potts (1806) 7 East 449 50
Mackender v. Feldia A.G. [1967] 2 Q.B. 590 150
Marcel Beller Ltd. v Hayden [1978] Q.B. 694 .... 82, 83, 85
Marles v. Philip Trant& Sons Ltd [1954] 1 Q.B. 29 78
Maxim Nordenfelt Guns and Ammunition Co. v. Nordenfelt [1893] 3 Ch. 122 115
Metcalfe v Parry (1814) 4 Camp 123 41
Meah v McCreamer (1986) 1 AER 943 59
Mercantile Mutual Insurance (Ltd) v Gibbs & Anor [2001] WASCA 271 .... 155, 156
Moss and others v Byrom 101 E.R. 605 .... 37, 40
Morck and Another v Abel (1802) 3 B & P 35 .... 48, 50
Murphy v Culhane [1977] Q.B. 94 66
National Coal Board v England [1954] AC 403 .... 56, 57, 66
Norwest Refrigeration Services Pty Ltd v Bain Dawes (1984) 157 CLR 149 155
Oom and others v Bruce (1810) 12 East 225 42
Parkin v Dick (1809) 2 Camp 221 33
ParkingEye Ltd v Somerfield Stores Ltd [2013] 2 W.L.R. 939 .... 103, 112
Parkinson v College of Ambulance Ltd and Harrison [1925] 2 K.B. 1 AT 13 111
Patrick v Ronson International Ltd [2005] EWHC 1767 123
Pearce v Brooks (1865–66) L.R. 1 Ex. 213 102
Pieschell v AllnuttSame v Lavie (1813) 4 Taunton 792 34
Pipon v Cope (1780) 1 Camp 434 41
Pitts v Hunt and Another [1991] 1 Q.B. 24 .... 57, 58, 63, 64
Planche and Another v Fletcher (1779) 1 Doug 251 .... 37, 39, 143, 145, 148
Potts v Bell and others (1800) 8 TR 548 38
Pollard and Another v Bell (1800) 8 TR 434 39
Raphael Brandon v Nesbitt (1794)6 TR 23 40
Ralli Brothers v CompañiaNavieraSota Y Aznar [1920] 2 K.B. 287 144
Redmond v Smith (1844) 7 M. &Gr 474 .... 30, 32, 120, 136
Reeves v Comr of Police of the Metropolis [1999] QB 169 56
Revill v Newbery [1996] QB 567 .... 58, 73, 74, 86
Re Mahmoud v Ispahani [1921] 2 KB 716 111
Regazzoni v. K. C. Sethia [1958] A.C. 301 .... 144, 145, 147
Re Emery's Investments Trusts [1959] Ch. 410 145
Re Claim by Helbert Wagg & Co. Ltd [1956] 2 W.L.R. 183 146
Richardson v Mellish (1824) 2 Bing 229 34
Rian Lane v Dive Two Pty Ltd [2012] NSWSC 104 122
Rian Lane v Dive Two Pty Ltd [2012] NSWSC 209 122
Royal Boskalis Westminster v Mountain [1999] Q.B. 674 146
Sadler v Dixon (1841) 8 M & W 895 .... 29, 31
Safeway Stores Ltd v Twigger [2010] EWHC 11 (Comm) at 974 70
Saunders v Edwards [1987] 1 W.L.R. 1116 .... 60, 72
Scott v Brown, Doering, McNab& Co [1892] 2 Q.B. 724 102
Sea Glory Maritime Co, Swedish Management Co SA v AL Sagr National
    Insurance Co [2013] EWHC 2116 (Comm) 32, 51, 149
Smith v Jenkins (1970) 44 A.L.J.R. 78 63

TABLE OF CASES

Solway v Lumley General Insurance Ltd &Ors [2003] QCA 136 155
Stone & Rolls Ltd v Moore Stephens and another [2008] 3 W.L.R. 1146 .... 60, 61
St. John Shipping Corporation v Joseph Rank Ltd [1957] 1 Q.B. 267 .... 103, 104
Stewart v Oriental Fire and Marine Insurance Co. [1985] Q.B. 988 .... 117, 118
Strongman LD. v Sincock [1955] 2 Q.B. 525 .... 110, 135, 181
Suart v Powell 109 E.R. 785 43
Switzerland Insurance Australia Ltd v Mowie Fisheries Pty Ltd [1997] FCA 231 154
Taylor v Bhail [1996] CLC 377 110
Tappenden v Randall 126 E.R. 1388 111
Thackwell v Barclays Bank Plc [1986] 1 All E.R. 676 .... 60, 76, 111
The Bamburi [1982] 1 Lloyd's Rep. 312 139
Tinsley Appellant v Milligan Respondent [1994] 1 A.C. 340 .... 61, 65, 107, 111
Tinline v White Cross Insurance Association Limited [1921] 3 K.B. 327 ...... 78, 124, 125
Toulmin v Anderson (1808) 1 Taunt 232 46
Town of Newton v Rumery, 480 US 386 (1987) 83
Tompson v Hopper (1858) E.B. &E. 1038 123
21St Century Logistic Solutions Limited v Madysen Limited [2004]
    EWHC 231 .... 101, 102
Vandyck and Others v Whitmore (1801) 1 East 475 37–9
Vandyck and others v Hewitt (1800) 1 East 96 .... 31, 34, 50
Vellino v Chief Constable of Greater Manchester [2002] 1 W.L.R. 218 .... 66, 69
Victorian Daylesford Syndicate v Dott [1905] 2 Ch. 624 .... 92, 93
Wainhouse v. Cowie, 4 Taunt 178 .... 31, 35
Waugh v Morris (1872–73) L.R. 8 Q.B. 202 .... 95, 99, 104
Webb v Chief Constable of Merseyside Police [2000] Q.B. 427 65
Wetherell v Jones 110 E.R. 82 .... 103, 104
Wilson v Rankin (1865–66) LR 1 QB 162 .... 35, 42
Wilson v Foderingham (1813) 1 M & S 471 44
Womersley v Peacock Unreported High Court of NZ 159
Yango Pastoral Co Pty Ltd v First Chicago Australia Ltd (1978) 139 C.L.R. 410 118

TABLE OF STATUTES

British Columbia Marine Insurance Act 1993 160
Financial Service Act 1986 119
Financial Services and Markets Act 2000... 119
Insurance Act 2015..2, 13, 24, 161–75
Insurance Companies Act 1974 .... 92, 117
Insurance Contract Act 1984 .... 157, 167
Insurance Law Reform Act 1977 .... 158, 159, 167
Insurance Contract Law Bill 2014 161
Marine Insurance Act 1906 .... 1, 9, 11, 13, 14, 15, 21, 23, 24, 25, 29, 42–51,
94, 129, 131–3, 136, 148, 149, 153, 161, 163,
165, 166, 169, 174, 179, 180, 183
Marine Insurance Act 1909 .... 14, 153, 156, 157
Road Traffic Act 1988.. 85, 87, 88, 89

INTRODUCTION

The illegality issue is a difficult and chaotic field in both marine insurance law and common law.

The doctrine of the warranty of legality in English maritime law originates from the eighteenth century and has influenced the jurisdictions of many Commonwealth countries which have developed their own marine insurance law with reference to English law, such as Australia, New Zealand, and Canada. In English law, as codified in section 41 of the Marine Insurance Act 1906: "There is an implied warranty that the adventure insured is a lawful one, and that, so far as the assured can control the matter, the adventure shall be carried out in a lawful manner".[1] The legality issue in marine insurance law is quite a difficult one. From the perspective of the consequence of a violation of this law, the effect of such a breach is somewhat controversial and harsh on the assured. On the one hand, since this section is an implied warranty, it requires the strict compliance of the assured, and the breach of such a warranty according to English law entitles the insurer to discharge his liability automatically from the time of such a breach with no regard to materiality and causation. On the other hand, the boundaries of the concept "lawful" in this section – which may cover not only statute and common law, but also technical rules and regulations, which in most circumstances are unfamiliar to the assured – are very wide. It is clear that, on the face of it, this section gives the insurer too much power and it is very difficult to balance the interests of the assured and the insurer.

Furthermore, from the perspective of the application of this warranty, it is very hard to ascertain how far the English courts can apply the illegality defence rules in common law to marine insurance cases, what factors should be considered by the courts when dealing with such issues, and what the function of section 41 under current circumstances and the restrictions on the application of this implied term is.

The chaos of the illegality issue has been noticed by the legal institutions in the UK and work to clarify it has been carried out. The Law Reform Committee and the Law Commission has published three consultation papers on this issue: Consultation Paper 154, which concerns the illegality defence in contract and transaction; Consultation Paper 160, which concerns the illegality defence in tort; and Consultation Paper 189, which is a consultative report on both areas. Most

---

1 Marine Insurance Act 1906, s 41

INTRODUCTION

recently, in 2010, the Law Commission published Paper No 320 mainly on the illegality issues in trust. Unlike the situation in common law, the illegality issue in marine insurance law has been considered by the Law Commission only in their consultation papers which relate to warranty. There are two former papers which contain the warranty of legality: Issues Paper 2 and Consultation Paper No 182. However, both these papers only contradict reform recommendations that have been proposed. In the most recent Law Commission paper, No 353,[2] the Law Commission proposed a universal reform recommendation on the express warranty as well as implied warranty in insurance and marine insurance law; the most important proposal is that breach of the warranty only suspends the insurer's liability and that the breach of warranty can be fixed, making the insurer liable from that point again. This new proposal has been recognised in clause 10 of the new Insurance Act 2015. However, this is clearly not the end of the story.

This book aims to analyse the problem of the current status of the warranty of legality in marine insurance law in the UK, and through a comparative study of the illegality defence in English common law and other jurisdictions, the research also attempts to explore a more reasonable approach in marine insurance law when dealing with illegality.

Firstly, this book will introduce the history and development of the warranty of legality in marine insurance law and try to explore whether section 41 really reflected the true intention of the authorities prior to 1906. The warranty of legality can be traced back to the late eighteenth century and this research study will illustrate what is the true scope of section 41 and how English law has developed into its current state.

Secondly, this book will also cover the illegality defence in English common law. The research will explore the origin of the illegality defence in both tort law and contract law and then clarify the illegality defence rules which are applied in current English law and the rationales underlying these rules. It will also explain whether the rules in common law can be applied to insurance cases. The differences between common law illegality and statutory illegality will also be examined.

The third objective of this book is to compare the differences between the illegality defences in common law and the warranty of legality in marine insurance. Through this comparison, this research will attempt to ascertain why the English courts adopt a different pattern from the illegality defences in common law when dealing with illegality in marine insurance.

The fourth objective is to find out whether the illegality defence in common law is eligible in marine insurance cases. Because of the marked differences between common law and marine insurance law, it is worth discussing whether the rules in common law can be applied to marine insurance cases freely and, if not, what are the obstacles to this application and what is the boundary to this application.

The fifth objective of this book is to explore the marine insurance law illegality defence in other Commonwealth jurisdictions which have similar rules to English

---

2 *Insurance Contract Law: Business Disclosure; Warranties; Insurers' Remedies for Fraudulent Claims; and Late Payment* Law Com No 353 (July 2014).

law, especially in Australian law, and to examine how the local courts resolve such problems, and whether this is valuable for the reform of English law.

The sixth objective is to explore and clarify English law when dealing with illegality under foreign law. This is a controversial issue in English law, since according to authorities, section 41 only applies to illegality under English law. This issue is becoming a more pertinent one, because of the increase in commercial relationships between nations, and the necessity therefore to understand foreign law illegality.

The final objective of this book is to explore ways in which the warranty of legality in marine insurance law can be reformed. This part will attempt to propose a reasonable way of reforming this piece of law, and also assess the reform which has been carried out by the Law Commission in the upcoming new Insurance Act.

This book is divided into three parts. The first part will concentrate on the general rule of warranty and warranty of legality in marine insurance law. The second part will focus on the illegality defence in common law. Finally, the third part will comprise a comparison of the warranty of legality and the illegality defence in common law and the illegality issue in other jurisdictions, ending with a possible pattern for reform.

The theme of Part 1 is to explore the origins of the warranty of legality in marine insurance law. The research in this part will examine the law in chronological order so as to reveal how the law evolved into its current position. In this part, the research will begin with an analysis of cases prior to 1906 and trace back to the eighteenth century. There are almost two hundred cases prior to 1906 which underlie this implied warranty. With this data and analysis, Part 1 will give a clear answer as to whether section 41 has reflected former authorities which precede this Act, what the meaning and boundary of the word "lawful" is, what "so far as the assured can control the matter" means, and also whether there exist any exceptions in former authorities. In addition, because of the specificity of this section, the work will be divided into two different sections: the first section will consider the first part of section 41, that is, that the adventure should be a lawful one; and the second part will consider the second part of the section, that is, lawful performance. The first part will pay particular attention to the differences between these two sections, which are of key importance as a matter of law. By doing so, this part will explore every detail of section 41 and its defects at the end of this part; this will be a preparation for the later comparison.

The theme of the second part is to investigate the illegality defence in tort law and contract law and summarise the *ex turpi causa* defence in common law. In this part, the work will be divided into two sections: firstly, the *ex turpi causa* defence in tort law will be examined; and secondly, the illegality defence in contract law will be investigated, and its origins and rules will be summarised separately. In the tort law chapter, the origin of the *ex turpi causa* defence will be considered first, as well as the categories of such a defence in tort law; then the applicable general rules of this defence will be introduced and the rationales which underlie such rules considered. Finally, the application of the *ex turpi causa* defence in insurance law will be introduced and summarised, looking especially at why the defence can be applied and how the defence has been applied to insurance cases and the special situations that exist in insurance law, such as the circumstances in motor insurance.

INTRODUCTION

The structure of the chapter which deals with the illegality defence in contract law will be same as that dealing with the tort law; the only difference is that this chapter will also discuss the differences between statutory illegality and common law illegality, and the differences between the illegality defence in tort law and contract law. The reason for discussing these differences is because section 41 in marine insurance is one kind of statutory illegality and the illegality issue in marine insurance circumstances will also contain tort illegality – such as collision or physical injury on the sea – and contract illegality – such as insurance on illegal subject, or violation of navigation rules during transport; therefore, the comparison with common law will provide a direction of how the warranty of legality in marine insurance should evolve.

The methodology of this part will still be based on the case analysis and opinions from a number of articles will also be considered; besides the comparison and case analysis, this part will also criticise the current rules in the illegality defence.

In Part 3, several issues will be covered. Firstly, this part will examine the differences between the illegality defences in common law and the warranty of legality in marine insurance. By exploring these differences, this section will attempt to answer the question of why the English courts have adopted different methods for dealing with the same issue. By answering this question, it is possible to examine the obstacles to applying the common law illegality defence to marine insurance cases, and the possibility of this application will also be considered.

The second section of this part will examine the illegality rules in marine insurance cases in other Commonwealth jurisdictions, including Australia, Canada and New Zealand; the law in Australia will be examined particularly carefully, since it is of great value to English law.

The third section of this part will examine the status of foreign law illegality in English law – a very difficult and special area of law which is becoming increasingly important. This section will begin with examining the common law rules when dealing with foreign law illegality before considering the current status of section 41 on this issue, and finally proposing a reasonable solution for when foreign law illegality in marine insurance circumstances is encountered.

The final section of the third part and also of the book is the reform of English law in section 41. This section will be based on the former analysis of the insufficiencies of section 41, the rules in common law and other jurisdictions and also the latest judgments to give a combined and more reasonable method when dealing with illegality issues in marine insurance. Naturally, the most recent reform by the Law Commission and the new Insurance Act on this section will also be introduced and the possible impact on this section of insurance law will be considered.

As a result of the research, the following points should be made clear:

(1) What the origins of the warranty of legality in marine insurance law are and whether section 41 truly reflects the judgments of former authorities.
(2) What the origins of the illegality defence in common law – namely in tort law and contract law – are and what the currently applicable rules are.

INTRODUCTION

Also, what the differences between statutory illegality and common law illegality are.

(3) The nature of section 41 and the differences between section 41 and the illegality defence in common law and the reasons behind such differences.

(4) Whether the common law illegality rules can be applied when dealing with illegality issues in marine insurance.

(5) What the law of illegality in other jurisdictions is and whether it is valuable to English law.

(6) What a reasonable way to reform section 41 in English law might be.

PART 1

THE WARRANTY OF LEGALITY IN MARINE INSURANCE LAW

CHAPTER 1

Marine insurance law of warranty in general

As one of the oldest parts of English marine insurance law, the foundation of the basic principles of warranty can be traced back to the eighteenth century.[1] After 300 years of development, the regime is mature, but also rigid. Since 2006, several consultation or issue papers have been published by the Law Commission in order to change this rigid and unfair regime of warranty law, or to abolish it.[2] In order to understand the necessity of reform and the specificity of warranty of legality, this book begins with an introduction of general warranty rules in marine insurance law. This introduction addresses marine insurance law, which relates to general warranty and includes express warranty and implied warranty. This part also introduces warranties in marine insurance law in general, including the origin, classification of warranties, construction rules, and waiver of warranty. Relevant sections in the Marine Insurance Act 1906 are also introduced; however, only the sections that relate to section 41 are considered.

1.1 Warranties in contract law

A warranty is one of the oldest terms in marine insurance law and in contract law. Contractual terms were clarified into condition and warranty by the end of the nineteenth century. For example, in the Sale of Goods Act 1893, s 12(2)–(3), there are implied warranties that a buyer shall have and enjoy quiet possession of the goods, and the goods shall be free from any charge or encumbrance in favour of any third party.[3] It has been suggested that warranties in contract law have been misused. For example, in some cases they have been used as a condition,[4] and in other cases as a promise of understanding of the contract from one party to another. The reason for such chaos is that people want to define different types of warranties with a single concept, which is not possible.

---

1 During the period when most fundamental principles of marine insurance law were written by Lord Mansfield.
2 Please see a series papers of the Law Commission, Issues Paper 2: Warranties (November 2006); Misrepresentation, Non-Disclosure, and Breach of Warranty by the Insured (June 2007) Law Commission Consultation Paper No 182; Consumer Insurance Law: Pre-Contract Disclosure and Misrepresentation (December 2009) Law Com No 319; The Business Insured's Duty of Disclosure, and the Law of Warranties (June 2012) Law Commission Consultation Paper No 204.
3 Sale of Goods Act 1893, s 12(2) and (3).
4 For example, in marine insurance cases which is discussed later.

In fact, aside from marine insurance law, which will be introduced later, warranties in general contract law that also embrace non-marine insurance contracts are described in *Chitty on Contracts* as "a term of the contract, the breach of which may give rise to a claim for damages but not a right to treat the contract as repudiated".[5] The differences between warranty and condition in general contract law are whether the breach of a contractual term addresses the root of the contract and whether it affects the substance and foundation of the venture that the contract intends to carry out.[6]

In a more recent case, *Hong Kong Fir Shipping Co Ltd v Kawasaki Kisen Kaisha Ltd*,[7] the court recognised another type of contract term, an "intermediate term"; a breach of this term entitles the injured party to select between terminating the contract and suing for damages. As a result of the judgment of this case, terms that will be viewed as a warranty have become rare. On the other hand, the word warranty does not necessarily imply warranty terms; it can also describe contractual terms, which are less important, as breaching them will not entitle the other party to terminate the contract. Furthermore, in circumstances where there is no warranty term in a contract, the injured party can also treat the breach of this condition as a breach of warranty and not repudiate the contract. Instead, the injured party will seek to benefit from the contract or sue for damage. This is known as suing on a "*warranty ex post facto*".[8]

1.2 Origin and development of warranties in insurance law and marine insurance law

This section addresses the difference between warranty and representation in the early development of warranty, and the difference between warranty in insurance and marine insurance law; there is no implied warranty in non-marine insurance law. In addition, this section focuses on the differences between warranty in contract law and warranty in marine insurance law. This section also explains how to create a warranty, namely express or implied. Warranty in marine insurance is similar to a condition precedent or a condition in contract law. As demonstrated above, the word warranty does not have a specific meaning in general contract law; it is simply a type of contract term. However, cases are not the same in insurance law and marine insurance law, and the meaning of the word "warranty" becomes increasingly meaningful.

The early development of warranty in marine insurance contracts can be traced back to policies that ancient Italian merchants drafted in the thirteenth century. The fundamental principle of warranty in insurance law was founded by a marine insurance case in England by Lord Mansfield. In *De Hahn v Hartley*,[9] there was a term of the policy that required 50 or more crew on board before sailing. However,

---

5 *Chitty on Contracts* (31st edn) at para 12–031.
6 *Bettini v Gye* (1876) 1 Q.B.D. 183.
7 *Hong Kong Fir Shipping Co Ltd v Kawasaki Kisen Kaisha Ltd* [1962] 2 Q.B. 26.
8 *Chitty on Contracts* (31st edn) at para 12–032.
9 *De Hahn v Hartley* 99 E.R.1130.

the ship sailed with only 46 men on board. When the court was determining whether such a clause on the margin of the insurance policy could be seen as a warranty, Lord Mansfield held that the requirement of sailing the ship with a certain number of men on board was a warranty. He stated that: "a warranty in a policy of insurance is a condition or a contingency, and unless that is performed, there is no contract".[10]

In another identical case, *Bean v Stupart*,[11] Lord Mansfield also concluded that a warranty is a condition on which a contract is based. This is not the case in warranty of legality, the rationale of which originates from a common law case, and the word "warranty" was not used in the first place.[12] Other express warranties originate from these two mentioned cases with their fundamental nature.[13] Lord Mansfield also outlined the implied warranty of seaworthiness in *Eden v Parkinson*,[14] in which his Lordship stated: "By an implied warranty, every ship insured must be tight, staunch, and strong; but it is sufficient if she be so at the time of sailing. She may cease to be in 24 hours after departure, and yet the underwriter will continue liable".[15]

Along with the early judgments of Lord Mansfield on warranty in marine insurance law, numerous authorities on this issue prior to 1906 also outlined several fundamental principles. Sir Mackenzie Chalmers later codified all of these principles in the Marine Insurance Act 1906, ss 33 and 34. All types of marine insurance warranties share these features, whether it is an express warranty or an implied warranty. Therefore, by summarising these unique features of marine insurance warranty, it may be helpful for readers to understand the severe nature of implied warranty in current law.

The most fundamental rule is the strict compliance principle, which is codified in section 33(3) of the Marine Insurance Act 1906. As stated in s 33(3): "a warranty, as above defined, is a condition which must be exactly complied with".[16] In addition, non-exact compliance is viewed as a breach of contract, unless such a breach occurs because of a change of circumstances that renders the warranty inapplicable to the circumstances of the contract, or when compliance with the warranty is rendered unlawful by a subsequent law.[17]

As observed by academics the exact compliance principle is not unique in marine insurance law.[18] What makes this principle different from a similar principle in general contract law is the severe consequence of breach.[19] However, it does not seem that in order to evade such a severe consequence, the English courts will offer latitude for the strictness of compliance of a marine insurance warranty by applying the *de minimis non curat lex* rule. This is because applying this rule will be

---

10 Ibid at 346.
11 *Bean v Stupart* (1778) 1 Douglas 11.
12 As shown in Chapter 2 and Chapter 3.
13 As discussed below.
14 *Eden v Parkinson* (1781) 2 Douglas K.B. 782.
15 Ibid.
16 Marine Insurance Act 1906, s 33(3).
17 Marine Insurance Act 1906, s 34(1).
18 Professor Baris Soyer, *Warranties In Marine Insurance* (2nd edn), p 133.
19 The consequences of breach of warranty are discussed later.

a violation of former authorities. According to the judgment in *De Hahn v Hartley*: "It is perfectly immaterial for what purpose a warranty is introduced, but, being inserted, the contract does not exist unless it be literally complied with".[20] Therefore, according to this statement, even though only one can of pork is short out of 1,000 cans of pork, which the assured is warrantied to carry, this will amount to a breach of warranty.

The second reason for not applying the *de minimis* rule is that such a rule can only be applied to a representation in general contract law and not to an express warranty in a marine insurance contract. This is because there is a difference between representation and express warranty. Lord Mansfield clarified this point in *De Hahn v Hartley*: "While a representation may be satisfied with a substantial and equitable compliance, a warranty requires a strict and literal fulfilment".[21] The third reason is that, although in some cases there is a rejection of a literal compliance test, this is because of the construction of warranty by the court.[22] Therefore, even though the outcome may be similar, the rationales underlying these two tests are different.

The next rule is that no causal link is required between the breach of warranty and the loss that is suffered by the assured. In addition, it does not matter whether the breach is material to the risk or not. This is the principle that has received the most criticism since it was written. In addition to *De Hahn v Hartley*, another conclusive authority on this issue is the House of Lords case *Thomson v Weems*. In this case, the insurer issued life insurance to the assured. In the policy form there was a question about whether the assured was temperate, and whether the assured had always been strictly so. The assured answered this question positively and declared that this was the basis of the contract. In an action on the policy after the death of Mr Weems, House of Lords unanimously held that the declaration of Mr Weems was an express warranty. In addition, it is not of any importance whether the express warranty is material or not, as there is no requirement for a causal link between the loss and the breach of warranty.[23]

The reason for the existence of this principle is addressed by Lord Goff in *The Good Luck*: "If a promissory warranty is not complied with, the insurer is discharged from liability as from the date of the breach of warranty, for the simple reason that fulfilment of the warranty is a condition precedent to the liability of the insurer. This, moreover, reflects the fact that the rationale of warranties in insurance law is that the insurer only accepts the risk provided that the warranty is fulfilled. This is entirely understandable; and it follows that the immediate effect of a breach of promissory warranty is to discharge the insurer from liability as from the date of the breach".[24]

This approach has been criticised on numerous occasions. As early as the 1980s, the English Law Commission began to notice that "it seemed quite wrong that

---

20 *De Hahn v Hartley* 99 E.R.1130.
21 *Arnould's Law of Marine Insurance and Average* (18th edn) at para 19–08.
22 For example, in *Berns & Koppstein Inc v Orion Ins Co Ltd* (1959) A.M.C.2455. See also para 19–08 of *Arnould's Law of Marine Insurance and Average* (18th edn).
23 *Thomson v Weems* (1884) 9 App. Cas. 671.
24 *Bank of Nova Scotia v Hellenic Mutual War Risks Association (Bermuda) Ltd* [1991] 2 WLR 1279; [1992] 1 AC 233 at 262.

an insurer should be entitled to demand strict compliance with a warranty which was immaterial to the risk".[25] In addition, it seems unjust to entitle the insurer to reject any claim no matter how irrelevant the breach is. Therefore, the English Law Commission proposed to insert a causal connection test in current English law in almost every issue paper or consultation paper that deals with insurance warranty, such as Issue Paper 2 in 2006 and Consultation Paper 182. However, the Law Commission rejected this reform proposal in its most recent issue paper, IC 353, based on increased investigation costs, complex litigation, uncertain outcomes, and difficulties of proof.[26] Therefore, since the new Insurance Act 2015 will come into effect in August 2016, there is no hope of an establishment of a causal connection test in English law in the near future.

The next feature of current insurance warranty law is that the breach of warranty cannot be remedied. This sentence is codified in the Marine Insurance Act 1906, s 34(2). However, according to the Insurance Act 2015, the breach of warranty can be remedied as of August 2016, and this old principle in marine insurance law will be replaced accordingly. According to this new Act, the insurer will be liable to the assured again after the breach has been restored.[27] Therefore, aside from a few occasions,[28] warranties in marine insurance contracts must be strictly complied with, whether they are express warranties or implied warranties.

Given the serious consequence of breaching warranty, the type of term or expression that amounts to a warranty is crucial. In addition, creating a warranty in a marine insurance contracts is a sophisticated technique, which the insurer would like to grasp. An express warranty can be a written warranty or an oral warranty, although the last category is unusual.[29] In marine insurance contracts, as cited in section 35(2) of the Marine Insurance Act 1906, an express warranty must be written in a policy or in documents that are incorporated by reference to a policy.[30] Although, compared to a non-marine insurance contract, the scope of documents that may contain a warranty term is narrow,[31] it is still important to distinguish a warranty from other express terms in a marine insurance contract.

Lord Goff in *The Good Luck* defined a warranty as follows: "any term of the insurance contract which, properly construed, is a condition precedent to the inception or continuation of cover".[32] It is impossible for English law to state what constitutes a warranty since there are various types of warranties between the assured and insurers. However, English law makes clear what does not constitute a warranty. First, a representation is not a warranty. This is found in Lord Mansfield's early judgments, which are introduced above. A representation, as recognised by Lord

---

25 Law Commission Consultation Paper 204 at p 136.
26 Law Commission IC 353: Insurance Contract Law: Business Disclosure; Warranties; Insurer's remedies for Fraudulent Claims; and Late Payment at 14.24.
27 Discussed below in Chapter 7.
28 For example, in cases of waiver of warranty by the insurer or the performance of warranty becomes illegal.
29 M Clark, *Insurance Contract Law*, para 20–2A.
30 Marine Insurance Act 1906, s 35.
31 Since in non-marine insurance contracts, a warranty can be reasonably contained in a proposal form prior to a policy.
32 *The Good Luck* [1992] 1 AC 233 at 263.

Mansfield, may be equitably or substantially answered, but a warranty must be strictly complied with.[33]

Therefore, a sole description of risk is not a warranty if it is not relevant to the risk or does not affect the underwriter's judgement of the risk. For example, if there is only one letter difference between the vessel that is insured and the vessel that is described in the insurance policy, then that difference will not be construed as a breach of warranty.[34] However, a few exceptions can turn a description of risk into an express warranty. In the first scenario, if there were clear indications that it was the intention of the contracting party that a description should have the effect of warranty, then that description would likely be rendered as a warranty.[35] However, one exception to this scenario is that "the language in the policy being that of the insurers, if there is any ambiguity; it must be construed most strongly against them".[36] In an employer's liability insurance case, *Woolfall & Rimmer Ltd v Moyle*,[37] the Court of Appeal construed whether the plaintiff assured had sufficiently complied with a condition in the insurance policy, which required the assured to take reasonable precautions to prevent accidents, Lord Greene MR held that this condition would only be applied to personal acts of the plaintiff assureds and could not extend to acts of everyone employed by them. Therefore, although this term named a condition in this insurance policy, it was still subject to proper construction by the court.

In the second scenario, if the description of risk is relevant to the risk of loss then the term is treated as a warranty as well. Lord Justice Bowen said in *Barnard v Faber*: "A term as regards the risk must be a condition".[38] The most significant case on this issue is *Yorkshire Insurance Company, Limited Appellants v Campbell Respondent*, to which several articles have referred. The marine insurance policy in this case stated, "all the words which the policy contains (except parts of the general form inapplicable to the particular transaction) are words of contract. Words qualifying the subject-matter of the insurance prima facie are words of warranty constituting, under s 39 of the Commonwealth Marine Insurance Act 1909 (a section in the same terms as s 33 of the English Marine Insurance Act 1906), a condition which must be complied with, whether it is material to the risk or not".[39] The policy stated that a proposal form that was signed on behalf of the respondent should be the basis of the insurance and should be incorporated therein. The subject matter that the policy insured, which the

---

33 *De Hahn v Hartley* 99 E.R.1130.
34 However, if a vessel's nationality is also stated after the name of this vessel then it will normally be considered as an express warranty, which can be seen from early judgments such as *Baring v Claggett* (1802) 3 B & P 201. However, the name of a vessel cannot indicate the nationality of the vessel and constitute an implied warranty, as seen in judgments by Lord Ellenborough, such as *Clapham v Cologan* (1813) 3 Camp. 382. Please also refer to *Arnould's Law of Marine Insurance and Average* (18th edn), ch 19 at 19–04.
35 Malcolm Clark, "Insurance Warranties: the absolute end?" [2007] L.M.C.L.Q at p 475; see also *Wheelton v Hardisty* (1857) 8 El & Bl 232, 300, per Bramwell B.
36 Malcolm Clark, "Insurance Warranties: the absolute end?" [2007] L.M.C.L.Q at p 475.
37 *Woolfall & Rimmer Ltd v Moyle* (1941) 71 Ll.L.Rep 15.
38 *Barnard v Faber* [1893] 1 Q.B. 340 at 344.
39 *Yorkshire Ins Co Ltd v Campbell* [1917] A.C. 218.

proposal form stated was a horse, was wrongly claimed to be "by Soult out of St. Paul mare". In addition, there was an express warranty that the horse was well and free from disease. However, the horse died from natural causes during the voyage. The assured sued to recover a total loss; however, the insurer appealed since the description of the horse was stated in the proposal form that was incorporated into the insurance policy. This description was rendered as a basic contract clause. Therefore, the description should constitute a warranty and must be strictly complied with. The Privy Council of the House of Lords gave a judgment for the insurer and stated, "words qualifying the subject matter of the insurance will be words of warranty, which in a policy of marine insurance operate as conditions".[40]

The final category of term, which may not constitute a warranty, is exception. How to distinguish an exception from a warranty is clear. As stated in *The Law of Insurance Contract*: "If the term is concerned with circumstances which give rise to a temporary increase in the risk, it is an exception"[41] . . . If, however, the term concerns circumstances in which there is or might be a permanent increase in the risk, it is a warranty".[42] Therefore, the insurer's liability will be discharged during the excepted period, and will be restored again after the excepted period. However, if a warranty is breached then the insurer's liability will be discharged until August 2016.

Given the introduction of what can constitute a warranty, it is clear that there is no particular form of a warranty in insurance (marine insurance), and the word warranty is not necessary. In fact, in cases where the word warranty is used in a contract, it may not be a warranty that is stipulated in the Marine Insurance Act 1906, s 33, such as warranties that indicate an exception to a policy, as stated in the previous paragraph.[43] The only question that matters is: What is the intention of the parties? In circumstances where the assured and the insurer clearly stipulate which term is a warranty and the consequences for breaching that warranty, there is no need for interference from the court. However, in cases where there is no clear instruction by the contractual parties, the court must decide whether a statement of fact or a promise constitutes a warranty.

English case law has generated an applicable test. The most significant case on this issue is *HIH Casualty & General Insurance Ltd v New Hampshire Insurance Co*.[44] The insurance in this case was pecuniary loss indemnity insurance. This insurance is designed to enable investors whose finance supports the production of films to recoup their investment. The purpose of this insurance was to indemnify the assured, "if at the end of a defined period there was a shortfall between the amount of finance provided and the revenue collected".[45] There is a term in both

---

40 *Yorkshire Ins Co Ltd v Campbell* [1917] AC 218 at 224.
41 Malcolm A Clarke, *Law of Insurance Contracts* (4th edn) – Service Issue 32–2 (April 2015) at 20–2B1.
42 Ibid.
43 For example, warrantied free of capture and seizure.
44 *HIH Casualty & General Insurance Ltd v New Hampshire Insurance Co* [2001] 2 Lloyd's Rep 161.
45 Ibid.

insurance and reinsurance contracts, which states that a certain number of films must be made.[46]

The preliminary issue, which was addressed by the Court of Appeal, was whether the six-film term was a warranty. Rix LJ held that in the absence of clear words of contract, there are three applicable tests: "One test is whether it is a term which goes to the root of the transaction; a second, whether it is descriptive of or bears materially on the risk of loss; a third, whether damages would be an unsatisfactory or inadequate remedy".[47]

By applying these tests, Rix LJ found that in this case, the six-film term is clearly "the essence of the risk underwritten: if the slate of (six) films is made with the moneys invested, the insurers will indemnify the investors against loss. That is what the insurance is all about";[48] this term is an insurance warranty. Therefore, it can be concluded from Rix LJ's tests that the most fundamental question that must be asked when deciding whether a term is a warranty or not is still: "Is the statement or promise material to the risk?"

1.3 Construction of warranties

After the identification of a warranty, the next controversial issue is how to construe a warranty. This issue is crucial to determining the parties' intentions by inserting a warranty, especially in the context of deciding whether a breach of the assured falls into the scope of a breach of warranty. This issue is controversial because the dispute between the rigid, literal construction of warranties' words and the reading of a warranty from the context of a policy was fierce under English law. Literal construction means that the court will construe the scope of warranty strictly according to the surface meaning of the words, without considering the circumstances of that time. Most cases of this kind are about warranties that require enough number or qualified crews on board.

The most acknowledged case, which has been introduced by numerous authorities and reference books, is *Brownsville Holdings Ltd v Adamjee Insurance Co Ltd ("The Milasan")*.[49] In this case, *The Milasan*, a 90ft motor yacht sank by the stern in calm water and good weather about 25 miles from Cape Spartivento, which is on the eastern Calabrian coast, on 23 July 1995. The insurers denied liability on several grounds. One of these grounds was that between the time that the last master left in September 1994 and the time that the new master was appointed on 1 July 1995, there was no professional skipper in charge and such absence was a breach of a warranty, which provided that "warranted professional skippers and crew [be] in charge at all times".[50]

Without further consideration of the circumstances under which the yacht sank, Aikens J held that "it was clear that the insurers were concerned to ensure that

---

46 Respectively 6 and 10.
47 See fn 44 at 182.
48 Ibid.
49 *Brownsville Holdings Ltd v Adamjee Insurance Co Ltd ("The Milasan")* [2000] 2 Lloyd's Rep 458.
50 Ibid.

the vessel was properly looked after all the time, both winter and summer and wherever she was – whether cruising or in a marina for the winter months; that was the rationale for the warranty; a skipper was someone who commanded a vessel of the type in question and the plural 'skippers' was used because the parties appreciated that 'skippers' might change during the policy period; 'professional skipper' referred to a person who had some professional experience that qualified him to be regarded as a 'skipper'; the 'skipper' together with the 'crew' had to be 'in charge' of the vessel 'at all times'; and the wording 'professional skippers and crew to be in charge' meant that the skipper and crew together were to take care of and manage the vessel the whole time as opposed to intermittently or at intervals; and all these requirements of the warranty had to be complied with".[51] Although in the judgment of this case, Aikens J concluded that "a practical construction must be given to the words of the warranty",[52] he still construed the policy solely by relying on the words of the policy rather than considering the fact that there was no breach of warranty during the loss.

One contrasted marine insurance policy that contained a similar warranty is found in *GE Frankona Reinsurance Ltd v CMM Trust No 1400 ("The Newfoundland Explorer")*.[53] The motor yacht *Newfoundland Explorer* was insured against a marine policy that contained a warranty stating that it was "warrantied fully crewed at all times". According to the proposal form, the vessel had one full-time crewmember and two occasional crewmembers. On 25 April 2004, the vessel was severely damaged by fire while alongside a berth in the marina at Fort Lauderdale. The cause of the fire was the overheating of the vessel's generator, which had been running under load since 23 April 2004 and was left running; at the time of the fire no crewmembers were aboard the vessel. The preliminary issues that had to be decided were whether the words "at all times" in the warranty meant 24 hours per day and the meaning of the word "crewed".

Gross J held that by the natural and ordinary meaning of the word, a vessel was "crewed" by the crew (whatever its number) performing such duties as are required on board. A vessel is not crewed if the crew was elsewhere. In the ordinary and natural meaning of the phrase "fully crewed at all times", while laid up alongside a berth, there had to be at least one crew member on board 24 hours per day; "at all times" meant what it said – the entire time, and not some of the time.

However, other than the literal construction, Gross J in this particular case also concluded that whether a vessel is fully crewed or not also depends on what she is doing: "manifestly, a vessel undertaking an ocean voyage will have different crewing requirements to a vessel laid up alongside a berth".[54] Therefore, the judgment of this case implied that words of warranties could have different meanings under different circumstances. However, these two cases were not conclusive, and

---

51 See fn 49 at 459.
52 *Brownsville Holdings Ltd v Adamjee Insurance Co Ltd ("The Milasan")* [2000] 2 Lloyd's Rep 458 at 467.
53 *GE Frankona Reinsurance Ltd v CMM Trust No 1400 ("The Newfoundland Explorer")* [2006] Lloyd's LR 704.
54 Ibid at para 15.

although it seemed that *The Newfoundland Explorer* was developing a new pattern, no certain rules on this issue were concluded until *Pratt v Aigaion Insurance Co SA ("The Resolute")*.[55]

In the case *Pratt v Aigaion Insurance Co SA ("The Resolute")*, the claimant entered into a contract of insurance on the vessel for 12 months from 23 June 2006, and contained the following warranty: "Warranted Owner and/or Owner's experienced skipper on board and in charge at all times and one experienced crew member".[56] On 10 December, the claimant and his crew of three took the vessel out to fish for a day and returned to North Shields. The crew readied the vessel for fishing the next day before one of them, who lived in North Shields, went home, and another visited a pub some 200 yards from the vessel. The vessel was lost in a fire. The inspectors concluded that the fire started in the galley, possibly either by operation or malfunction of the deep fat fryer or the fridge. The defendant insurer relied on the crewing warranty to decline his liability.

By referring to *Hussain v Brown*,[57] Sir Anthony Clarke MR held that the ordinary contractual principles of construction were subject to further considerations in the context of continuing warranties in insurance contracts. The apparent literal meaning of the words in a warranty were to be restricted if they produced a result that was inconsistent with a reasonable and business-like interpretation of such a warranty, and any ambiguity had to be construed against the insurers.[58]

The warranty required that the owner or his skipper be on board and in charge. The natural inference was that an experienced skipper was to be on board because underwriters wanted protection from the risks that a skipper would be needed to guard against. That suggested that the primary purpose of the warranty was to protect the vessel against navigational hazards. Thus, the purpose of the warranty, read as a whole, was to protect the vessel in circumstances in which at least two members of the crew (i.e. the skipper and one other) could be expected to be on board. The phrase "at all times" could not receive its literal meaning. Thus, the question was about how far it should be qualified. In those circumstances, it was to be construed *contra proferentem*, against the insurer. Therefore, considering the warranty as a whole, it does not discharge the insurer's liability under such circumstances. Since the Court of Appeal endorsed the construction rule in *The Resolute*, it is believed that this rule can be generally applied in marine insurance cases.[59]

---

55 *Pratt v Aigaion Insurance Co SA ("The Resolute")* [2009] Lloyd's Law Rep 225.
56 Ibid at 225.
57 *Hussain v Brown* [1996] 1 Lloyd's Rep. 627, which held that, based on the draconian nature of a continuing warranty and the severe consequence of breach in a case where the insurer's interests have not been stipulated in clear terms, warranties would be construed against the insurer rather than give them more protection.
58 Former English authorities held that whether or not there is ambiguity, the court seeks to avoid a literal construction of warranties which would give absurd results: *Connecticut Mutual Life Ins Co v Moore* (1881) 6 App Cas 644 (life).
59 *Arnould's Law of Marine Insurance and Average* (18th edn), ch 19 at p 883.

1.4 Classifications of warranty

There are different classifications of warranty. According to the continuity of warranty, there is present warranty and continuing warranty;[60] according to the presentation of warranty, there is express warranty and implied warranty. The simplest way to describe the differences between present warranty and continuing warranty is that present warranty is a statement of affairs which already existed at the date of the policy. Continuing warranty, however, is a promise of the assured's obligations during the currency of the policy. However, according to English authorities, there is no clear boundary between a present warranty and a continuing warranty. The characteristics of these two warranties can be changed subject to a court's construction. Therefore, it is not always the case that a statement of fact which prior the contract can constitute to a present warranty.

One judgment that implied this principle is found in *Hussain v Brown (No 1)*.[61] Lloyd's fire policy covered the claimant's commercial premises. Question nine of the proposal form asked: "Are the premises fitted with any system of intruder alarm?" The claimant answered "Yes" to this question. By the time the risk was presented to the underwriters, the security alarm had been fitted and modifications had been carried out. On 24 November 1992, there was a fire at the plaintiff's premises in Bury and the plaintiff claimed under the insurance. The plaintiff admitted that the alarm system was inoperative before and at the time of the fire. The underwriters alleged that the answer given to question nine in the proposal form amounted to a continuing warranty, and there was a breach of warranty by the assured.

The first judgment held that question nine was only a state of affairs. In the later appeal by the underwriter, the Court of Appeal dismissed the appeal and held that questions contained in proposal forms, albeit in the present time, cannot be interpreted as warranties about the future. According to Saville LJ, three points were clear: first "there is no special principle of insurance law requiring answers in proposal forms to be read, prima facie or otherwise, as importing promises to the future. Whether or not they do depend upon ordinary rules of construction, namely consideration of the words the parties have used in the light of the context in which they have used them and selection of that meaning which seems most closely to correspond with the presumed intentions of the parties".[62] Saville LJ also held that by construing the simple words of question nine "there was nothing in the words of the simple question posed or to be gleaned from the context which began to suggest that what an affirmative answer entailed was an undertaking as to the future".[63]

Third, as concluded by Saville LJ, because of the draconian consequences of breaching a continuing warranty, if the underwriter wanted such protection then it was up to them to stipulate this in clear terms. Therefore, it is clear that since a continuing warranty imposes more responsibility on the assured, the court will normally be careful to construe a state of current affairs into a continuing warranty.

---

60 May also be called "promissory warranty".
61 *Hussain v Brown* [1996] 1 Lloyd's Rep. 627.
62 Ibid, fn 63.
63 *Hussain v Brown* [1996] 1 Lloyd's Rep. 627.

However, as noted before, this is not always the case, and normally the warranty would be construed against the intention of the insurance policy in a commercial context.

In the case *Agapitos v Agnew*,[64] the insured vessel *Aegon* was lost by fire on 19 February 1996, at the time moored at Neo Molo, Drapetsona, undergoing conversion from a roll-on roll-off car ferry to a passenger cruise ship. Sparks from hot work that was carried out on board the vessel caused the fire. The policy under which the vessel was insured contained two warranties: first, the assured warrantied to comply with the London Salvage Association approval of location, fire-fighting, and mooring arrangements and all recommendations; second, the assured warrantied no hot work.

In this particular case, the assured's Salvage Association Survey had to be obtained after any arrival or removal of the vessel. On 9 January 1996, the vessel was towed back to Drapetsona. Therefore, according to the insurance policy, the assured needed to obtain another survey. However, the assured failed to do this, since the inspector of L.S.A did not visit the vessel prior to the casualty. Another crucial fact is that on 6 February 1996, underwriters agreed to extend cover for two months from 9 February, subject to the condition that the L.S.A certificate must be updated. Therefore, the underwriter maintained a breach of warranty by the assured. The assured, however, contended that such a warranty only promised that a Salvage Association certificate would be obtained by 9 February 1996. However, Moore-Bick J disagreed with this proposition and held that "the warranty is to be construed as a warranty of an existing state of affairs, not as an undertaking as to the state of affairs existing on 9 February".[65]

The main reason given by Moore-Bick J for this judgment was that the insurer in this case required the assured to obtain the certificate for every change of location or hot work, and in this particular case, the certificate was only valid for a limited period or particular project. The underwriter would like to impose a continuous requirement on the assured to obtain a certificate for every change of circumstances. Therefore, such a warranty must be a continuing one rather than a present one. It is clear that, in addition to the words of the warranty,[66] the purpose of the clause is an issue that must be construed carefully. Consequently, if the purpose of the warranty is to require the assured to comply with a particular requirement throughout the entire risk, then such warranty is a continuing one.[67]

1.5 Implied warranties other than warranty of legality

In former parts of this chapter, rules that relate to express warranties are considered. In addition to express warranties, there are different kinds of implied warranties in marine insurance contracts. This section provides a brief introduction

---

64 *Agapitos v Agnew* [2003] Lloyd's Rep IR 54.
65 Ibid at para 27.
66 As stated in *Hussain v Brown* [1996] 1 Lloyd's Rep 627.
67 Please also see *Eagle Star Insurance Co Ltd v Games Video Co (GVC) SA ("The Game Boy")* [2004] 1 Lloyd's Rep 238 which shares the same character as in *Agapitos*.

of implied warranties in the Marine Insurance Act 1906, except for warranty of legality, which is considered later.

The first implied warranty is warranty of neutrality. As described in section 36 of the 1906 Act, there are two parts of this implied warranty. First, if ship or goods are expressly warranted neutral, there is an implied condition that the property shall have a neutral character at the commencement of the risk, and as far as the assured can control the matter, its neutral character shall be preserved during the risk. Second, where a ship is expressly warranted neutral, there is also an implied condition that the ship shall carry the necessary papers to establish her neutrality. If any loss occurs through breach of this condition, then the insurer may void the contract.[68]

Similar to warranty of legality, which will be considered in Chapter 2, the warranty of neutrality originates from the late eighteenth century during the wars between France and America. At that time, it was crucial for underwriters to consider whether the ship or goods that were insured would be captured during transit; capture would normally mean a total loss. Therefore, in order to reduce such a loss, underwriters would insert an express clause in the policy, stating that the ship or goods is warranted neutral, or as stated in the construction of warranty, an express warranty of a neutral nation will be stated. However, the application of this implied warranty and disputes about this warranty were dramatically reduced after the Napoleonic war. Therefore, in modern marine insurance law, the function of this implied warranty is more symbolic than practical.

Implied warranty is a present warranty and not a continuing warranty. Therefore, this warranty only means that "at the time the risk commences the property warranted neutral be really owned by neutrals, it will be no breach of warranty if these parties become belligerents by the subsequent breaking out of hostilities between the state of which they are subjects and another state".[69] Another implied warranty, which is more important, is warranty of seaworthiness. In general, this implied warranty requires that in a voyage policy, the ship shall be seaworthy for the purpose of the particular adventure that was insured at the commencement of the voyage.[70] In a voyage that consists of different stages, the ship needs to be seaworthy at the commencement of every stage for the purpose of this particular stage. In a time policy, there is no such implied warranty at any stage of the adventure. However, the insurer is not liable for any loss related to unseaworthiness if a ship is sent to sea in an unseaworthy state with the privity of the assured.[71]

Like other implied warranties in marine insurance, warranty of seaworthiness also originated from the early nineteenth century authorities. It is clear that this warranty is a condition precedent to the policy attaching and it requires strict compliance by the assured;[72] even if the loss cannot be traced back to the breach of this warranty, the insurer is not liable and the breach cannot be remedied. These

---

68 Marine Insurance Act 1906, s 36.
69 *Arnould's Law of Marine Insurance and Average* (18th edn), ch 19 at 19–30.
70 Even while the ship is in port, Marine Insurance Act 1906, s 39(2).
71 Marine Insurance Act 1906, s 39.
72 For example, in *Wedderburn v Bell* (1807) 1 Camp 1.

fundamental principles are found in *Dixon v Sadler*[73] and *Quebec Marine Insurance Co v Commercial Bank of Canada*.[74]

The basic rules of implied warranty of seaworthiness were fully set out in the *Dixon* case. The substantial question of *Dixon v Sadler* is: In a time policy, does the throwing of the ballast overboard by the master and crew, whereby the ship became unseaworthy, excuse the underwriter?

In its first judgment, which was later confirmed, the judge stated: "In the case of an insurance for a certain voyage, it is clearly established that there is an implied warranty that the vessel shall be seaworthy, by which it is meant that she shall be in a fit state . . . to encounter the ordinary perils of the voyage insured, at the time of sailing upon it. If the assurance attaches before the voyage commences, it is enough that the state of the ship be commensurate to the then risk; and . . . it would be enough if the vessel were, at the commencement of each stage of the navigation, properly manned and equipped for it. But the assured makes no warranty to the underwriters that the vessel shall continue seaworthy, or that the master or crew shall do their duty during the voyage; and their negligence or misconduct is no defence to an action on the policy, where the loss has been immediately occasioned by the perils insured against".[75]

In the second judgment of this case, the Court of Exchequer also confirmed that such a warranty is not a continuing one: "we think, upon the later authorities, the rule is established, that there is no implied warranty on the part of the assured for the continuance of the seaworthiness of the vessel, or for the performance of their duty by the master and crew during the whole course of the voyage".[76] Therefore, due to this judgment, it is clear that there is no breach of this warranty in a time policy insurance, even though during the voyage, the crews' conduct rendered the vessel unseaworthy.

Another typical case that can reflect the nature of such warranty is the *Quebec Marine Insurance Co v Commercial Bank of Canada*.[77] This case on the other hand related to voyage policy. In this case, at the commencement of this voyage, a defect in the vessel's boiler was found that was not apparent in the rivers. However, when she got into the sea, the vessel disabled due to a defect and was compelled into port to repair. After being repaired and detained for days, she proceeded to sea, but was lost because of bad weather.

The court concluded that first, that in a voyage policy there is, by implication of law, a warranty of seaworthiness, which had not been complied with, as the vessel sailed with a defect of such a nature that, so long as it remained unremedied, it made her unseaworthy for the voyage, or stage of the voyage, she entered upon, and that although the defect was afterwards repaired, though before loss, it avoided the policy.

---

73 *Dixon v Sadler* 151 E.R. 172.
74 *Quebec Marine Insurance Co v Commercial Bank of Canada* (1870), L.R.3 P.C.
75 *Dixon v Sadler* 151 E.R. 172 at 414.
76 Ibid at 899.
77 Ibid, fn 74.

Second, the enumeration of excepted losses contained in the policy from "loss from unseaworthiness did not exclude the implied warranty of seaworthiness, as it did not expressly specify an intention to exclude it. There may be different stages of seaworthiness in cases where different stages of navigation involve the necessity of different equipment or states of seaworthiness; but the vessel must be properly equipped, and in all respects seaworthy for each of the stages at the time when she enters upon each stage, otherwise the warranty of seaworthiness is not complied with.

Unlike express warranty, there are no similar rules to identify warranties and construction of warranties. However, there are rules in this particular implied warranty that relate to the conduct of the assureds and that amount to breach of seaworthiness. Section 39 indicates that there is no universal standard for seaworthiness. A vessel only needs to be seaworthy for its particular voyage. In *Steel v State Line Steamship Co*, when the court was dealing with whether the loss of wheat was caused by the unseaworthiness of the ship, Lord Cairns stated that: "the ship should be in a condition to encounter whatever perils of the sea a ship of that kind, and laden in that way . . .".[78] His Lordship further concluded that: "in a contract of this kind there is implied an engagement that the ship shall be reasonably fit for performing the service which she undertakes".[79]

In *Daniels v Harris*, when addressing whether the on-deck cargo rendered the insured voyage unseaworthy, Brett J held that: "The required condition of the ship has been held to be different when the ship was to enter under policy in port from what it must be when going to sea under the same policy".[80] Therefore, in the case of a policy of insurance on deck cargo, it is not a compliance with the warranty of seaworthiness that the ship is fit to encounter ordinary rough weather safely because the deck cargo may be readily jettisoned in such weather. Thus, from these two cases, it is clear that seaworthiness is a relative concept. When dealing with whether a vessel is seaworthy or not, the nature of the ship and the nature of the voyage that is insured must be considered.[81]

A vessel can be rendered as unseaworthy by various factors, such as insufficient crew on board[82] or if the ship is unfit for ocean navigation.[83] These factors can be summarised into two groups. The first group relates to the condition of the ship. The second group relates to the condition of the goods,[84] and was considered in *Daniels v Harris*. Regarding the first group, the Marine Insurance Act 1906 requires that: "a ship is deemed to be seaworthy when she is reasonably fit in all respects to encounter the ordinary perils of the seas of the adventure insured".[85] Therefore, as

---

78 *Steel v State Line Steamship Co* (1877) 3 App. Cas. 72 at 77.
79 Ibid.
80 *Daniels v Harris* (1874–75) L.R. 10 C.P. 1.
81 This principle was further applied in *Garnat Trading & Shipping (Singapore) Pte Ltd v Boaminh Insurance Corp* [2011] 1 Lloyd's Rep IR 366.
82 As in *De Hahn v Hartley* (1786) 1 Term Rep 343.
83 *Burges v Wickham* 122 E.R. 251.
84 Namely, the ship shall be fit for the carriage of the particular cargo. For example, in *Sleigh v Tyser* [1900] 2 Q.B. 333, where there was no sufficient cattle-men on board the vessel which carried cattle, it was rendered unseaworthy.
85 Marine Insurance Act 1906, s 39(4).

concluded by Arnould, for seaworthiness, a "ship should be well furnished, tight, sound, staunch, and strong; competent, that is, in her hull to resist the ordinary attacks of wind and weather on the voyage insured, and properly rigged, stored and provisioned for such voyage".[86] In addition, there should be sufficient and competent crew on board.

1.6 The effect of breach of warranty: The law before 12 August 2016

The Insurance Act 2015 will come into force on 12 August 2016 since the consequences of breach of warranty have been dramatically reformed; the new law is discussed in detail in Chapter 7, whereas in this section the old doctrines are briefly introduced. What amounts to a breach of warranty is discussed above. In general, a warranty, whether express or implied, must be strictly complied with, although such strict compliance may be subject to limited exceptions.[87] Section 33(3) of the Marine Insurance Act 1906 clearly states the consequences of breach of warranty. The simple reason for such consequences is that the fulfilment of warranty is a condition precedent. Therefore, as stated above, the insurer is automatically discharged from liability from the date of breach. However, this discharge does not have the effect of voiding the contract *ab initio*. Nor does it have the effect of bringing the contract to an end.[88] Therefore, it is clear that breach of warranty will not prejudice claims that incurred before the breach.[89] Although the consequence of breaching warranty is severe, such consequence is still subject to express provision in the policy.[90] One typical example is found in International Hull Clauses 2003. Clause 13.2.1 states, "if the vessel is at sea at such date, such automatic termination shall be deferred until arrival at her next port".[91] Therefore, a breach of warranty will not leave the vessel without cover on the sea.

Another important express provision is the held cover clause. A held cover clause can enable the assured to remain under cover as soon as the assured discovers the breach of warranty, and it requires the insurer to hold the assured covered. It is not necessary for marine insurance policies to use the words "held cover". Any clauses that are designed to have the same effect can be held cover clauses, such as clause 10.1 of the Institute Cargo Clauses 2009. Therefore, for an assured to enjoy the held cover clause and mitigate the harsh consequence for breaching a warranty, a notice of breach of warranty must be given as soon as a breach is discovered. In addition, there is no need to express this requirement in the policy. In the House of Lords case, *Thames and Mersey Marine Insurance Company, Limited v*

---

86 *Arnould's Law of Marine Insurance and Average* (18th edn), ch 20 at 20–21.
87 Please see Marine Insurance Act 1906, s 34(1). Strictly speaking, there are no excuses for non-compliance with a warranty, unless there is no breach of warranty by construing the contract. However, there is a debate over this issue and limited exceptions are found in *Insurance Contract Law*, ch 20 at 20–6B. Special exceptions for warranty of legality are introduced in the next chapter. Please also see *Arnould on Marine Insurance and General Average* (18th edn) at 19–16.
88 Please see *Bank of Nova Scotia v Hellenic Mutual War Risks Association (Bermuda) Ltd ("The Good Luck")* [1992] 1 A.C. 233 at 262–263.
89 *Arnould on Marine Insurance and General Average* (18th edn) at 19–12.
90 Marine Insurance Act 1906, s 33(3).
91 International Hull Clauses 2003, cl 10.1.

H.T.Van Laun & Co, when Lord Halsbury L.C. examined the function of the held cover clause in the policy, he stated: "as I do, to imply an obligation, in order to obtain the advantage which it confers upon the assured, that the assured should communicate as to the arranging of the premium within a reasonable time after obtaining advices . . .".[92]

Therefore, giving notice to the insurer within a reasonable time can be seen as an implied obligation of the assured. However, the scope of reasonable time is unclear. Similar to construction of warranty, how to define a reasonable time is still subject to the consideration of the circumstances of each case. Therefore, in cases where giving notice immediately is essential to the contract, a slight delay will render the assured uncovered.[93] The word "immediately" in this case was construed "as meaning with all reasonable speed considering the circumstances of the case".[94]

According to different express provisions of insurance policies, the time of giving notice can be dramatically different. For example, in cases where the parties agreed that it shall be held and covered at a premium to be arranged "provided due notice be given by the assured on receipt of advice of such deviation", if the assured is not advised of the deviation until after the loss of the vessel then a notice that is given by him after the loss will be sufficient to satisfy the proviso.[95] However, in the absence of such an express term, a notice of facts that may amount to a breach of warranty must be given immediately, as long as the assured is aware of such facts, rather than after the breach.

It is clear that a held cover clause is not a new policy; it still affects the same policy. Therefore, in cases where a breach of warranty changes the nature of the risk, which results in the consequence that the risk cannot be covered in the market at a reasonable commercial rate, then the held cover clause will cease to be applied. Therefore, in *Liberian Insurance Agency Inc v Mosse*, after the loss when it was found by the court that the subsistence of the goods insured were under a condition such that no underwriter would offer a reasonable commercial rate of premium on it, the assured failed to rely on the held cover clause.[96] The final point is that the burden of proving a breach of warranty is on the underwriter.

1.7 Waiver of warranty

Section 34(3) of the Marine Insurance Act 1906 expressly states: "A breach of warranty may be waived by the insurer". The waiver rule in maritime law is settled. The most conclusive case on this issue is *Motor Oil Hellas (Corinth) Refineries SA v Shipping Corporation of India ("The Kanchenjunga")*. The first dispute issue of this case was whether the owners had waived their right not to comply with the charterer's orders to proceed to Kharg Island. Lord Goff held that there are two types

---

92 *Thames and Mersey Marine Insurance Company, Limited v H.T. Van Laun & Co* [1917] 2 K.B. 48 at 51.
93 *Re An Arbitration between Coleman's Depositories, Limited and the Life and Health Assurance Association* [1907] 2 K.B. 798.
94 Ibid at 806.
95 *Mentz, Decker & Co v Maritime Insurance Company* [1910] 1 K.B. 132.
96 *Liberian Insurance Agency Inc v Mosse* [1977] 2 Lloyd's Rep. 560.

of waiver: the first one is by election, which means "the contract gives the other party the right to elect to treat the imperfect performance as if it were a fulfilment of the contract (even if he knows that in fact it is not), and to claim damages if any result from the imperfection".[97] The second type is by estoppel, which "occurs where a person, having legal rights against another, unequivocally represents (by words or conduct) that he does not intend to enforce those legal rights; if in such circumstances the other party acts, or desists from acting, in reliance upon that representation, with the effect that it would be inequitable for the representor thereafter to enforce his legal rights inconsistently with his representation, he will to that extent be precluded from doing so".[98]

In the context of breaching warranty, there is no possibility of waiver by election since the insurer's liability is discharged automatically and no positive action is needed by the insurer. Therefore, other than an express waiver clause in the insurance policy, the only implied waiver category is by estoppel. The similarity between these two types of waivers is clear; each of them requires an unequivocal representation. However, the differences between them are more important. The differences, as concluded by Lord Goff, can be summarised as follows: first, in the context of a contract, the principle of election applies when a state of affairs comes into existence, where one party becomes entitled to exercise a right, and has to choose whether to exercise that right or not. His election must be an informed choice that is made with knowledge about the facts giving rise to the right. His election once made is final; it is not dependent on reliance by the other party. On the other hand, equitable estoppel requires an unequivocal representation by one party that he or she will not insist upon his legal rights against the other party, and such reliance by the representee will render it inequitable for the representor to revoke his representation. Second, the character of representation in these two cases can be different. The insurer who is making his election is communicating his or her choice of whether to exercise a right that has become available. The insurer, to an equitable estoppel, is representing that he or she will not enforce his or her legal rights in the future. The insurer's representation is therefore in the form of a promise, which though unsupported by consideration, can have legal consequences.[99]

English law has established certain requirements in order to constitute a waiver by estoppel. First, there must be an unequivocal representation on the part of the underwriters, by words or by conduct, that they will not enforce their strict legal rights with respect to the breach. Second, it must be shown that the assured has acted or desisted from acting in reliance upon that representation. Third, the court must be satisfied that given the circumstances, it would be inequitable to allow the underwriters to revoke their representation and treat the breach of warranty as discharging their liability.

---

97 *The Stork* [1954] 2 Lloyd's Rep. 397.
98 *Motor Oil Hellas (Corinth) Refineries SA v Shipping Corporation of India ("The Kanchenjunga")* [1990] 1 Lloyd's Rep 391.
99 *Motor Oil Hellas (Corinth) Refineries SA v Shipping Corporation of India ("The Kanchenjunga")* [1990] 1 Lloyd's Rep 391 at 399.

The underwriter's knowledge is not important; the conduct of the underwriter is more crucial. Thus, the underwriter's knowledge of the unseaworthiness of the ship cannot constitute a waiver unless he or she insured the ship with such knowledge.[100] Pure silence by the insurer is clearly not enough.[101] The parties have the freedom to waive breach of warranty by express provisions. However, such express waive is unusual in current marine insurance practice.[102]

---

100 *Weir v Aberdeen* (1819) 2 B & Ald 320.
101 *Arnould on Marine Insurance and General Average* (18th edn) at 19–40.
102 Ibid at 19–41.

CHAPTER 2

Illegal performance of marine insurance contracts

2.1 Introduction to the warranty of legality in marine insurance law

Warranty is unanimously recognised as a complex and difficult area in marine insurance law. There are basically two types of warranties under current marine insurance law, namely, express warranties and implied warranties. The implied warranty only exists in marine insurance.[1] Several species of implied warranty have been discussed and introduced into the market, such as warranty of seaworthiness,[2] no implied warranty of nationality[3] and warranty of legality. The main purpose of this chapter is to introduce and discuss the development and the true scope of the warranty of legality.

The main origin of this warranty was based on early judgments during the eighteenth and nineteenth centuries. The main purpose of introducing this principle was to balance the conflict between public and private interests. Another purpose of this principle in common law, as cited by Lord Mansfield, was that no court will lend its hand to the illegal party and no one can benefit from his own illegality.[4]

There are two sections in the Marine Insurance Act 1906 which relate to legality issues, s 41 and s 3(1). Section 41 states that:

> There is an implied warranty that the adventure insured is a lawful one, and that so far as the assured can control the matter, the adventure shall be carried out in a lawful manner.

Section 3(1) states that: "every lawful marine adventure may be the subject of a contract of marine insurance". The words of those sections are straightforward and can be summarised into two points: firstly, the warranty of legality can be divided into two sections: the legality of the adventure itself and the legality of the performance of that adventure, these two distinct sections are closely connected; secondly, a lawful adventure is the foundation of a marine insurance contract, and therefore without the lawful adventure a marine insurance contract will not exist.

The importance of the warranty of legality is incontestable, there are four points to support this argument: firstly, as can be concluded from former cases the legality

---

1 Rhidian Thomas, *The Modern Law of Marine Insurance* (vol 2), p 167.
2 For example, *Dixon v Sadler* (1841) 8 M & W 895.
3 For example, *Eden v Parkinson* (1781) 2 Doug KB 732.
4 As will be seen in the case *Holman v Johnson* (1775) 1 Cowp. 341.

of the adventure and performance is the foundation of the insurance contract;[5] secondly, since the legality issue is regulated as a warranty in marine insurance law, the insurance policy can be terminated by the insurer from the time of that breach and such consequence is clearly severe; thirdly, by examining the judgments of cases prior to s 41, this section seems unable to cover former case law and several factors may influence the consequence of illegality which happens under marine insurance: such factors and the assured's connection with it shall be considered;[6] fourthly, the implied warranty means that there is no need to express the requirement of legality of adventure in the marine insurance policy: by taking the severe consequence of the breach of warranty into account, it is important for the assured to be familiar with this warranty and strictly comply with it.

In this chapter, both legality of the adventure and the legality of the legal performance will be discussed, and since there are significant differences between these two kinds of warranties, this chapter will first introduce the origin and formation of these two sections separately, and then clarify the species and scope of this warranty; lastly, this chapter will discuss the insufficiency of section 41 based on former case law and common law and attempt to solve the question of whether section 41 truly reflects the former common law or not and attempt to explore the true scope of section 41.

2.2 Origin and formation of the warranty of legal adventure in marine insurance law

The origin of the warranty of legal adventure is still open to debate, as hardly any books or articles have clarified this ambiguity. In *Arnould's Law of Marine Insurance and Average*, the case *Redmond v Smith* seems to be considered as one of the possible sources of the marine insurance and illegality issue;[7] however, earlier cases related to illegality can be traced back to the late eighteenth century.

2.2.1 The origin of the warranty of legal adventure

As stated before, most illegality cases were decided in the eighteenth and nineteenth centuries, during the Napoleonic Wars. Although there were several cases which related to the legality adventure issue, none of them can be regarded as the sole origin of s 41. Therefore, the cases prior to the 1906 Act should be considered carefully.

The first case which relates to legality in marine insurance can be traced back to 1797, namely *Farmer v Legg*.[8] This case related to the slave trade: losses happened in consequence of an insurrection, which was the result of improper command and navigation. The principal question of this case was whether the ship had been navigated according to the 31 Geo.3; c.54, a statute which regulated

---

5 *Redmond v Smith* (1844) 7 M.&Gr. 474 "where is a voyage is illegal an insurance upon it is invalid".
6 As will be seen in Section 2.4 below.
7 *Arnould's Law of Marine Insurance and Average* (18th edn), para 21.03.
8 *Farmer v Legg* (1797) 7 TR 186.

the qualification of the master who participated in the slave trade; according to this statute the adventure was lawful only if the master fulfilled the requirements of the statute. By failing to provide a certificate which complied with the statute, the plaintiff was nonsuited, because by failing to do so the whole adventure was unlawful and the policy upon it was rendered void.

The case *Farmer v Legg* was one of the earliest cases which related to the illegality of adventure. Another case which can be treated as a combined origin of this piece of legislation is *Law v Hollingsworth*,[9] which was codified three months earlier than *Farmer v Legg*. In *Law v Hollingsworth*, the plaintiff failed to recover the loss of the vessel because there was no qualified pilot on board when the loss happened; this was prohibited by the statute of that time, even though there was no connection between the violation and the loss. Although the judgment of this case mainly concentrated on whether there was a pilot on board, no words such as "warranty" or "legality" were mentioned, and it can easily be concluded that the absence of such pilot was a violation of the law, and the legality of the adventure was essential to the validity of the insurance policy. One of the grounds for discharging the responsibility of the underwriter, raised at the trial, was: "it being an implied condition in every policy that the ship shall be navigated according to the law."[10] This was the first time that the legality issue was clearly raised in marine insurance cases. Although the judgment used the word "condition", the consequence of the breach of that "condition" was almost the same as a breach of warranty under current marine insurance law.

Other cases mainly happened in the early nineteenth century during the period of war with France. There were several restrictions on navigation during that period, therefore the policies relating to vessels which sailed in contravention of convoy Acts were held void[11] as well as voyages which were against the provisions of the East India Company Acts, or the South Sea Company Acts,[12] or the general Navigation Act; and in the judgments of these cases the word "illegal" was commonly used because of violation of these laws. The consequences and punishments on illegal voyages were severe; in most cases the assured could not recover the losses and in some particular cases they even could not recover the premium.[13]

The phrase "implied warranty" was first raised in *Sadler v Dixon*, a case that dealt with the loss of a vessel. In the judgment of that case, Tindal CJ cited *Law v Hollingsworth* and stated that the requirement of statute 5 Geo. 2 "was an implied contract on the part of the assured"[14] and: "The decision of that case may be maintainable, on the ground of an implied warranty to observe the positive requisitions of an act of Parliament".[15] Therefore, in this case, in the absence of the express requirement of legality, the legality issue was rendered as an implied one in contract. However, these cases only stated that an illegal adventure could taint the insurance policy,

---

9 *Law v Hollingsworth* (1797) 7 TR 160.
10 Ibid.
11 *Hinckley v Walton* (1810) 3 Taunt 131.
12 *Wainhouse v Cowie*, 4 Taunt 178.
13 Such as in *Vandyck v Hewitt* (1800) 1 East 96.
14 *Sadler v Dixon* (1841) 8 M & W 895.
15 Ibid.

but the reason behind it was never clearly explained; furthermore, there were no clear general rules on illegality issues, until the judgment of *Redmond v Smith*. In this case, the defendant insurer issued a policy on a ship which covered any loss and misfortune which should be lawful to the assured. The ship foundered and sank on its voyage to London. By refusing to pay the losses, one of the defendant's pleas to the court was that the failure of the payment of seamen's wages on the said voyage was contrary to 5 & 6 W. 4, c. 19 and rendered the voyage wholly illegal. By analysing former cases, Tindal CJ considered the defendant's argument and stated in his judgment that "A policy on an illegal voyage cannot be enforced; for it would be singular, if, the original contract being invalid and therefore incapable to be enforced, a collateral contract founded upon it could be enforced. It may be laid down, therefore, as a general rule, that, where a voyage is illegal, insurance upon such voyage is invalid."[16] This statement not only explained the reason why the adventure must be lawful but also explained the consequence of an insurance which was based upon an illegal adventure, i.e. no valid contract of insurance was ever created.

This is the first authority which clearly expounded the legal basis of the legality issue; however, the judgment of this case was based on several former cases. Thus both the terms "implied warranty" and "lawful" can be supported by former cases.

Consequently, judgments of these series of cases were codified in the 1906 Act, and the requisition of lawful adventure was regulated as one of the implied warranties.

2.2.2 Explanation of the word "lawful"

According to the first part of s 41, the adventure insured must be a lawful one. However, there is no clear definition of the word "lawful". Besides the clarification of the word lawful, the definition of which kinds of conduct can be regarded as a breach of the lawful adventure warranty is also an ambiguous issue which needs to be resolved. In addition, the statute has omitted to mention the formation of such illegality and some special situations.

An adventure can be rendered illegal as a result of breach of statute, breach of the King's or Council's order or breach of public policy and common law. Some books calculate the EU legislation or international instruments as one of the species which can be covered by the word lawful; however, this point is still uncertain under current circumstances: firstly, according to former judgments, the adventure must be illegal under English law and the mere illegality under foreign law is not necessary to render the whole adventure void; secondly, for EU legislation and international instruments to be effective in the UK, the legislation must be incorporated into domestic law. Therefore, in order to render an adventure illegal under EU law, the former two points must be fulfilled.[17]

---

16 *Redmond v Smith* (1844) 7 M & G 474.
17 This argument has been supported by the most recent case, *Sea Glory Maritime Co, Swedish Management Co SA v AL Sagr National Insurance Co* [2013] EWHC 2116 (Comm) at para 291.

(a) Illegal adventure by statute

A marine adventure can be rendered illegal by statute, and this is the most straightforward and common method to decide whether an adventure is legal or not.

In the early cases prior to the 1906 Act, numerous marine insurance policies were rendered illegal because of violation of statutes. In the case *Farmer v Legg*, the adventure was rendered illegal because the ship had not been navigated according to the 7th section of 31 Geo.3, c.54. In the case *Law v Hollingsworth* the adventure was rendered unlawful because the pilot on board was not properly qualified according to the provisions of 5 Geo.2, c.20.

However, there are various circumstances which need to be emphasised: firstly, the words in statutes may not always be straightforward or without doubt, therefore the intention of the statutes needs to be examined in such cases. This principle was firstly cited in the case *Farmer v Legg*, and in that case the fundamental issue was to find out what exactly the Act required the assured to perform during the slave transportation. Therefore in the judgment, Ashhurst J stated that: "In a case where the words of an Act of Parliament are doubtful, we must see what were the mischiefs against which the Legislature meant to guard, and endeavour to find out the most probable means of effecting that purpose".[18] Another approach to understanding the intention of the statute is to examine the aim of the policy of the statute, namely "whether the intention of parliament was to ban such contracts or merely to impose fines upon those transgressing its terms".[19]

Secondly, not every violation of statute may render the policy void. This is the case when the requirements of statutes can never be complied with under some special circumstances. In the case *Suart v Powell* the supply of seamen on a vessel was completely impossible so as to comply with the proportion of English seamen required by the Navigation Acts. The court rendered this voyage legal because of the unavoidable circumstances the vessel encountered. However, the courts still need plenty of evidence to prove such unavoidable circumstances, which will be discussed later.

(b) Illegal adventures by King's or Council's order

A policy can be rendered illegal by King's or Council's order; this kind of illegality is unique in the late eighteenth and nineteenth centuries during the Napoleonic wars. The most significant case was *Parkin v Dick*;[20] this was a case which related to the prohibition of exportation. According to His Majesty by proclamation or order in Council which originated from the stat.33 Geo.3, c.2, the exportation of naval stores was prohibited and therefore the whole contract was rendered illegal and void. Two points need to be noticed: firstly, this kind of illegality mainly happened in earlier cases and rarely happens under current circumstances. Secondly, the King's or Council's order also originates from statute. Therefore, this kind of violation can be seen as a derivate of the statutory illegality.

---

18 *Farmer v Legg* (1797) 7 TR 186.
19 Soyer, *Warranties in Marine Insurance* (2nd edn).
20 *Parkin v Dick* (1809) 2 Camp 221.

(c) Illegal adventures because of violation of public policy and common law

An insurance policy can be rendered illegal because of violation of public policy. There are various kinds of public policy principles under common law, such as the assured cannot rely on his own illegality to get compensation and the assured cannot profit from his own illegality. However, in early marine insurance cases, adventure which was rendered illegal by public policy was rare. This section of the book will only consider the public policies which relate to lawful adventure.

There is no clear definition of public policy, neither in marine insurance law nor in contract law. Cases which can be classified into this category are illegal activities not covered by clear statutory regulations; trading with the enemy was a case which fell within this scope. For instance, in the case *Vandyck v Hewitt*,[21] the insurance policy was rendered illegal based on the decisions of two former cases, therefore, even though there was no statute which forbade trading with the enemy at that time, the former judgments were viewed as public policy in this case and were therefore the foundation of the judgment. Furthermore, when there is an absence of statute, public policy was used as an ancillary instrument by courts. In the case *Kensington v Inglis*[22] when the court decided whether the insurance was illegal or not, one of the elements which the court took into account was whether this insurance contravened the public policy of this country.

However, public policy was not limited by former judgments; judges could create new public policy according to the facts of different cases, thus in the case *Pieschell v Allnutt Same v Lavie*[23] it was decided that not every communication with the enemy could render the insurance void, which was a supplement to former judgments.

The positive effect of the application of public policy when deciding cases of illegality is obvious: statutes are unable to list every kind of illegality, therefore the applications of public policy increases flexibility. However, on the other hand, public policy is a very unstable foundation of judgments, just like Burrough J said "against arguing too strongly upon public policy; it is a very unruly horse, and when once you get astride it you never know where it will carry you".[24]

2.2.3 Formation of illegal adventure

The objective of this section is to explore the different stages of unlawful adventure under marine insurance law. Illegal conduct which happens in different stages may lead to different results, even though this rarely happened in early cases.

There are basically two forms of illegal adventure: firstly, the adventure or voyage insured is itself expressly prohibited by law; secondly, the voyage itself is lawful, however the adventure is tainted by performance before its commencement.

So far as the first type of illegal adventure is concerned, where the adventure itself is illegal, it is undoubtedly true that some kinds of voyages were expressly

---

21 *Vandyck v Hewitt* (1800) 1 East 96.
22 *Kensington v Inglis* (1807) 8 East 273.
23 *Pieschell v Allnutt* (1813) 4 Taunton 792.
24 *Richardson v Mellish* (1824) 2 Bing 229 at 252.

prohibited by law. Therefore a voyage to an enemy port during wartime was rendered illegal and the insurance upon it was void;[25] a voyage which transported English manufacture to any port to the Eastward of the Cape was rendered illegal by statute as well.[26] Furthermore, a voyage without sufficient proportion of English seaman on board was rendered illegal as well, unless it was impossible for the assured to provide enough seamen.[27]

So far as the second type of illegal adventure is considered, according to early cases, there were basically three kinds of performance which may render an adventure illegal before its initiation.

Firstly, sail without licence or convoy which needed to be acquired before the commencement of voyage. In the early nineteenth century, several statutes required ships to sail with convoy or licence and the absence of this would render it illegal. There were various kinds of licences such as the licence to sail without convoy and the licence to trade with the South Sea Company or with an enemy. Both the licence or convoy need to be granted or arranged before the commencement of a voyage, as stated in the judgment of *Wainhouse v Cowie*: "the first answer is, every person shipping goods must know and see that a sufficient licence is given";[28] this phrase clearly indicated that a licence needs to be granted before a voyage. In the case *Wainhouse v Cowie* a licence which was granted for a previous voyage would not render the next voyage legal, and a licence for a specific voyage was unable to legalise a voyage to a different destination, as in this case: a licence to Gibraltar did not legalise a voyage to Malta.[29] This was the same in convoy cases; in the case *Cohen v Hinckley*[30] it was decided that "a ship cannot legally sail from port to port without convoy". Therefore the voyage in that case which was from Portsmouth to Falmouth without a convoy was rendered illegal as well.

Secondly, the loading operation before a voyage can render a lawful voyage illegal. In the case *Cunard v Hyde*[31] the adventure was rendered illegal before its initiation because the master did not load the timber below the deck and sailed without certificate which was requested by statute. Therefore, even though a voyage from North America to the UK was not prohibited by law, the loading operation before the voyage tainted it. This case was frequently compared with the case *Wilson v Rankin*; this was also a case which related to the illegal stowage of goods. The main difference between the two cases is that, in the *Cunard* case the illegality happened before the commencement of the voyage, but in the *Wilson* case the illegality happened during the voyage, and this minor distinction resulted in two different judgments. In the latter case, the illegal performance which was carried out by the master did not affect the assured's right to claim for compensation under the insurance policy; however, in the *Cunard* case, the whole adventure was rendered

---

25 *Hagedorn v Bazett* (1813) 2 M & S 100.
26 *Gray v Lloyd* (1811) 4 Taunt 136.
27 *Suart v Powell* (1830) 1 B& A 266.
28 *Wainhouse v Cowie* (1811) 4 Taunt 178.
29 *Wainhouse v Cowie* (1811) 4 Taunt 178.
30 *Cohen v Hinckley* (1809) 2 Camp 51.
31 *Cunard v Hyde* (1858) EB & E 670.

illegal and the assured could not claim compensation under it. Thus, this is also one of the reasons why illegal performance before initiation of adventure and illegal performance during adventure should be considered separately.

Thirdly, if there is no sufficient or competent crew on board before the commencement of a voyage, the voyage can be rendered illegal as well. In the case *Clifford v Hunter*,[32] the captain who was very ill before sailing rendered the whole voyage illegal, because he was incompetent to take charge of the vessel which resulted in the losses.

Besides the three scenarios which have been introduced, there are numerous kinds of performance before the commencement of an adventure; nevertheless, the former three cases can demonstrate the existence of the second kind of formation of illegal adventure.

There may be confusion between the second formation of illegal adventure and the illegal performance of the 1906 Act. However, there are two differences between them.

First of all, even though both kinds of illegality include the performance of the assured, the second form of illegal adventure mainly happens before the commencement of the adventure; however, the second part of section 41 regulates unlawful activities after the initiation of the adventure.

Secondly, the requirement on the performance of the assured is different, which leads to different results after violation. In the second part of section 41, it requires that "so far as the assured can control the matter, the adventure shall be carried out in a lawful manner". However, there is no such defence for the assured before the commencement of the adventure. Thus, if the assured performs illegally before the commencement of an adventure, the whole policy upon it is rendered void; however, if the illegal performance happens during the adventure, there are various kinds of defences for the assured.

The proposal to divide the lawful adventure into two kinds of formation is to enable the courts and contractual parties to consider the legality of adventure in a more specific way, and may provide the possibility to provide more defences for the assured to avoid the automatic discharge rule in warranty. However, based on former authorities, the second formation of unlawful adventure means that the adventure can only be performed in an illegal way, or the contractual parties intend to perform such adventure illegally; therefore, unless there are some particular circumstances, the second formation of unlawful adventure always renders the whole policy void.

2.3 Origin and scope of the warranty of legal performance in marine insurance law

This section will discuss the origin and scope of the second kind of illegality, the illegality of performance. The origin of such illegality is open to doubt as well. There are no clear authorities on this issue. However, the origin and scope of the illegal performance may share some identical characteristics with illegal adventure.

---

32 *Clifford v Hunter* (1827) M & M 103.

2.3.1 Origin of the warranty of legal performance in marine insurance law

The origin of the second part of section 41 almost developed at the same time as the warranty of legal adventure. The origin of this piece of legislation can also be traced back to the late eighteenth century.

The case which may be seen as the origin of this legislation is *Planche v Fletcher* in which the issue of the legality of the performance of the assured was first raised by the court. In this case, the defendant argued that by exporting enemy property during the time of war the whole adventure was rendered illegal because of the performance of the assured, and the insurance upon it was void. However, by considering the facts of the case, Lord Mansfield overruled the defendant's argument based on two points; the first was that: "What had been practised in this case was proved to be the constant course of the trade, and notoriously so to everybody".[33] The second is that every man in England and France expected the commencement of a war and the underwriter was aware of that, therefore, the assured was not bound to give the insurer notice of this and since the insurer was aware of the risk and insured such risk, he was liable in case of capture. This can be seen as the first case in marine insurance law in which the legality of performance issue was first considered by a court. In this case, even though there was no fact proved, the phrase "so far as the assured can control the matter" indicated that the adventure should be carried out in a lawful manner. In the cases *Farmer v Legg* and *Law v Hollingsworth* it can also be seen that the court required the adventure to be carried out in a lawful manner as well, otherwise the adventure would be rendered illegal. Former cases mainly concentrated on or related to trade with the enemy during war time. Therefore if an adventure was carried out to trade with an enemy or to profit the enemy, such conduct could render the voyage illegal, regardless of whether such adventure was carried out prior to the commencement of hostilities or not.[34] If the assured carried out the adventure not in strict compliance with the King's licence, the adventure was rendered illegal as well.[35]

However, not every illegal performance which happens during the course of the voyage can render the adventure illegal, which is the origin of the phrase "so far as the assured can control the matter". The first case which relates to this issue is *Moss v Byrom*.[36] In this case, a loss happened because of the illegal capture of an American ship. The underwriter in this case argued that because an illegal letter of marque was taken on board and because of the illegal capture of a vessel, the policy was put to an end and the underwriter should not be liable for any losses. However, by denying such argument, the court cited that the action of the master was a barratry and even though the capture was partly for the owner's benefit the underwriter was still liable for damage in consequence of that conduct, since the act was no longer under the control of the assured.

These early cases which relate to this piece of legislation only developed the basic rule of legal performance. Most of the cases in the early development of

---

33 *Planche v Fletcher* (1779) 1 Doug 251.
34 *Furtado v Rogers* (1802) 3 B & P 191.
35 *Vandyck v Whitmore* (1801) 1 East 475.
36 *Moss v Byrom* 101 E.R. 605.

this section were similar. The fundamental principle which the courts follow was the same as the principle in legal adventure, which is that the insurance contract based upon an illegal adventure is void.[37]

In the later development of legal performance in marine insurance law, several exceptions had been cited by common law and more factors had been taken into consideration when deciding such cases which will be discussed later.

It can be seen that the foundation of the origin of this piece of law is the same as the origin of lawful adventure; however, the main difference is that, in the warranty of lawful performance, the adventure which is insured is lawful and can be performed legally, but the assured chose an illegal method to perform it.

2.3.2 Species and formation of illegal performance

The aim of this part is to examine the scope and species of illegal performance in marine insurance law which is based on cases prior to section 41. It will first illustrate different kinds of illegal performance in former cases and then clarify and analyse several ambiguities and exceptions in case law, such as the phrase "so far as".

So far as the first issue is concerned, it is similar to illegal adventure, a lawful adventure can be performed illegally because of violation of statute, King's or Council's order, treaty between nations and public policy.

(a) Violation of statute

An adventure which is lawful in its inception can become illegal because the performance of the assured is a violation of statute. This is the most common kind of illegality; an adventure may be rendered illegal because of violation statute either by the assured himself or his agent.

An example of an adventure rendered illegal because of violation of statute is the case *Vandyck v Whitmore*.[38] In this case a voyage was rendered illegal because of the lack of a valid licence, which was regulated by the stat. 34 Geo. 3, c. 9 as the legal method of performance. However, one difference between the violation of statute in illegal adventure and illegal performance is that, in the illegal adventure scenario, if the adventure is clearly prohibited by statute then the insurance is void, nevertheless in illegal performance scenarios, the factors which may influence the performance of the assured will be considered, as will be introduced later.

(b) Violation of King's or Council's order and licence

This kind of illegality is common in cases which relate to trade with an enemy or trade with the subjects of an enemy. Therefore any trade with an enemy is rendered illegal if such licence has not been obtained or no valid licence has been granted; in the case *Potts v Bell*, it was cited that according to the principle of common law, trading with an enemy without King's licence was illegal in British subjects.[39] The trading with enemy case in this illegality category is similar to the

---

37 *Furtado v Rogers* (1802) 3 B & P 200.
38 *Vandyck v Whitmore* (1801) 1 East 475.
39 *Potts v Bell* (1800) 8 TR 548.

illegality of unlawful adventure. In fact, this kind of illegality is a combination of illegal adventure and illegal performance because the statute which the assured violated was the legal method with which to perform such adventure. Thus, the adventure is only legal by trading with King's licence and without such licence or without a valid licence the whole adventure is rendered illegal. In the case *Vandyck v Whitmore*[40] the adventure was rendered illegal because the King's licence granted was for a limited time and any trade beyond this period was illegal. However, a valid King's licence or Council's Order is not enough to legalise such adventure; the assured also need to ensure the spirit of this document. Therefore, in the case *Atkinson v Abbott*,[41] the adventure was not rendered illegal because the judge found that the assured was "without any purpose of defeating the Order of Council or trading with an enemy". Otherwise, even if such document has been granted, if the assured intended to violate the law the adventure would be rendered illegal as well.

(c) Violation of treaties between nations

This kind of violation was not very common in early judgments. The first reason was that commercial treaties between nations were not very common during that period and secondly, as cited in the case *Planche v Fletcher* "one nation does not take notice of the revenue law of another".[42] Therefore it appears that if the UK is not one party of a treaty and the content of the treaty has not been enacted into UK law, then a court will not follow such treaty and render an adventure illegal accordingly, as in the case *Pollard v Bell*,[43] where the legality of an insurance policy was not falsified by the judgment of a foreign court. However, there are some exceptions: in the case *Bell v Carstairs*[44] an American assured could not recover their loss against the British underwriter because the ship was not properly documented according to the existing treaty between France and America and this was the efficient cause of the loss. Compared with the former two cases, the courts decided to follow the treaty and render the adventure illegal based on two points: firstly, the assured subject in this case was an American property, therefore, it should be regulated by the treaty of their state, whereas all the assureds in the two former cases were British; secondly, the document which was not on board was material to the adventure. Therefore, there was no reason why an English court could not use foreign treaties when dealing with a foreign assured's case. And this was also the case in *Baring v The Royal Exchange Assurance Company* where Le Blanc J cited that: "And if they expressly condemn a prize for a breach of treaty, that is binding on our Courts where the same question arises upon the propriety of that condemnation".[45] Thus violation of treaty was clearly one kind of illegal performance under English law.

---

40 *Vandyck v Whitmore* (1801) 1 East 475.
41 *Atkinson v Abbott* (1809) 11 East 135.
42 *Planche v Fletcher* (1779) 1 Doug 251.
43 *Pollard v Bell* (1800) 8 TR 434.
44 *Bell v Carstairs* (1811) 14 East 374.
45 *Baring v The Royal Exchange Assurance Company* (1804) 5 East 99.

(d) Violation of common law and public policy

Violation of common law was very common in the early judgments of illegal cases. This was the case because firstly, in the early period the performance of illegality in most cases was the same, such as trading with the enemy or sailing without documents; secondly, the statutes in the early period were incapable of covering many kinds of illegality. Therefore, there were several early cases which followed the judgments cited before. In the case *Potts v Bell* the judge rendered the adventure illegal because the authorities cited by the insurer "were so many, so uniform, and so conclusive, to show that a British subject's trading with an enemy were illegal".[46] This provided a reliable source for the English court to decide illegality cases.

So far as the violation of public policy is concerned, there is still no clear scope of how public policy relates to illegal performance. Just like the comment on violation of public policy in illegal adventure, public policy in illegal performance is a very unruly horse as well. As there is no clear definition of public policy in marine insurance law, the kinds of cases that can be contained in this category are vague. According to early cases, new public policy can be created by the courts. In the case *Raphael Brandon v Nesbitt*, after analysing former cases and statutes, the court rendered the adventure illegal on the ground that "an action will not lie either by or in favour of an alien enemy",[47] which originated from judgments of former cases and was cited as a new public policy by the court. Therefore a public policy may be a supplement to common law or a summary of common law.

2.3.3 Scope of "so far as the assured can control the matter"

The phrase "so far as the assured can control the matter" can be divided into two different parts: firstly, the difference of who commits the illegality can lead to different consequences and secondly, not every illegality which is committed by the assured can render the adventure illegal. Thus the scope of this phrase should be discussed from two aspects: firstly, illegality which involves the agent of the assured; secondly, illegality which is committed by the assured only. This section will consider the first scenario only, and the second scenario will be covered in the insufficiencies of section 41.

According to early judgments, when the courts dealt with the first scenario, several factors were taken into consideration, such as the connection between the losses and the assured, the relationship between the assured and his agent, and the intention and the knowledge of the assured and his agent.

The law clearly indicates that, if there is no connection between the conduct of the assured's agent which led to the loss and the assured, then such cases will not be regarded as violation of this warranty. In the case *Moss v Byrom*[48] the captain illegally took a prize during a voyage and violated the instructions of the assured, then even though the vessel was lost because of such illegality, the assured was

---

46 *Potts v Bell* (1800) 8 TR 561.
47 *Raphael Brandon v Nesbitt* (1794) 6 TR 23.
48 *Moss v Byrom* 101 E.R. 605.

entitled to recover against the insurer. This is also the case in *Metcalfe v Parry*; in this case it was decided that "to invalidate a policy on ship on the ground that she sailed without convoy, it is necessary to prove that this happened with the privity of the owner".[49] But this is not always the case according to former cases; in the case *Pipon v Cope*[50] even though the smuggling committed by the crew had no connection with the assured and the losses were not caused purely because of such illegality (the loss happened because of a collision in harbour), the assured was not entitled to compensation. This was because the assured failed to prevent the repeated acts of smuggling by the crew which increased the risk to the insurer and discharged the insurer's responsibility accordingly. Therefore, so far as the assured can control the matter, the assured has a duty to pay due diligence on the performance of the crew, otherwise even if there is no connection between the assured and the loss, the assured may not be entitled to claim for insurance.

The relationship between the assured and his agent is another factor which is significant when deciding upon the breach of this warranty. The agents of the assured may include the crew on the ship or the broker of the assured. In former cases if losses happen because of the barratry of the crew then in most circumstances the assured is entitled to claim such losses. In the case of *Heyman v Parish* Lord Ellenborough decided that if barratry was proved and no surprise upon the defendant then the assured could recover such loss.[51] The assured is also not liable for the negligence of his agent; for instance, in *Busk v The Royal Exchange Assurance Company*[52] once the assured had provided a sufficient crew on board, the negligence of the crew which caused the loss did not vitiate the assured's right to claim for loss. However, the mere act of barratry will not result in such consequence; only the barratry which commits an illegality will not prejudice the assured's right.[53] In contrast, if the illegality committed by the crew is in obedience to the orders of the assured, then such act may contribute to the violation of such warranty. In the case of *Hobbs v Hannam*[54] which dealt with smuggled goods on board, the court found that the smuggled goods were brought on board because of the orders of the agent of the assured and the master implicitly obeyed; in this case the order from the agent was considered as the order from the assured. Therefore, in this case even though the assured himself did not participate in the illegal performance, the illegality which was committed by his agent rendered the loss irrecoverable. Thus, so far as the assured can control the matter, the insurer is liable for the losses which are caused by barratry and not liable for the illegality which is caused because of the orders of the assured or his agent. However, it is clear that the *Hobbs* case was wrongfully decided, since it is unfair for the assured, if orders from any of his agents are considered as his orders; thus, in the case *Carstairs, Executors of Lyon v Allnutt* it was decided that "it is not enough to shew that the ship sailed without

---

49 *Metcalfe v Parry* (1814) 4 Camp 123.
50 *Pipon v Cope* (1780) 1 Camp 434.
51 *Heyman v Parish* (1809) 2 Cowp 149.
52 *Busk v The Royal Exchange Assurance Company* (1818) 2 B &Ald 73.
53 Compare *Cory and Sons v Burr* (1881–82) LR 8 QBD 313.
54 *Hobbs v Hannam* (1811) 3 Camp 93.

convoy by the instrumentality of an agent of the assured, unless it appear that the agent had authority from his principal for this purpose".[55]

Furthermore, if it turns out that the assured has no knowledge of the illegality then the assured should not be liable for the loss; this is another factor which is beyond the assured's control. Thus, in the case *Wilson v Rankin*[56] without the knowledge that the master carried the timber on deck, the assured still had the right to claim for loss. In the case *Oom v Bruce*[57] which dealt with insurance on enemy subjects, the agent of the assured still carried out the insurance even after the commencement of hostilities between Britain and Russia. Lord Ellenborough, however, decided that the insurance was not rendered illegal, because the assured carried out the insurance without any knowledge of the illegality and the hostilities between the nations, and the agent of the assured was entitled to the return of the premium. Another case which was based on the judgment of *Oom* and goes much further is *Henting v Staniforth*. In this case, a voyage was illegal from its inception because the ship sailed before the licence was granted, which was unknown to the assured who resided abroad. When deciding whether the voyage was illegal and whether the assured was entitled to recover back his premium Lord Ellenborough decided that: "The illegality depended upon a fact, viz. the posteriority of the licence to the ship's departure, which was not known to the parties, and was contrary to the opinion and expectation that the plaintiff might reasonably entertain".[58] Therefore, the assured had a right to suppose that the voyage would be legal. And therefore, "he (the assured) is not a party to a violation of the law and is entitled to recover back his premium".[59] From this point of view, the knowledge of the illegality of the adventure is not within the scope of the matter which the assured can control. However, one factor which is crucial when deciding such cases is that the assured's intention has to be proved, which will be discussed later.

Based on the introduction of the origin of this piece of law and the former judgments which formulate the phrase "so far as the assured can control the matter", it is clear that the intention of this phrase is to provide a defence for the assured during the voyage, because the assured is not able to control everything during the course of a transaction. However, according to former analysis there are still two obligations for the assured to comply with: firstly, the assured should have no connection with the losses, either by physical performance or indirect performance, such as orders on agent; secondly, during a voyage, the assured should observe due diligence on the adventure and his agent.

2.4 The insufficiencies of section 41 of the 1906 Marine Insurance Act

After the analysis of the origin and the phrases of warranty of legality in marine insurance law, the objective of this section is to resolve the questions raised in the

---

55 *Carstairs, Executors of Lyon v Allnutt* (1813) 3 Camp 497.
56 *Wilson v Rankin* (1865–66) LR 1 QB 162.
57 *Oom v Bruce* (1810) 12 East 225.
58 *Hentig v Staniforth* (1816) 5 M & S 124.
59 Ibid at p 125.

introduction: whether section 41 of the 1906 Act truly reflects the judgments of former cases, and what is the true scope of section 41? To answer these questions, two issues need to be expounded: firstly, the insufficiencies of section 41 and secondly, whether this section should be regulated as a warranty.

The insufficiencies of section 41 can be summarised as: the language of this piece of law is abstract. There is no clear description of defences for the assured in either of the two pieces of legislation and the elements which may influence the consequences of the case have been ignored by the legislation as well. Furthermore, some specific circumstances which may not render the adventure illegal have not been covered by the law. Therefore, from this point of view, the legislation has not inflected the former cases properly and can be proved as follows.

Firstly, not every illegality can render the whole policy void. This is a very important defence for the assured which has been ignored by the 1906 Act. This exception exists in several circumstances: (1) statute itself may clearly provide such exception: for instance, it has been demonstrated that sailing without convoy contributes to an illegal voyage; however, according to the stat.43 Geo.3, c.57, unless the party interested in the insurance was privy to or instrumental in the sailing without convoy, the statute may not avoid such policies.[60] (2) If the circumstances which prevent the assured fulfilling the lawful requirement are permanent and unchangeable, then such illegal act will not render the insurance policy void. For instance, the case *Suart v Powell*[61] the assured is not guilty if a due proportion of such seamen cannot be procured in any foreign port. (3) If the entire cargo belongs to different parties which have no partnership between them, and are covered by distinct policies then the illegality of part of the cargo may not taint the others. In the case *Hagedorn v Bazett*,[62] the illegality of the cargo which was exported to Russia did not render the cargo which was exported to Hamburg illegal, even though the cargo was carried in the same vessel. And this is also the case when the illegality happens during the performance of an adventure; for example, in the case *Keir v Andrade* the assured was allowed to export 150 barrels of gunpowder, but the assured exported 300 barrels instead. The vessel was captured and caused the loss; the insurer alleged that the exportation of the extra 150 barrels was a violation of statute and consequently illegal and contaminated the whole adventure. However, the court divided the cargo into two parts and "the adding 150 barrels afterwards did not vitiate the application of the licence to the first".[63] Therefore the whole adventure was not illegal and the insurance on the first 150 barrels was valid. (4) The voyage may not be rendered illegal if the intention of the parties and law has been taken into consideration, which will be discussed later.

The exceptions which may not render the whole policy void vary from case to case; it is impossible to enumerate them and there are no general rules related to this defence. This exception depends upon how the courts construe the law and what facts the courts take into consideration. Consequently, this kind of defence

---

60 *Cohen v Hinckley* (1808) 1 Taunt 249.
61 *Suart v Powell* 109 E.R. 785.
62 *Hagedorn v Bazett* (1813) 2 M & S 100.
63 *Keir v Andrade* (1816) 6 Taunt 504.

is not stable; however, when the courts decide similar cases they may take the decisions of former cases into account.

Secondly, the intention of the parties which had been taken into account by several former cases has been ignored by section 41 as well. The intention of parties has provided a defence for the assured in illegality issues. The intention of parties was considered by Lord Ellenborough CJ in two cases: in the case *Ingham v Agnew*, the voyage was rendered illegal not because there was no licence on board as required by the law, but because the parties had no intention to obey it: "it appears that at the very time the parties obtaining that licence meditated a voyage up the Mediterranean. The voyage was therefore illegal and the insurance void".[64] In another case, *Wilson v Foderingham*, the defendant refused to pay the freight because he argued that the voyage had been tainted by illegality, namely sailing without convoy. Even though this was not a marine insurance case, determination of the legality of the voyage is the foundation of carriage contracts as well. In this case the voyage was rendered legal because as cited by Lord Ellenborough CJ: "If this contract had been made upon an understanding that it was intended to contravene the provisions of the Act of Parliament, perhaps the voyage might have been illegal, as being an act contemplated to be done in violation of a law of the State; but this contract was entered into, as we must presume until the contrary be shown, in perfect innocence, and with the purpose of effectually complying with the Act of Parliament".[65]

Therefore two kinds of intention of parties have been considered by Lord Ellenborough CJ, namely the intention of the parties when entering the contract and the intention of the parties when executing the contract; if the assured enters into the insurance policy without the intention to commit the adventure illegally, then the illegal performance may not render the policy void. However, if both of the parties enter into the contract with intention to commit it illegally, then even though it can be performed legally, the contract is void.

However, this may only provide limited protection to the assured, because on the one hand, it is inconvenient to estimate the moral intention of the assured as admitted by Lord Ellenborough CJ himself: "it would lead to this inconvenience, that in every case we should have to estimate the moral rectitude of the captain";[66] and on the other hand, it is hard to prove this either by the assured or insurer. Besides these two reasons, the courts tend to adopt a severe attitude towards illegality issues and frequently ignore this factor. However, such intention issue should raise the attention of the courts when dealing with illegality in marine insurance cases, and this has been considered by the judges in the most recent case *Sea Glory*.

The intention factor had also been considered in illegal performance circumstances; in the case *Atkinson v Abbott* which dealt with shipping goods to enemy territory, the intention of the assured and his agent had been considered by the Lord when deciding this case. In this case, an insurance policy was issued on a voyage to a neutral port in Sweden which the assured had no intention of visiting;

---

64 *Ingham v Agnew* (1812) 15 East 522.
65 *Wilson v Foderingham* (1813) 1 M & S 471.
66 Ibid at p 472.

the object of the voyage was to supply the British fleet in Denmark which was a hostile country then. The ship was captured by a Danish vessel and the assured claimed for damage. When deciding whether the intention of the assured and the voyage was fraud or illegal the Lord analysed that because "the object of it was to supply the British fleet and forces engaged in the expedition to Copenhagen with provisions"[67] and the voyage was "without any purpose of defeating the Order of Council or trading with an enemy",[68] the object of the voyage was not illegal, therefore the voyage was not illegal either in intention or act. It is clear that the intention of the assured in this case was considered a very important element. However, this is not always the case when the assured has no intention to violate the law. In the case *Denison v Modigliani*, even though it was alleged by the assured that the letter of marque which had been taken on board was "not being intended to be made use of and not having been acted upon in the voyage out"[69] the court decided that the conduct of the assured has raised the risk insured and the whole adventure was illegal.

Thirdly, the intention of the law has been ignored by section 41 as well. Under some circumstances, the courts need to clarify the ambiguities of legislation. For example, in the case *Farmer v Legg* it was cited that: "In a case where the words of an Act of Parliament are doubtful, we must see what were the mischiefs against which the Legislature meant to guard, and endeavour to find out the most probable means of effecting that purpose".[70] And "we (the court) must decide according to the intention of the Legislature which is to be collected from the general object of the Act and from the particular words used in it".[71] Therefore, the objection of the court is to protect the intention of the legislation rather than simply follow the requirements of the legislation.

Another circumstance in which the intention of the law may provide a defence for the assured is that the court is obliged to find out which punishment the law intends to impose upon the guilty assured, namely whether the consequence of illegality is the voiding of contract or simply a penalty. In the case *Redmond v Smith*, after analysis of the facts of the case, even though the illegality of the assured was confirmed, the court rejected the plea of the insurer which requested the invalidity of the policy. As cited by the court, "the object of the legislature was to protect seaman from imposition".[72] And even though the illegality sustained according to the law "he (the master) shall be liable to a penalty; but there is nowhere said that such non-compliance shall make the voyage illegal".[73] Thus, despite the illegality that existed in the voyage, it was not severe enough to make the voyage illegal and vitiated the insurance upon it.

According to these two cases, it seems that the court has developed a reliable defence for the assured in illegality cases, which has not been covered by section 41.

---

67 *Atkinson v Abbott* (1809) 11 East 140.
68 Ibid at p 140.
69 *Denison v Modigliani* (1794) 5 TR 582.
70 *Farmer v Legg* (1797) 7 TR 191.
71 Ibid at p 192.
72 *Redmond v Smith* (1844) 7 M & G 457 at p 475.
73 Ibid at p 474.

However, in order to achieve the correct application of this defence the function and character of the law shall be considered. Namely, whether the character of the law is suitable for the court to rely upon in order to forbid an insurance contract and vitiate the policy. Not every violation of any legislation can render an insurance contract illegal. This is because, firstly, the assured is not obliged to be familiar with every piece of UK law, for some law is of little use or clearly unfair; secondly, even though the legality is not necessarily closely connected with the loss, the law which the courts use to determine the illegality needs to demonstrate an illegal act, otherwise this may provide an improper defence for the insurer.

For instance, in the case *Toulmin v Anderson* which was wrongfully decided, the loss of the vessel and goods on board was because of the barratry of three Spaniards on board. Neither the goods on board nor the voyage was illegal according to the law of that time. Even though the first objection of the insurer was that the voyage was illegal according to statute 15 Car.2, c.7, s.6, the court did not deliver a legal opinion upon that subject.[74] The second objection raised by the insurer which the judgment relied upon was that the vessel did not obtain a licence from the South Sea company before the initiation of the voyage and the policy was subsequently rendered void by the court because of this objection. Nevertheless, this judgment was clearly inequitable because of two points. Firstly, as stated by the judge, the statute relied upon was "the almost forgotten charter of the South Sea Company".[75] Therefore, whether the legislation is still valid and suitable to be applied on such a specific case was a question to be clarified by the court. According to the argument of the plaintiff, two recent Acts of Parliament tended to legalise such voyage; however this had been ignored by the court.[76] Thus, not only might the assured not be familiar with the statute but also such statute might not be appropriate to be applied on such voyage. Secondly, the judgment was not fair to the assured because the legislation the court relied upon had no connection with the illegality. The function of the statute as stated by the court is that it "gives to the South Sea Company in the strongest terms possible an exclusive right to trade in the South Seas". According to the facts of the case, it was clear that the assured did not intend to violate this exclusive right of trade, therefore the legislation the court relied upon cannot properly demonstrate such illegality which existed in this case. Consequently, even though the objective of the law had been considered by the court, the legislation the court applied was incorrect which led to an incorrect judgment.

Fourthly, another insufficiency which has not been mentioned before is that in some cases the breach of warranty of legality has no connection with the losses. It is well known that under current marine insurance law, to establish a breach of warranty there is no need for a connection between the breach and the loss, which has been demonstrated by numerous cases. However, in illegality cases it may not be appropriate to adopt the same rule. Firstly, it was cited that the object of legislation shall be taken into consideration, therefore if the illegality does not

---

74 *Toulmin v Anderson* (1808) 1 Taunt 232.
75 Ibid.
76 Ibid at p 233.

contravene what the law intends to protect and does not result in loss, it is clear that such illegality will not be supported by the court.[77] Secondly, based upon the analysis of exceptions in section 41, the objective of this section is to protect the insurer from losses caused by illegality on the part of the assured rather than to preclude any illegality in an adventure, otherwise there will be no exceptions. Therefore, if the illegality of an adventure has no connection with the losses or the illegality which causes the losses is not committed by the assured, then there is no need to trigger this piece of law. Furthermore, under common law illegality rules, there is a causation requirement between the losses and the illegality which has been proved by several cases and the Law Commission Report.[78]

Therefore it can be summarised from this part that, firstly, section 41 of the 1906 Act does not reflect the judgments of former cases well; secondly, the 1906 Act and common law impose a severe consequence on the assured when in breach of such warranty and only provide limited defences for the assured; this is clearly unconscionable and is the reason to discuss whether section 41 should be regulated as a warranty issue.

2.4.1 Should the warranty of legality be regulated as an implied warranty in section 41?

According to the authorities and cases which have been listed above, it can be established that marine insurance contracts which involve illegality will be regarded as void. Based on the earlier analysis above, it can be concluded that section 41 of the 1906 Act does not reflect the former case law properly. Therefore a question may arise, why is the legality rule of marine insurance regulated as an implied warranty in the Marine Insurance Act 1906 rather than a condition, innominate terms or express warranty in marine insurance? The phrase "implied warranty" used in the judgment of some cases is not enough to answer this question. This is a question which the drafter of the Act, Sir Mckenzie Chalmers, himself did not answer. And another question is whether this classification is reasonable. To answer these two questions is another way to resolve the question, whether section 41 has reflected former case law properly. To answer these two questions, the different kinds of terms in ordinary contract law and insurance law shall be introduced first.

In general contract law, contract terms can be divided into three classes: condition, breach of which entitles the innocent party to repudiate the contract; warranty, breach of which enables the innocent party to claim for damage only; innominate terms, the breach of innominate terms may entitle the innocent party to repudiate the contract or claim for damages, which mainly depends on the seriousness of that breach.

However, the concepts of condition and warranty in insurance contracts have different meanings. According to *Clinvaux's Law of Insurance*, an insurance condition is "either an obligation on the assured to act in a particular way, or a contingency – which may be outside the control of the assured – upon which the

---

77 *Redmond v Smith* (1844) 7 M& G 457.
78 For example, the *Gray v Thames* and Law Commission Paper No 189.

validity of the policy or of any claim may depend."[79] And the insurance warranty is "a pre-contractual promise by the assured that a given fact is true, or that a given fact will remain true, or that he will behave or refrain from behaving in a particular way."[80]

The consequences of breach of condition and warranty terms in insurance law are different from the consequences in ordinary contract law as well. The consequence of breach of condition in insurance law is more like the breach of innominate terms in ordinary contract law although some special circumstances may exist; and the consequence of breach of warranty in insurance contract is basically automatic termination of the insurance contract.[81]

One of the minor differences between the non-marine insurance contracts and marine insurance contracts is that the implied warranty is unique to marine insurance and all the warranties in non-marine insurance must be expressed.[82] Therefore as one of the two implied warranties which has been regulated by the Marine Insurance Act 1906,[83] it is necessary to answer the question why the warranty of legality is an implied warranty.

According to former judgments, the reasons why warranty of legality is regulated as an implied one in section 41 can be concluded into the following two points.

Firstly, this is the foundation of marine insurance contracts. Other kinds of warranties may not be required in every marine insurance contract; however the warranty of legality must be fulfilled before the inception of the adventure and maintained during the adventure in order to make the legislation effective. This requirement originates from a fundamental principle which has been long decided in English law: "the courts will not permit a person to enforce his rights under a contract of any kind if it is tainted by illegality",[84] which is a general principle first cited in the case *Holman v Johnson* by Lord Mansfield. This is a case related to smuggling of tea into England; in the judgment Lord Mansfield cited that "The principle of public policy is this; *ex dolo malo non oritur actio*. No Court will lend its aid to a man who founds his cause of action upon an immoral or an illegal act."[85] Later it was also decided in the marine insurance case *Morck v Abel* that "no man can come into a British court of justice to seek the assistance of the law who founds his claim upon a contravention of the British laws"[86] and no man shall benefit from his own criminal conduct. In the absence of any Marine Insurance Act in the nineteenth century this is the public policy which many cases were based on and it is common sense in the insurance market. Therefore there is no need to express the legality of adventure and performance in marine insurance contracts, since all the prohibitions have been clearly cited by statutes and public policy.

---

79 *Colinvaux's Law Of Insurance* (9th edn, 2010), p 331.
80 Ibid, p 331.
81 The specific consequences of breach of warranty will be discussed below.
82 *Euro-Diam Ltd v Bathurst* [1988] 2 All ER 23.
83 The other is the implied warranty of seaworthiness.
84 *MacGillivray on Insurance Law* (11th edn), p 356.
85 *Holman v Johnson* (1775) 1 Cowp 341.
86 *Morck v Abel* (1802) 3 B & P 35.

Secondly, the main function for the warranty to be expressed in an insurance policy is to make clear the intention of the parties to the court, which enables the court to decide the consequences of the breach of that specific term easily. However, in practice the court can hardly ignore the illegality issues. In the case *Gedge v Royal Exchange Assurance Corp*[87] the judgment of that case stated that "the court cannot properly ignore the illegality or give effect to the claim even if the illegality be not pleaded or relied on by the defendants". In this case the court did not ignore the illegal transaction even though there was no express prohibition in the insurance contract. Therefore, there is no necessity for the legality requirement to be expressed.

The legality requirement can be regulated as an implied one because of the two points mentioned; however whether the legality requirement should be regulated as a warranty is another question, since there are five differences between the warranty of legality and other ordinary warranties:

(1) Compared with other kinds of warranties, warranty of legality cannot be waived either by agreement or by estoppel, for such waiver will negate the effect of legislation and such act will be contrary to public policy as stated in the first point. And it is also because the court will not ignore the illegality which exists in a contract.

(2) The most important principle in warranty is the strict compliance principle as stated in section 33 of the 1906 Act: once a warranty is breached, the insurance contract is automatically terminated regardless of whether the assured can control or is aware of the matter or not. However as clearly stated in section 41 "so far as the assured can control the matter", it indicates that if the adventure which is performed illegally is out of the control of the assured, such circumstance will not be considered as a breach of this implied warranty. In the warranty of legal adventure cases, as has been stated before, there are several circumstances where illegal adventure may not be rendered as a breach of warranty as well. Thus, these regulations clearly contradict the well-known principle in warranty.

(3) The difference also exists in the doctrine of divisibility of warranty. It is clear that in most cases if a warranty has been breached then the loss of the whole cargo under the same policy cannot be covered. However, in some special occasions of the legality cases, the cargo under the same policy can be divided. In the case *Hagedorn v Bazett*, a licence on a voyage to the Baltic had been granted; however, part of the cargo on the ship belonged to Russia which was regarded as an enemy by England at that time, therefore a question arose at the trial, whether this licence could be extended to protect the whole property or only a part of it, because at that time trade with enemy was regarded as illegal by English courts. By deciding the insurance policy only did not cover the goods of Russia (which was illegal), Lord Ellenborough CJ stated that "the mere accidental circumstance of several persons having employed one common agent, does not communicate to the others the vice belonging to the property of one

---

87 *Gedge v Royal Exchange Assurance Corp* [1900] 2 Q.B. 214.

of the assured; but that the contract may be distributed".[88] Therefore, in this case, even though part of the goods was illegal such illegality did not taint the whole insurance policy. However, this was a very special case; if it can be established that the subject matter insured is covered by the same policy, and belongs to the same assured, the partial illegality may taint the whole policy.[89] However, the former case law on this issue contradicted each other: in the case *Keir v Andrade*,[90] even though all of the gunpowder was covered under the same policy and belonged to the same assured, the illegality of half of the goods did not render the lawful part of the goods illegal.

(4) The issue on return of premium is different as well between the warranty of legality and other kinds of warranties. Under insurance law, premiums paid by the assured are recoverable either on the present warranty or continuing warranty, because the insurer will not face any liabilities for losses since the insurance contract has come to an end after the breach. There are no clear words related to the return of premium in section 41 of the 1906 Act; however in the early judgments which relate to illegality prior to the 1906 Act, the premium paid on an illegal insurance cannot be recovered. In the case *Vandyck v Hewitt*, the insurance policy which was to cover trading with the enemy was considered as illegal and the premium paid on it could not be recovered; the judge stated "where it was considered that money deposited upon an illegal wager, and paid over to the winner, [it] could not be recovered back from him".[91] Furthermore, it was later decided in the case *Morck v Abel* that "a foreigner cannot recover back the premium paid by him upon a policy of insurance, if the voyage be in contravention of the British laws".[92] This judgment has been supported by a number of cases such as *Chalmers v Bell*[93] and *Lubbock v Potts*.[94] This is also the reason why section 84(3) of the Marine Insurance Act 1906 indicates that there is no return of premium if there has been illegality on the part of the assured, which is clearly not a happy one.

(5) The last point is the difference which exists in the consequence of breach between the warranty of legality and other ordinary warranties. It can be established by numerous cases prior to the 1906 Act that the consequence of an insurance which is tainted by illegality is that the insurance contract is void rather than merely unenforceable after the breach, therefore not only the losses which happen after that breach are unrecoverable but also the losses which happen before that breach. However, this is clearly not the case in breach of ordinary warranties. Under ordinary warranty regulations the breach of a continuing warranty will not influence the insurer's

---

88 *Hagedorn v Bazett* (1813) 2 M & S 100.
89 *Cunard v Hyde* (1859) 2 E& E 1.
90 *Keir v Andrade* (1816) 6 Taunt 498.
91 *Vandyck v Hewitt* (1800) 1 East 96.
92 *Morck v Abel* (1802) 3 B & P 35.
93 *Chalmers v Bell* (1804) 3 B & P 604.
94 *Lubbock v Potts* (1806) 7 East 449.

liabilities which occur prior to the date of breach. Therefore the consequence of breach of warranty of legality is clearly not the same as other kinds of breach of warranties.

Above are the five differences which exist between the warranty of legality and other kinds of warranties. Therefore, based on the analysis above, it is clear that section 41 of the 1906 Act does not reflect the special character which exists in the judgment of former cases, and consequently it is not appropriate to regulate the requisition of lawful adventure and performance as a warranty in marine insurance law.

2.5 Conclusion on nature of section 41

Based on the analysis of former case law above, it can easily be concluded that section 41 of the Marine Insurance Act 1906 does not reflect former case law properly. And the true scope of the legality issue in marine insurance law has more abundant meanings. The true scope of legality in marine insurance law is to protect the legitimate interests of the insurer and prevent the assured from profiting from his own fault. However, section 41 only cited the two basic principles in practice and the possible defences for the assured have been ignored. Furthermore, based on the severe consequence of breaching legality rules, it is inappropriate to regulate these rules as warranty as well. Therefore, based on the most recent case *The Nancy*,[95] it seems that the application of common law illegality rules is the more proper method when dealing with marine insurance illegality issues.

---

95 *Sea Glory Maritime Co, Swedish Management Co SA v AL Sagr National Insurance Co ("The Nancy")* [2013] EWHC 2116 (Comm).

PART 2

BACKGROUND TO COMMON LAW ILLEGALITY

Following the introduction to the origins of the warranty of legality in marine insurance law, it is commonly agreed that the illegality rules adopted by the court when dealing with statutory illegality and the illegality in performance are different.

However, it is clear that the illegality rule in marine insurance law is not the only one which has made a difference between statutory illegality and illegality in performance. Moreover, the illegality rules in marine insurance also have a common law background. From the earliest case, *Holman v Johnson*, which is the origin of the illegality defence in English law, until the latest case, *Bilta v Nazir*, the illegality defence has been commonly used in both tort law and contract law to decline the claimant's compensation, on the ground that the claimant's right to compensation has been barred because of his illegal conduct. Unlike the warranty of legality in marine insurance law, the illegality defence in common law cannot render the contract void automatically, and the engagement of this defence is subject to various factors.

Furthermore, as will be seen below, the common law illegality defence is commonly applied to insurance law, especially motor insurance and liability insurance. Since the warranty of legality has been viewed as improper and outmoded, it is important to review the origins and the application of the illegality defence in common law and non-marine insurance circumstances, to re-analyse the original intention of the construction of this defence and how the defence has evolved. This will provide evidence needed for the modification of the warranty of legality in marine insurance.

This part will be divided into two chapters. The first chapter will consider the illegality defence, namely the *ex turpi causa* defence, in tort law and in insurance law, and the second chapter will consider the illegality in contract law and insurance contracts. At the end of the second chapter, there will be a comparison between the two kinds of illegality and an exploration of the differences between them. This chapter will begin with an examination of the origins of the illegality defence in tort law.

CHAPTER 3

The illegality defence in tort law and the *ex turpi causa* defence in insurance

3.1 The illegality defence in tort law

3.1.1 The origin of the illegality defence in tort law

The illegality defence, or illegality rules, in tort law in England and Wales often refer to the defence which is used by the defendant (who may be the tortfeasor) to bar the claimant who has acted in an unlawful manner from claiming loss or compensation from him. And it may also bar the guilty claimant from claiming compensation for his loss or claiming a penalty from the third party. The claimant may be a victim purely because of the conduct of the defendant or because of his own conduct; or he may be a victim because of the illegal act which was committed by both the defendant and himself. In both circumstances, the illegality of the act committed by the claimant, no matter how trivial or severe, may provide a defence for the defendant and the third party.

The Latin word *ex turpi causa*, which is commonly used to refer to the illegality defence in tort law, is also known as *ex turpi causa non oritur actio*. The origin of such a maxim in tort law derived from the case of *Holman v Johnson*, cited by Lord Mansfield in 1775, which concerned the smuggling of tea into England during the performance of a sale contract. In this case it was decided that the court would:

> not lend its aid to a man who founds his cause of action upon an immoral or an illegal act if, from the plaintiff's own stating or otherwise, the cause of action appears to arise ex turpi causa, . . . there the court says he has no right to be assisted. It is upon that ground the court goes; not for the sake of the defendant, but because they will not lend their aid to such a plaintiff.[1]

However, whether the decision can be viewed as the origin of the illegality defence in tort law[2] has been implicitly argued by former authorities since this principle was decided in a contract law case and the relationship between the defendant and claimant in contract law and tort law is not the same.

Firstly, it was contended that there is a limited application of the defence in tort. With regard to the *National Coal Board v England* case, a tort law case related to

---

1 *Holman v Johnson, alias Newland* (1775) 1 Cowper 341 at 343.
2 G Williams, "Contributory Negligence and Vicarious Liability" (1954) 17 MLR 365 (plaintiff a wrongdoer is not one of the general defences recognised in tort).

the compensation to the claimant which involved his illegality, according to Lord Porter, although the maxim is generally applied to contract cases, it could equally be applied to tort cases.[3] Furthermore, according to Lord Asquith, although: "The vast majority of cases in which the maxim has been applied have been cases where, there being an illegal agreement between A and B either seeks to sue the other for its enforcement or for damages for its breach. That, of course, is not this case";[4] and: "Cases where an action in tort has been defeated by the maxim are exceedingly rare". Lord Asquith finally agreed that "the plaintiff cannot be precluded from suing simply because the wrongful act is committed after the illegal agreement is made and during the period involved in its execution".[5]

However, it was finally agreed in the case *Clunis v Camden and Islington HA* that the public policy that the court will not lend its aid to the litigant who relies on his own criminal or immoral act is not confined to particular causes of action.[6] In this case, the defendant submitted that "the rule of policy embraced by the Latin maxim *ex turpi causa non oritur actio* does not apply to causes of action founded in tort".[7] However, by referring to several former judgments, the Court of Appeal finally cited: ". . . whether a claim brought is founded in contract or in tort, public policy only requires the court to deny its assistance to a plaintiff seeking to enforce a cause of action if he was implicated in the illegality and in putting forward his case he seeks to rely upon the illegal acts".[8] In other words, this public policy should be applied to tort law cases as it is to contract law cases. Although this judgment was questioned by Buxton LJ: "The limits of this defence are very difficult to state or rationalise, it being recognised as sitting more easily in the law of contract than of tort".[9] It was finally agreed in the case *Hewison v Meridian Shipping Services PTE Ltd* that "One thing at least is clear: the defence of illegality is available in the case of tort".[10] In the case *Gray v Thames Trains Ltd*, the judge also confirmed that "The principle derives originally from the judgment of Lord Mansfield in *Holman v Johnson*".[11] In the most recent case *Les Laboratoires Servier v Apotex Inc*, Lord Mansfield's judgment is still seen as the origin of the *ex turpi causa* defence in tort; however, it is also indicated that "it does not provide a simple measuring rod for determining the boundaries of the principle".[12]

3.1.2 Which kinds of claimant's illegality may trigger the illegality defence?

There are various kinds of illegal conduct which may bar the claimant from claiming compensation from the defendant. These types of conduct fall into several categories and can be analysed from two points of view: firstly, the illegality of an

---

3 *National Coal Board v England* [1954] AC 403 at 419.
4 Ibid at 428.
5 *National Coal Board v England* [1954] AC 403.
6 *Clunis v Camden and Islington HA* [1998] Q.B. 978 at 987.
7 Ibid at 986.
8 Ibid at 987.
9 *Reeves v Comr of Police of the Metropolis* [1999] Q.B. 169.
10 *Hewison v Meridian Shipping Services PTE Ltd* [2002] EWCA Civ 1821.
11 *Gray v Thames Trains Ltd* [2009] 1 A.C. 1339.
12 *Les Laboratoires Servier v Apotex Inc* [2014] 3 WLR 1257 at para 57.

act conducted by the claimant subjectively, which also includes the joint enterprise context; and secondly, the illegality of an act conducted by the claimant as a consequence of a former tort committed by the defendant. This part will only discuss the categories of the claimants' illegal acts; the rationales for these acts will be considered later.

(a) The illegal act conducted by the claimant subjectively
This category covers the illegality of an act committed by the claimant in the course of an illegal joint venture with the defendant, as well as the illegal activities which are committed by the claimant only:

(i) In the first circumstance, it is clear that when both the claimant and the defendant have been involved in the illegality, it will be impossible for the court to determine the standard of care in some certain circumstances. Thus, if the claimant is seeking compensation as a consequence of the joint illegal conduct with the defendant, such a claim may be dismissed on the basis that the claimant's own criminal conduct precludes him from recovering damages. This rule was first introduced by Lord Asquith in the case *National Coal Board v England*: at the end of his judgment, he made an example of the illegal joint venture: "If two burglars, A and B, agree to open a safe by means of explosives, and A so negligently handles the explosive charge as to injure B, B might find some difficulty in maintaining an action for negligence against A".[13] In a latter case, *Ashton v Turner*, after three young men had spent an evening drinking, two of them committed a burglary and sought to escape in the second defendant's car while the first defendant was driving it. The claimant plaintiff was badly injured in the ensuing car accident because of the reckless and illegal driving of the first defendant; the plaintiff subsequently claimed damages from the first defendant and the second defendant, who was alleged to have permitted the first defendant to use the car in a dangerous way and without insurance. The court dismissed the plaintiff's claim on the ground that "as a matter of public policy, the law might not recognise that a duty of care was owed by one participant in a crime to another in relation to an act done in the course of the commission of the crime and that, on the facts, the defendants did not owe a duty of care to the plaintiff during the burglary or the subsequent flight from the scene of the crime".[14] This rationale was upheld in a subsequent case, *Pitts v Hunt*. The facts of this case were similar to those in *Ashton v Turner*: both the defendant and the claimant were drunk before driving and the claimant had even encouraged the drunken defendant to drive in the reckless way which caused the accident, so the plaintiff's claim for compensation was dismissed on that ground. Firstly, "the plaintiff's action arose directly *ex turpi causa* and not from his having suffered a genuine wrong to which unlawful conduct was

---

13 *National Coal Board v England* [1954] AC 403 at 429.
14 *Ashton v Turner* [1981] Q.B. 137.

incidental";[15] and secondly, "there being a distinction between joint illegal enterprises where on the facts the court could determine the appropriate standard of care and those where it could not".[16] Clearly in this case the defendant did not owe the claimant that duty of care.

However, one possible exception may occur if the conduct of the claimant is so trivial that the court might not take it into account; the seriousness of the illegal conduct will be considered later. In the case *Lane v Holloway*, it was decided that the insult to the defendant's wife by the claimant was not a matter which the court may take into account "when awarding him compensatory damages for physical injuries which he has sustained as the result of the wrong which has been unlawfully inflicted on him".[17] Such conduct did not amount to contributory negligence. (The abandoning of the duty of care test will be considered in the "duty of care" section below.)

(ii) The second claim concerns a tort claim arising purely because of the illegal conduct of the claimant.

The reason for loss in this circumstance is purely because of the illegality of an act of the claimant and the claimant's claim for compensation can be dismissed because of that.

One typical case which relates to this issue is *Cross v Kirkby*.[18] In that case, the claimant tried to attack the defendant hunter with a broken baseball bat but was seriously injured by the defendant during the struggle afterwards. By overruling the former court's judgment, the Court of Appeal finally decided that the self defence of the defendant stood and the claimant was therefore precluded from recovering his own losses because of his own illegal and criminal act.

However, this principle is barred in various situations. Not every illegal act which originates from the claimant may bar him from compensation. The first exception is that there must be sufficient illegal conduct by the claimant; the mere knowledge of the intention to commit an illegal act is not enough. In the case *Revill v Newbery*,[19] which was also discussed in the *Cross* case, the defendant discharged a loaded shot-gun in the direction of the claimant who he thought was attempting to break in. The claimant was injured and his claim for compensation was allowed based on the fact that the claimant did not display any intention of resorting to violence with the defendant.

Secondly, the claimant's illegal conduct must be serious enough. If the illegality of the act of the claimant is so trivial, as in the case of *Lane v Holloway*,[20] even though the tort claim against the defendant is because of the claimant's civil wrong, the defendant's illegality defence may also fail as well.

---

15 *Pitts v Hunt* [1991] 1 Q.B. 24.
16 Ibid at 25.
17 *Lane v Holloway* [1968] 1 Q.B. 379.
18 *Cross v Kirkby* [2000] WL 530.
19 *Revill v Newbery* [1996] Q.B. 567.
20 *Lane v Holloway* [1968] 1 Q.B. 379.

(b) The illegality of the act committed by the claimant because of the defendant's former "tort".

The plaintiffs under this circumstance always allege that their illegal conduct is because of the defendant's former tort conduct and seek to claim compensation from the defendant based on this. They allege that but for the defendant's "tort" they would not have committed the crime. The most significant cases are *Meah v McCreamer*[21] and *Meah v McCreamer (No 2)*.

The two cases are based on the same fact. The plaintiff suffered a head injury and a personality disorder because of the defendant's negligent driving which was the reason for his sexual assault and rape conviction four years later. In the first judgment, the plaintiff was entitled to damages for injuries causing a personality change which resulted in his imprisonment. However, in the second judgment, the plaintiff's seeking to recover damages from the defendant which he had paid to his victims as compensation was dismissed by the court, on the grounds that, first, the victims of the plaintiff could not have claimed against the defendant because of remoteness and because there was no duty of care which the defendant owed them and, secondly, on the ground that it would be contrary to public policy for the claimant's damage to be allowed.

The second judgment is easy to comprehend and is uncontroversial. However, the first judgment was the subject of a great deal of criticism. According to Law Commission Report 160, "it is widely thought that, had the illegality point been argued, the claim would have been disallowed".[22] However, as had been decided in former cases, the court should have taken the illegality issue into consideration, whether the defendant had raised such a defence or not. Thus, cases of such character should not be allowed from the very beginning.

A similar case which relates to this issue is *Clunis v Camden and Islington HA*.[23] In this case, the plaintiff who suffered a mental disease stabbed a stranger to death after he left a hospital and was receiving post-care treatment in the community. After he had been found guilty of manslaughter and detained in a secure hospital, he brought an action against the local hospital for negligence under tort. One of the grounds for dismissing the claimant's appeal was that the claim was based on the plaintiff's own illegal act. However, this decision was not as simple as it appears. The policy underlying this kind of case, namely the reliance principle, is that the claimant cannot rely on his own illegality; this will be discussed later.

Thus, based on the former three cases, the defendant is not responsible either for the loss because of detention or indemnity to the third party because of the illegality of the act committed by the claimant. Therefore, when dealing with circumstances where the claimant has committed an illegal act because of the defendant's former tort action, there is no need to consider the seriousness of the defendant's tort or the causation link between the illegality and the losses; as long as the claimant needs to rely on his illegality to plead for compensation, such an

---

21 *Meah v McCreamer* (1986) 1 AER 943.
22 Law Commission Consultation Paper No 160.
23 *Clunis v Camden and Islington HA* [1998] Q.B. 978.

application will be denied, although such a decision is subjected to several exceptions which will be introduced later.

3.1.3 The principle based on which the claimant's claim is barred because of illegality

(a) Tendencies in the development of public policy and the abolishment of the public conscience test

It seems that the court of England has adopted increasingly strict principles which underlie the illegality defence.

With regard to the first of these principles, the maxim of *ex turpi causa*, this only regulates that no cause of action may be founded upon an immoral or illegal act. However, the test is too loose when deciding tort cases. In the early judgments, the principles adopted by the court were always too general and the phrase public policy was commonly used.

In the case *Gray v Barr*,[24] the defendant who killed the plaintiff's husband by accident sought an indemnity from his insurer under his insurance policy because of the tort claim brought against him by the plaintiff. It was decided by the court that the defendant's claim should not be allowed under the insurance policy, because allowing this claim would be contrary to public policy.

However, the boundary of the concept of public policy was not clear under tort law. Because of the unsteady and unpredictable nature of illegal conduct, the court used to rely on the flexibility of the application of public policy, and the well-known public conscience test was introduced when dealing with illegality cases. According to Hutchison J in the case *Thackwell v Barclays Bank Plc*,[25] the conscience test "involved the court looking at the quality of the illegality relied on by the defendant and all the surrounding circumstances, without fine distinctions, and seeking to answer two questions: first, whether there had been illegality of which the court should take notice and, second, whether in all the circumstances it would be an affront to the public conscience if by affording him the relief sought, the court was seen to be indirectly assisting or encouraging the plaintiff in his criminal act".[26]

The essence of this judgment was to give the court discretion when dealing with illegality cases. It is not only that the courts have to decide whether there is an illegality which the courts should not lend its aid to, but also to decide whether such a refusal is fair to the claimant. This test was supported by several later cases and it was considered by Lord Nicholls in the case *Saunders v Edwards* that "the test is a useful and valuable one". The use of this test required the court to "weigh, or balance, the adverse consequences of granting relief against the adverse consequences of refusing relief. The ultimate decision calls for a value judgment".[27]

However, this adoption seems to leave a great deal to the discretion of the court. As has been analysed in the case *Tinsley v Milligan* the essence of this test "was

---

24 *Gray v Barr* [1971] 2 Q.B. 554.
25 *Thackwell v Barclays Bank Plc* [1986] 1 All E.R. 676.
26 Ibid at 680.
27 *Stone & Rolls Ltd v Moore Stephens* [2008] 3 W.L.R. 1146 at 1153.

no more than the assumption of a judicial discretion as to whether or not in any particular case, despite the illegality or immorality, to grant or refuse relief".[28]

This test was finally rejected in the judgment of the case *Tinsley v Milligan*. It was held in this case that "[a]lthough the public conscience may be the underlying reason for the principle that is not to say that 'affront to the public conscience' is either a desirable or indeed a workable test. A clear and strict rule maximises the deterrent effect, whilst flexibility gives hope. The 'public conscience' test is inherently uncertain in its application. The very uncertainty of this test will serve only to encourage more protracted and uncertain litigation in future cases. Moreover, it is particularly important for property law to be clear and not dependent upon unpredictable judicial decision making".[29] The court decided that "he (the 'guilty' claimant) is entitled to recover the losses if he is not forced to plead or rely on the illegality, even if it emerges that the title on which he relied was acquired in the course of carrying through an illegal transaction".[30] Therefore the mere existence of illegality does not necessarily bar the claimant's claim for compensation.

Later, in the judgment of *Stone & Rolls Ltd v Moore Stephens*, by supporting the House of Lords' decision, Rimer LJ further decided that the statement of the principle is not confined to property disputes "[b]ut it is one I regard as applying generally and which Langley J conveniently described as a 'reliance' test".[31] Thus, for tort and contract claims, the public conscience test is no longer used.

However, English courts are still struggling on whether the public conscience test shall be abolished or not. In the most recent Supreme Court case of *Hounga v Allen*[32] this controversial issue emerged again. In this case, the illegal migrant Miss Hounga was employed by Mrs Allen with the knowledge that Miss Hounga entered into the UK illegally. After the employment, Miss Hounga was repeatedly abused and exploited by Mrs Allen and was eventually dismissed. Miss Hounga brought a claim against Mrs Allen based on discrimination since she is a Nigerian national. The Court of Appeal held that, since the employment contract was illegal, such illegal contract prohibited Miss Hounga from claiming against Mrs Allen.[33] However, such decision was overturned by the majority judgment of the Supreme Court. On behalf of the majority of the Supreme Court Lord Wilson delivered the judgment. The principle on *ex turpi causa* as concluded by Lord Wilson is flexible and although the first aspect which needs to be considered is the public policy which underlies such defence, such defence is still under change subject to the change of circumstances in each individual cases.[34] In addition to this basic principle, the other basis of *ex turpi causa* is the duty of courts to preserve the integrity of the legal system.[35]

---

28 Ibid at 1153.
29 *Tinsley Appellant v Milligan Respondent* [1994] 1 A.C. 340 at 345.
30 Ibid at 376.
31 *Stone & Rolls Ltd v Moore Stephens* [2008] 3 W.L.R. 1146 at 1154.
32 *Hounga v Allen* [2014] 1 WLR 2889.
33 *Hounga v Allen* [2012] IRLR 685.
34 *Hounga v Allen* [2014] 1 WLR 2889 at para 42.
35 *Hall v Herbert* [1993] 2 SCR 159.

Therefore, based upon the detailed assessment of the context of the current case Lord Wilson concluded that, to allow Miss Hounga's claim would not compromise the integrity of the legal system and the defence which would defeat Miss Hounga's claim scarcely existed.[36] Moreover, Lord Wilson found that the UK's public policy is to prevent human trafficking and is in favour of the protection of its victims, therefore, the Court of Appeal's decision was counter to the public policy and: "The public policy in support of the application of that defence, to the extent that it exists at all, should give way to the public policy to which its application is an affront".[37]

However, the minority of the Supreme Court came to the same decision via another approach. Lord Hughes together with Lord Carnwath provided that the principle when dealing with *ex turpi causa* should still follow the decision of *Tinsley* and *Stone & Rolls* and *Gray v Thames Trains*, that is since there is no close connection between the illegal immigration and the discrimination, to allow Miss Hounga's claim would not amount to the court condoning what it otherwise condemns.[38] Lord Hughes clearly did not agree with Lord Wilson's decision by stating that: "public policy very obviously underlies the rules upon illegality as it affects civil claims, but I do not think that the cases establish a separate trumping test of public policy".[39]

It is clearly that, based upon former analysis, to consider whether the illegality defence should sustain or not, based upon the "weigh[ing] or balanc[ing of] the adverse consequences of granting relief against the adverse consequences of refusing relief" contradicts the House of Lords decision on *Tinsley*. Therefore, the majority position in *Hounga v Allen* is highly problematic and it should be seen as a misplacement of judicial focus by Lord Wilson, since in the later Supreme Court case of *Les Laboratoires Servier v Apotex Inc*[40] the public conscience test is clearly denied by the Supreme Court, although by a different Lordship.

However, even though the public conscience test has been rejected, more specific formulations have found favour. These include the duty of care principle, the reliance principle, the causation principle, the protection of the integrity of court (the non-condonation and consistency), the seriousness of illegality principle, the proportionality principle and the intention of statute principle, and will be introduced later.

(b) Should the "no duty of care" principle be applied?

The duty of care principle was introduced when dealing with the joint enterprise circumstances above. However, whether the duty of care should be recognised as a principle which underlies the illegality defence is an unresolved question. Nevertheless, no matter whether this principle will be used any longer, it used to be one of the principles adopted by the English courts.

---

36 *Hounga v Allen* [2014] 1 WLR 2889 at para 45.
37 Ibid at 52.
38 *Hounga v Allen* [2014] 1 WLR 2889 at 67.
39 Ibid.
40 Which has been analysed from p 102.

The duty of care principle is a principle in tort law. In tort law circumstances, one party owes a duty of care to the other party; therefore, if the claimant's loss has been caused by the negligence of the defendant, then the claimant can sue the defendant for damages on this ground. In the circumstances where there is illegality, this means that, because of the illegal conduct of the claimant, the defendant owes no duty of care to the claimant and the claimant cannot sue for damages on this ground. The no duty of care principle was first created in an Australian case. In the case *Godbolt v Fittock*, the judge held that: "In my opinion, when co-adventurers in a joint criminal venture of a nature comparable with that in question in the present appeal use a motor vehicle in the pursuit of their common purpose, damages are not recoverable by one, being a passenger, against another, being the driver, in respect of injuries suffered as a result of want of due care in driving on a journey which is directly connected with the execution of the criminal purpose".[41] In another case, *Smith v Jenkins*, the judge decided that the dismissal of the action of the plaintiff was based on "a refusal of the law to erect a duty of care as between persons jointly participating in the performance of an act contrary to the provisions of a statute making their act a crime punishable by imprisonment".[42]

This principle was further discussed in the Australian case *Jackson v Harrison*: "A more secure foundation for denying relief, though more limited in its application – and for that reason fairer in its operation – is to say that the [claimant] must fail when the character of the enterprise in which the parties are engaged is such that it is impossible for the court to determine the standard of care which is appropriate to be observed".[43] Moreover, there are also resources in English law, like the judgment in the early case, *National Coal Board v England*, which was discussed above.

There are two main English cases which have adopted this rationale – the *Ashton v Turner* and the *Pitts v Hunt* cases,[44] which have already been discussed. In the *Ashton* case, the no duty of care is the only principle applied; however, in the *Pitts* case, although the court unanimously agreed that the illegality defence was triggered, the judges' decision had a different basis. In Lord Balcombe's view, the defendant owed the plaintiff no duty of care. However, Lord Beldam reached the same decision on the basis that the claimant and the defendant's conduct had violated the statute's intention to promote road safety and he criticised the no duty of care test as follows: "As this ground is also based on public policy, it is not I think in the circumstances of this case significant. That both the plaintiff and rider owed a duty to other road users to exercise reasonable care is clear. I am not convinced of the wisdom of a policy which might encourage a belief that the duty to behave responsibly in driving motor vehicles is diminished even to the limited extent that

---

41 *Godbolt v Fittock* (1963) 63 S.R.(N.S.W.) 617.
42 *Smith v Jenkins* (1970) 44 A.LJR. 78.
43 *Jackson v Harrison* (1977–1978) 138 CLR 438, 455.
44 For a more detailed analysis on this issue, see Charles Debattista, "Ex Turpi Causa Returns to the English Law of Torts: Taking Advantage of a Wrong Way Out" (1984) 13 *Anglo-Am. L. Rev.* 15, although some arguments are out of date from today's view.

they may in some circumstances not owe a duty to each other, particularly when those circumstances involve conduct which is highly dangerous to others".[45]

Although the no duty approach, according to the Law Commission Report No 160, ". . . has found considerable support in Australia, it has found little further judicial support in England and Wales, and has been subject to academic criticism".[46] The criticisms include: (1) the burden of proof may shift from the defendant to prove the defence established to the claimant to prove why the claim should not fail. If such a principle was applied, it would change the character of the illegality defence; (2) this approach would raise unnecessary complexity in a law which is already uncertain enough; (3) this approach could not be applied to other fields of tort and it seems insufficient to explain all the relevant authorities; and (4) there are no obvious criteria by which one can determine precisely when the court finds it impossible to set a standard of care.[47]

However, it cannot be assumed that this principle has been abandoned by the English courts. In the most recent case, *Joyce v O'Brien*, both the claimant and the defendant committed a crime together and during the escape from the scene, the claimant was injured by the defendant when he secured the stolen ladder, because of the careless driving of the defendant. The claimant sought to recover damages for injuries sustained in the course of criminal behavior. Although, his claim was rejected on the ground of the wider rule cited in the case *Gray v Thames*, the judge still recognised the ground that: "The law will not recognize the existence of a duty of care owed by one participant in a crime to another participant in the same crime in relation to an act done in connection with the commission of that crime".[48]

However, it is clear from this case that there is a limited use of this principle since this principle can be seen as merely one specific application of the wider rule in *Gray v Thames*,[49] and according to this case, the courts should focus on the causation rule rather than the duty of care rule.

(c) The reliance principle

The reliance principle is an old and commonly used principle in tort as well as in contract law. However, there is always a dispute as to whether this principle has the same effect in tort cases as in contract and property cases.[50]

The most general and early judgment related to this principle is the sentence "the court will not lend its aid to a man who founds his cause of action upon an immoral or an illegal act" in the case of *Holman v Johnson*. Therefore, if a claimant tries to recover losses against the defendant which relies on his own criminal or immoral act then the illegality defence for the defendant will be triggered and the claimant's action will fail. Following the *Holman* case, the reliance principle

---

45 *Pitts v Hunt* [1991] 1 Q.B. 24 at 46–47.
46 The Law Commission Consultation Paper No 160, p 23.
47 See N. Enonchong, *Illegal Transactions* (1998); *Clerk and Lindsell on Torts* (19th edn, 2006); and Dr Benjamin Andoh, *Illegality as a Defence to Negligence in English Law*.
48 *Joyce v O'Brien* [2013] EWCA Civ 546.
49 See *Gray v Thames*: the "narrow" and "wider" rules which were cited in this case will be discussed below.
50 The dispute arose since the judgment of *Tinsley v Milligan* and is discussed below.

was further recognised in *Bowmakers Ltd v Barnet Instruments Ltd*. In this case, the plaintiffs obtained a judgment against the defendant for the damages to the conversion of the property which belonged to the plaintiffs. The defendant raised the illegality of the contract as a defence. The principle laid down by the Court of Appeal is that "No claim founded on an illegal contract will be enforced by the court, but as a general rule a man's right to possession of his own chattels will be enforced . . . provided that the plaintiff does not seek, and is not forced, either to found his claim on the illegal contract, or to plead its illegality in order to support his claim".[51] Therefore, even if there was illegality involved in this case, as long as the claimant did not rely on it to find the claim, the illegality defence would not work. However, one exception stated by the judge is that it cannot be prohibited to deal with the goods in question: "An exception to this general rule arises in cases in which the goods claimed are of such a kind that it is unlawful to deal in them at all".[52]

This principle was upheld by the House of Lords in the case *Tinsley v Milligan*, which was discussed above. According to Lord Browne-Wilkinson: "In my judgment the time has come to decide clearly that the rule is the same whether a plaintiff founds himself on a legal or equitable title: he is entitled to recover if he is not forced to plead or rely on the illegality, even if it emerges that the title on which he relied was acquired in the course of carrying through an illegal transaction."[53]

As concluded by the Law Commission Report, "it seems that a claim in tort will fail if, in order to make out such case, the claimant must rely on an illegal act. It might seem that, conversely, the claim will not fail if the claimant does not have to rely on the illegal act".[54]

The second circumstance of the reliance principle was proved in the case *Webb v Chief Constable of Merseyside Police*. In this case, the police argued that the return to the claimant of the money which had been seized – which was suspected of having been used in a drug transaction – may constitute the completion by him of a crime. The judge in this case admitted that the court "should not make an order which facilitates a criminal to complete his crime".[55] However, as long as the claimant was not reliant upon the money to complete a crime, the court would not deny such a claim.

However, it should be remembered that the reliance principle is not a conclusive test; the judgment of *Tinsley* does not mean that if the claimant does not rely on his illegality to plead his claim, the illegality defence will not be triggered, since there are also other rationales which underlie the principle.

(d) The causation principle
Compared with the reliance principle, the causation principle can be seen as a more general and widely used principle. This principle requires a causation link

---

[51] *Bowmakers Ltd v Barnet Instruments Ltd* [1945] K.B. 65.
[52] Ibid at 70.
[53] *Tinsley v Milligan* [1994] 1 A.C. 340.
[54] Law Commission Consultation Paper No 160, p 19.
[55] *Webb v Chief Constable of Merseyside Police* [2000] Q.B. 427 at 446.

between the illegal conduct and the loss which the claimant intends to recover. The principle can be viewed as a special type of the reliance principle; it is not only important for the claimant to rely on the illegal conduct principle, but it is also important that the claimant's loss should be caused by such illegality. This difference was indicated by Lord Asquith in the case *National Coal Board v England*: "But if A and B are proceeding to the premises which they intend burglariously to enter, and before they enter them, B picks A's pocket and steals his watch, I cannot prevail on myself to believe that A could not sue in tort (provided he had first prosecuted B for larceny). The theft is totally unconnected with the burglary".[56] Therefore, even if under such circumstances the guilty claimant's need to sue for his loss relies on the burglary fact, since the illegal fact has no connection with the loss he suffered, the illegality defence is not sustained.

The basis of this principle is that, for the illegality defence to work, the claimant's conduct must in some category connect to the illegality; thus, if the claimant's loss links with his illegal or criminal act, the illegality defence maybe triggered. In other words, the illegality which the defendant uses as a defence must be committed by the claimant or be connected to the claimant's act.

The first category of the causation principle emerges in cases which relate to assault or criminal cases. In the case *Murphy v Culhane*, the plaintiff's husband was killed by the defendant during a criminal affray which was initiated by the deceased against the defendant. The plaintiff claimed damages against the defendant. The defendant's appeal, based on the maxim of *ex turpi causa*, was allowed because, firstly: "(1) . . . by taking part in a criminal affray the deceased might have deprived himself of a cause of action arising from its consequences";[57] and secondly: "That even if the plaintiff was entitled to damages they might fall to be reduced because the deceased's death might have been partly the result of his own 'fault'."[58] As Lord Denning concluded: "If Murphy was one of a gang which set out to beat up Culhane, it may well be that he could not sue for damages if he got more than he bargained for. A man who takes part in a criminal affray may well be said to have been guilty of such a wicked act as to deprive himself of a cause of action, or, alternatively, to have had taken upon himself the risk".[59]

Another case which shares a similar fact is *Cross v Kirkby*, the facts of which were analysed above. In this case, Judge LJ formulated the test of "inextricably linked" which was afterwards adopted by Sir Murray Stuart-Smith in *Vellino v Chief Constable of the Greater Manchester Police*. In the judgment of the Lord Justice, he concluded that "In my judgment, where the claimant is behaving unlawfully, or criminally, on the occasion when his cause of action in tort arises, his claim is not liable to be defeated *ex turpi causa* unless it is also established that the facts which give rise to it are inextricably linked with his criminal conduct".[60] It was also in this case that Beldam LJ said: "I do not believe that there is any general principle

---

56 *National Coal Board v England* [1954] AC 403 at 429.
57 *Murphy v Culhane* [1977] Q.B. 94.
58 Ibid at 95.
59 Ibid at 98.
60 *Harry Cross v William Dickinson Kirkby* [2000] WL 530 at para 103.

that the claimant must plead, give evidence of or rely on his own illegality for the principle to apply. Such a technical approach is entirely absent from Lord Mansfield's exposition of the principle. I would, however, accept that for the principle to operate the claim made by the claimant must arise out of criminal or illegal conduct on his part ... In my view the principle applies when the claimant's claim is so closely connected or inextricably bound up with his own criminal or illegal conduct that the court could not permit him to recover without appearing to condone that conduct".[61]

One of the more recent cases which applied this principle is *Gray v Thames Trains Ltd*. In this case, the claimant suffered a disorder because of the train accident which was caused by the negligence of the defendant. The claimant killed a man because of this disorder and was detained in a hospital. The claimant then claimed for loss of earnings since the date of the accident. The House of Lords dismissed the claimant's appeal on the ground of consistency as well as on the ground that the loss of the claimant was the consequence of the claimant's own unlawful act. Moreover, in this case, it was decided by Lord Hoffmann that there are wider principles and narrow principles in the illegality cases: "In its wider form, it is that you cannot recover compensation for loss which you have suffered in consequence of your own criminal act. In its narrower and more specific form, it is that you cannot recover for damage which flows from loss of liberty, a fine or other punishment lawfully imposed upon you in consequence of your own unlawful act".[62] It is clear that the causation principle was applied in both the wider and narrow rule, since, as observed by Lord Hoffmann, "the wider rule may raise problems of causation, which cannot arise in connection with the narrower rule. The sentence of the court is plainly a consequence of the criminality for which the Claimant was responsible. But other forms of damage may give rise to questions about whether they can properly be said to have been caused by his criminal conduct".[63]

The causation principle has also been applied in joint adventure cases; it seems that when dealing with such cases, the crucial question to ask is whether the cause of the claimant's loss is illegal. Therefore, in the case *Delaney v Pickett*, when packs of drugs were found on the claimant and the defendant in a motor car accident caused by the negligent driving of the defendant, when dealing with whether the defendant's illegality defence was sustained against the claimant's plea for loss caused by injury, the judges decided that: "Viewed as a matter of causation, the damage suffered by the claimant was not caused by his or their criminal activity. It was caused by the tortious act of the defendant in the negligent way in which he drove his motor car. In those circumstances the illegal acts are incidental and the claimant is entitled to recover his loss".[64]

This decision was followed in the case *Joyce v O'Brien*. In this case, the judge dealt with a circumstance where both of the parties had knowledge of the illegality and the increase in the risk of injury because of this illegality. The judge decided that

---

61 Ibid at para 76.
62 *Gray v Thames Trains Ltd* [2009] 1 A.C. 1339.
63 Ibid at 1342.
64 *Delaney v Pickett* [2011] EWCA Civ 1532.

"where the character of the joint criminal enterprise is such that it is foreseeable that a party or parties may be subject to unusual or increased risks of harm as a consequence of the activities of the parties in pursuance of their criminal objectives, and the risk materialises, the injury can properly be said to be caused by the criminal act of the claimant even if it results from the negligent or intentional act of another party to the illegal enterprise".[65] Therefore, it can be seen that the causation principle has been more commonly used, and the use of this principle is combined with other factors such as the intention and knowledge of the parties.

(e) The consistency principle

The consistency principle is also known as a part of the integrity of the legal system test. This principle is not recognised as one of the main principles in English tort law either by the Law Commission Paper No 160 or No 189. This rationale is mainly adopted by Canadian courts and requires the law to aspire to be a unified institution. As delivered in the judgment of *Hall v Hebert* by the Canadian Supreme Court: "the parts of which – contract tort the criminal law – must be in essential harmony. For the court to punish conduct with the one hand while rewarding it with the other would be to create an intolerable fissure in the law's conceptually seamless web".[66]

However, this consistency test was unanimously recognised as a good law by the House of Lords in the case *Gray v Thames Trains*. In the judgment of this case, it was concluded that "allowing the appeal, that, by reason of the need to avoid inconsistency in the justice system, as a manifestation of the public policy expressed by the maxim *ex turpi causa non oritur actio* a civil court would not award damages to compensate a claimant for an injury or disadvantage which the criminal courts had imposed on him by way of punishment for a criminal act for which he was responsible".[67]

This rationale was explained by Lord Hoffmann in the narrower rule of the public policy which relates to the illegality defence in tort: "In its narrower and more specific form, it is that you cannot recover for damage which flows from loss of liberty, a fine or other punishment lawfully imposed upon you in consequence of your own unlawful act. In such a case it is the law which, as a matter of penal policy, causes the damage and it would be inconsistent for the law to require you to be compensated for that damage".[68] Mummery LJ's judgment in *Clunis* was also referred to by Lord Hoffmann, who concluded that: "The reasoning of Mummery LJ reflects the narrower version of the rule. The inconsistency is between the criminal law, which authorises the damage suffered by the plaintiff in the form of loss of liberty because of his own personal responsibility for the crimes he committed, and the claim that the civil law should require someone else to compensate him for that loss of liberty".[69]

---

65 *Joyce v O'Brien* [2013] EWCA Civ 546.
66 *Clerk and Lindsell on Torts* (19th edn, 2006), pp 149–150.
67 *Gray v Thames Trains Ltd* [2009] 1 A.C. 1339.
68 Ibid at 1370.
69 *Gray v Thames Trains Ltd* [2009] 1 A.C. 1372.

Thus, according to Lord Hoffmann, even though the consistency principle was not recognised by the Law Commission paper, this test was already being used in English courts when deciding illegality cases. In fact, this is the case in various English cases: the claimant who has committed a kind of illegal act recognised by the court is highly unlikely to recover damages from the defendant. This is the case in the *Clunis* case and also in *Cross v Kirkby*.[70] Moreover, if the claimant has been penalised because of his illegal conduct, he is unlikely to recover damages in insurance law as well.

Another part of the integrity of the legal system test, referred to in the Law Commission Report, is the condonation test, which basically states that the court could not permit the illegal claimant to recover without appearing to condone or indirectly assist and encourage the claimant's illegal conduct.

However, this test has raised the question of when it would apply and what the effect on the claimant's other cause of action, if this principle is applied, would be, especially with regard to the claimant's insurance right against his insurer.

However, this principle is unlikely to be considered by the courts as the primary principle when dealing with illegality cases, since this principle is mainly to be applied when dealing with whether compensation or insurance should be paid to the guilty party, rather than to decide whether the party is guilty or not.

(f) The seriousness of illegal conduct

It has long been decided in English law that, for the illegality defence to be sustained, there is a requirement that the claimant's illegality should be sufficiently turpitudinous and reprehensible. In the case *Vellino v Chief Constable of Greater Manchester*, it was decided that a case of criminal conduct has to be sufficiently serious to merit the application of the illegality defence;[71] and in the case *Hewison v Meridian* shipping, it was also decided that for the defence to be applied, the claimant's conduct must be clearly reprehensible.[72]

In the case *Lilly v 8PM* both Lords Phillips and Rodger suggested that the seriousness of the illegality, or at least the culpability of the claimant, is a relevant factor in determining when the rule should apply.[73] Furthermore, in the case *Stone & Rolls Ltd v Moore Stephens*, Lord Phillips concluded that one of the three requirements to trigger the illegality defence is that: "The illegality must involve turpitude. The defence may not apply where the claimant's illegality consists of an offence of strict liability of which he is unaware".[74]

Knowledge is another factor which may influence the seriousness of illegality. In the case *Burrows v Rhodes*, it was decided that "if an act is manifestly unlawful, or the doer of it knows it to be unlawful, as constituting either a civil wrong or a criminal offence, he cannot maintain an action for contribution or for indemnity against the liability which results to him therefrom"; it was further decided that

---

70 *Harry Cross v William Dickinson Kirkby* [2000] WL 530.
71 *Vellino v Chief Constable of Greater Manchester* [2002] 1 W.L.R. 218.
72 *Hewison v Meridian Shipping* [2003] I.C.R. 766.
73 *Lilly v 8PM* [2009] EWHC 1905.
74 *Stone & Rolls Ltd v Moore Stephens* [2009] 1 A.C. 1391.

". . . it can never, in my judgment, be successfully contended that a claim for indemnity can be maintained where the doer of the act knew at the time, or must be presumed to know, of circumstances which make the act either a private wrong or a public crime".[75]

This rationale was adopted by the *Safeway Stores* case. In the first judgment of the case *Safeway Stores Ltd v Twigger*, it was decided "that the *ex turpi causa* principle was not restricted to cases where the claimant relied on his own criminal conduct in bringing the claim but applied to non-criminal conduct where there was a sufficient element of moral turpitude or reprehensibility".[76]

However, the application of the seriousness principle is vague on several points. Firstly, it is difficult to decide which kind of conduct is serious enough to trigger the defence, as was pointed out in the case *Hewison v Meridian shipping*: "where to draw the line between what is serious and what is trivial is not always easy".[77] Secondly, since the discretion of the courts on the illegality issue was denied in *Tinsley*, will the court be entitled to consider the seriousness of illegality according to the facts of each individual case? Thirdly, even if the claimant's illegal conduct is trivial, if the claimant commits such illegality intentionally, then will such conduct trigger the *ex turpi causa* defence?

The most recent authority which considered all these three questions is *Les Laboratoires Servier v Apotex Inc*. In this case the claimant argued that it was contrary to public policy for the defendant to recover damages for being prevented from selling a product whose manufacture in Canada would have been illegal there as an infringement of the claimant's Canadian patent. In its first instance, judgment of which was delivered by Arnold J, it was decided that the illegality defence which was raised by the claimant was sustained, as according to Arnold J ". . . what degree of seriousness is sufficient will depend on the circumstances of the case. In my view the key factor in most cases is likely to be the claimant's state of knowledge at the time of committing the act in question. If the claimant knew the material facts, and particularly if he committed the act in question intentionally, then the rule is likely to apply".[78]

This case was later appealed. And in the judgment of the Court of Appeal which was delivered by Etherton LJ, he decided that the illegality defence in this case should not sustain, firstly because the defendant "honestly and reasonably believed the Canadian patent to be invalid"[79] and secondly, because Etherton LJ had not been satisfied that the infringement of the Canadian patent was a relevant illegality. Therefore, the defendant's appeal was approved. It is clear that, in this judgment, not only the knowledge of the illegality was considered, but whether the illegality is severe enough to trigger the illegality defence was considered as well. And the criteria to decide whether an act is turpitude or not will all depend on the precise circumstances.[80]

---

75 *Burrows v Rhodes* [1899] 1 Q.B. 816.
76 *Safeway Stores Ltd v Twigger* [2010] EWHC 11 (Comm) at 974.
77 *Hewison v Meridian Shipping* [2003] I.C.R. 766.
78 *Les Laboratoires Servier v Apotex Inc* [2011] EWHC 730.
79 *Les Laboratoires Servier v Apotex Inc* [2013] Bus LR 80.
80 Ibid.

However, Servier appealed again: in its latest judgment, which has been delivered by the Supreme Court, Lord Sumption reviewed the development of the common law rules on the illegality defence; again, he criticised the public conscience rule and proportionate rule, and decided that these two rules should be abolished as a result of the uncertainty that may result. He upheld the wider and narrow rule, since these two rules did not contradict the judgment of *Tinsley*. He concluded that the most essential question which needs to be answered before the application of the *ex turpi causa* defence is what kinds of acts contribute to turpitude, namely, what kinds of acts can be seen as not only criminal but also immoral and illegal. By reviewing former authorities, the resolution which has been proposed by Lord Sumption is that for an act to be immoral or illegal, it must be "contrary to the public law of the state and engage the public interest".[81] And the act should be criminal or quasi-criminal and engage the public interest in the same way, because public interest is the foundation of the illegality defence. Lord Sumption clearly stated that torts, breaches of contract, statutory and other civil wrongs should not trigger the illegality defence and deprive the "guilty parties'" ordinary remedies, since all these acts offend against interests which are essentially private, not public.[82] Furthermore, an exception has been added by Lord Sumption: in the circumstances where the claimant is not privy to the facts making his act unlawful, his act cannot be seen as turpitude. For example, if the claimant has no knowledge of the facts which are making his conduct unlawful.[83]

Lord Toulson, on the other hand, delivered a wider rule, that is, all torts of strict liability are not severe enough to trigger the illegality defence. According to Lord Toulson "There are very few reported cases in which the doctrine of illegality has been applied to tort".[84] The only contrary case he cited in his judgment is *Brown Jenkinson & Co Ltd v Percy Dalton (London) Ltd* and the reason why judges in this case decided the plaintiff's tort triggered the illegality defence is because the plaintiff was fraudulently minded, otherwise, the plaintiff would not be failed as according to former authorities. In Lord Toulson's view, *ex turpi causa* is not a fixed rule or policy; on the other hand it is a defence which is based on public policies,[85] and policies which need to be considered vary from case to case. He quoted three recent authorities to support his view, *Gray v Thames Trains Ltd*,[86] *Stone & Rolls Ltd v Moore*[87] and *Stephens and Hounga v Allen*.[88] All these three authorities support one argument that *ex turpi causa* is not based upon a single justification but on a group of reasons, which vary in different situations, namely the public conscience or/and proportionate test (this will be introduced later). Indeed, at the end of his Lordship's judgment, Lord Toulson suggested that the rule which has been cited by *Tinsley v Milligan* should be re-analysed in detail.

---

81 *Les Laboratoires Servier v Apotex Inc* [2014] 3 WLR 1257 at para 25.
82 Ibid at para 28.
83 *Burrows v Rhodes* [1899] Q.B. 816.
84 *Les Laboratoires Servier v Apotex Inc* [2014] 3 WLR 1257 at para 56.
85 Ibid at para 61.
86 *Gray v Thames Trains Ltd* [2009] AC 1339 at 1370, para 30.
87 *Stone & Rolls Ltd v Moore Stephens* [2009] 1 AC 1391 at para 25.
88 *Hounga v Allen* [2014] 1 WLR 2889.

It is clear from former analysis of the case that, although the two judges came to the same conclusion, the rationales which underlie their judgments are different. From Lord Sumption's view, the principle which was launched by *Tinsley* is still good law, although he quoted the same phrase from the *Gray* case as Lord Toulson did; they explain Lord Hoffmann's phrase from different perspectives. In Lord Sumption's view, Lord Hoffmann dealt with the dilemma by defining as a matter of law when the illegality defence applied and when it did not, and the narrow and wider rule which was cited in *Gray* "did not seek to deal with the dilemma by leaving the court to make a value judgment about the seriousness of the illegality and the impact on the parties of allowing the defence".[89] And this is the reason why he held the disposition of this case by Etherton LJ as incorrect. In fact, by Lord Sumption's judgment, there is no existence of a seriousness test; there are only two kinds of immoral conduct, and in any case which may involve such conduct, the defence would be triggered.

However, in Lord Toulson's opinion, the policies which underlie the *ex turpi causa* principle can be and should be expanded and modified as according to the facts of each individual case. That means there is no fixed rule on which kind of act is turpitude; it will based on the analysis of the fact of each individual case. He held that Etherton LJ's approach is a good law. However, which kinds of factor shall be taken into consideration when deciding whether an act is serious enough or not have not been considered by Lord Toulson.

Although both judgments are valuable to current law and each of them has its own merit, Lord Sumption's test is more practical. The aim to consider the seriousness factor is to decide which kind of conduct is severe enough to trigger the defence. Lord Sumption clearly defines the boundary of this issue. It brings certainty to this aspect and resolves the dilemmas of former authorities, as can be seen from the beginning of this section. Although there will still be discussion on the judgment of *Tinsley*, one thing is for sure: a tort which is committed with no contravention of public interest and unintentionally will not trigger the defence.

(g) The proportionality principle
This principle was first raised in the case *Saunders v Edwards*. It was concluded by Bingham LJ that, when the illegality issue is raised, the court should avoid two unacceptable situations: "On the one hand it is unacceptable that any court of law should aid or lend its authority to a party seeking to pursue or enforce an object or agreement which the law prohibits. On the other hand, it is unacceptable that the court should, on the first indication of unlawfulness affecting any aspect of a transaction, draw up its skirts and refuse all assistance to the plaintiff, no matter how serious his loss nor how disproportionate his loss to the unlawfulness of his conduct."[90]

There are basically two kinds of the principle of proportionality. Firstly, the court will balance the actions of the defendant and secondly, the court may need to refer

---

89 *Les Laboratoires Servier v Apotex Inc* [2014] 3 WLR 1257 at para 19.
90 *Saunders v Edwards* [1987] 1 W.L.R. 1116 at 1134.

to the illegality conduct of the claimant and the amount of loss the claimant will suffer if the claimant's claim is disallowed.

As to the first kind of proportionality principle, if the conduct of the defendant is far more culpable than the claimant's then it is unlikely that the illegality defence will be applied. The most typical case with regard to this issue is the *Revill v Newbery* one, introduced previously. It is clear that the defendant's conduct of discharging the gun is far more culpable than the claimant's intention of breaking in. Thus, the claimant's claim for compensation of injury was allowed.

The second kind of proportionality principle was raised by Ward LJ in the case *Hewison v Meridian Shipping Ltd*.[91] In this case, the claimant seaman suffered from epilepsy, which should have prohibited him from working as a seafarer. However, by concealing his disease, he worked for the defendant employer for several years until 1997, when he suffered an epileptic seizure while at work which resulted in his being dismissed by the defendants. The claimant claimed damages on two grounds: first, on the ground of the negligence and breach of statutory obligation of the defendant and secondly, on the ground of earnings which he would have received until his retirement age but for the accident.

Both in the first judgment and the second judgment, the first claim of the claimant was allowed and the second was rejected. The reason for this kind of decision, as concluded by Clarke LJ, is that ". . . an English court should not deprive a claimant of part of the damages to which he would otherwise be entitled because of the defendant's negligence or breach of duty by reason only of some collateral illegality or unlawful act".[92] However: "It is common ground that there are cases in which public policy will prevent a claimant from recovering the whole of the damages which, but for the rule of public policy, he would otherwise have recovered".[93] Therefore, it is clear that the court weighed the seriousness of the illegality of the claimant and the loss which he suffered, and although he could not rely upon his illegality to claim more damages, his damage because of the negligence of the employer was allowed despite his unlawful conduct. In Ward LJ's decision, he noted that this kind of proportionality is not quite the same as the first one.

However, the limitation of this principle, especially the first type of the principle, was also noted by the court. As pointed out by Beldam LJ, it is not permissible in every case for the court to weigh up the degree of illegality by the claimant on the one hand and the defendant on the other hand to decide which one of them should be allowed to recover.[94] It was also noted in the *Hewison* case that applying the first type would be "reintroducing through the back door the public conscience test which we are not allowed to apply".[95] Therefore, as applied in this case, the proportionality rule is subject to many other kinds of principles such as the reliance principle and the causation principle.

---

91 *Hewison v Meridian Shipping Ltd* [2002] EWCA Civ 1821.
92 Ibid at 43.
93 Ibid at 28.
94 *Cross v Kirkby* [2000] WL 530.
95 *Hewison v Meridian Shipping Ltd* [2002] EWCA Civ 1821 at 72.

However, as the public conscience test has been overruled and the discretion of the courts has been reduced, it seems that the proportionate test would very rarely be applied if the other principles have been considered first. In the case *Joyce v O'Brien*, the judge overruled the claimant's appeal, which was based on the proportionality principle. Since in this case, what the claimant committed was a real crime with real moral culpability, and even though the proportionality principle still existed, the learned judge concluded that this doctrine will only be applied in minor traffic offences.[96] And furthermore, in the most recent judgment of the case *Les Laboratoires Servier v Apotex Inc*, it was considered by Lord Sumption that the proportionate test contradicts the intention of Lord Mansfield in the *Holman* case and application of this test will only cause uncertainty in this area of law.[97]

(h) The intention of the statute principle

The essence of this principle is that, when deciding whether the claimant is barred by the illegality defence, the intention of the statute and Parliament should be taken into consideration. The court will need to examine the intention of an Act when claimants commit some illegality which is recognised by statute. Therefore, in the case *Cakebread v Hopping Brothers*, which dealt with contributory negligence during work, and the court, when overruling the employer's argument that the negligence was solely caused by the workman, stated that: "The policy of the Factories Act makes it plain that such a defence as that put forward here would be inconsistent with the intention of Parliament."[98]

In a later case, *National Coal Board v England*, when dealing with whether the plaintiff's damages as a result of injury could be compensated, the House of Lords held that even though the plaintiff had committed an unlawful act under the statute, there was nothing "in the statute which creates the obligation indicating the intention that no action shall be brought at common law in respect of its breach, the ordinary rules of the common law of tort are applicable, including the doctrine respondent superior".[99]

This was also the case in the *Revill* case, as one of the grounds the court relied on when rejecting the defendant's illegal defence was that "Parliament has decided that an occupier cannot treat a burglar as an outlaw and has defined the scope of the duty owed to him".[100]

3.2 The application of the tort illegality defence to insurance law

The essence of this section is that, since the illegality defence *ex turpi causa* is applied in tort law, then: firstly, this defence will also be applied in insurance law; secondly, if this defence is applied in a tort case, then this application will affect the claimant's right against his insurer, and the insurer can use the illegality defence

---

96 *Joyce v O'Brien* [2013] EWCA Civ 546.
97 *Les Laboratoires Servier v Apotex Inc* [2014] 3 WLR 1257.
98 *Cakebread v Hopping Brothers* [1947] K.B. 641 at 654.
99 *National Coal Board v England* [1954] A.C. 403 at 422.
100 *Revill v Newbery* [1996] Q.B. 567 at 577.

in tort to deny the insurance claimant; and thirdly, if the illegality rule can be applied, then the extent to which this rule influences the insurance compensation and the existence of any exceptions in this circumstance, needs to be considered.

The illegality defence is always used by the insurer against the assured. This section of the book will examine two kinds of situations in insurance law when the illegality defence in tort law has been applied: firstly, if the claimant under the tort case is the insured under an insurance policy and has committed some kind of illegal act, then the illegality defence will influence the claimant assured's right under the insurance policy; and secondly, if the defendant under the tort is the assured under an insurance contract and involved in some kind of illegality, particularly in the circumstances of liability insurance, then the role of illegality in this insurance contract needs to be considered as does the question as to whether, if the defendant is denied compensation under the insurance contract, this would be fair to the claimant and would there be any other method for the claimant to be compensated in this circumstance. This section will examine how the illegality defence in tort works in insurance law and whether the restrictions which apply in tort also have the same effect in insurance law. Furthermore, the Law Commission's suggestions regarding this point will be introduced.

3.2.1 Why the ex turpi causa *defence is important in insurance*

The existence of the *ex turpi causa* principle in tort law does not mean that this rule can be applied automatically in insurance law. Therefore, for the *ex turpi causa* defence to be applied in insurance cases, the rationale underlying this application should be analysed.

Firstly, the illegality defence is important because of the nature of the insurance. As indicated by authorities, in the early development of insurance law, insurance, especially liability insurance, was considered to be immoral. For example, life insurance can be viewed as an encouragement to suicide and murder and fire insurance may encourage people to gamble with their own interests; as concluded by Mary Coate McNeely: "throughout its history the insurance device has been alternately hailed as a promoter of communal welfare and damned as a generator of evil".[101] Thus, illegality in insurance law is strictly forbidden in order to avoid such situations and to protect the interests of the insurer, especially in marine insurance, as has been explained before. It is an ordinary principle of insurance law that an assured cannot by his own deliberate act cause the event upon which the insurance money is payable.[102] This decision clearly shares the same character as Lord Mansfield's judgment in *Holman*.

Secondly, such defence is important because of the shortage of laws on the illegality issue in insurance law. Except in regard to marine insurance law, there is no implied warranty of legality in general insurance law, which means that the assured's right cannot be denied as soon as an illegality emerges. Besides the Motor Insurance Act and the Insurance Industry Act, there is no general rule which relates to

---

101 "Illegality as a factor in liability insurance" (1941) *Columbia Law Review* 26.
102 *Beresford v Royal Insurance Company* [1938] A.C. 586 at 595.

insurance illegality, since the illegality issues in insurance law arise mainly because of contract claims and tort claims, and thus both the consequence of the illegality under tort and contract should be taken into consideration. Thus, it is clear that whether the insurer is liable to the assured will largely depend on whether the illegality defence will be sustained under tort rules.

Thirdly, the reason why there is an illegality defence in insurance law is also because of the consistency of law. The consistency test in tort law has already been discussed; by applying that test it would be very difficult for judges to grant the guilty assured's claim when such conduct is barred in a tort case. As to the defendant's liability insurance, whether the insurer is liable to loss will totally depend on the tort conduct committed by the defendant. If the defendant has been held as having committed a crime, then insurers will deny their liabilities under the insurance contract, even though such a decision would leave the third party in a difficult situation.

Fourthly, if the claimant's illegal conduct has been judged as immoral or reprehensible under tort law, then such illegality will be rendered as not an adventure which the insurance intends to cover, and therefore the claimant's compensation will be denied.

The fifth possible ground for this application is deterrence. As explained in *Thackwell v Barclays Bank Plc*, the illegality defence is available for deterrence purposes "where the court, in finding for the plaintiff, would be indirectly assisting or encouraging the plaintiff in his criminal, fraudulent or illegal activity".[103] However, this rationale was questioned by the Law Commission as whether the rationale, which is of limited function in tort, will also apply to insurance, since the tort and insurance claims are often concerned as different from each other and the effect of deterrence on the claimant in terms of compensation is of course limited since "a person who is not deterred from these activities by the threat of criminal sanction will be deterred by the possibility that he or she may not receive compensation for any loss suffered in the course of or as a result of committing the offence".[104] There used to be an argument that, by applying the illegality defence in insurance law, this would have a deterrence effect on the assured, since every time the assured may plan to commit some kind of illegal act, the assured would be afraid of losing the insurance compensation. However, this argument has been the target of criticism, since in life insurance cases, the criminal activity committed by the assured is always an offence in criminal law, and it would not be believable that the assured would be afraid of the loss of recovery rights under the insurance policy.

However, if the assured buys an insurance policy with the clear objective of benefitting from the insurance, then the deterrence rationale would clearly have an effect on him since deterrence will prevent other people from entering into the same arrangement or performing the same illegal act. This was the case in *Beresford*; since suicide was a crime at that time, the denial of compensation under the insurance policy would clearly act as a deterrent to other policy holders who wanted to benefit from their life insurance policy.

---

103 *Thackwell v Barclays Bank Plc* [1986] 1 All ER 676 at 689.
104 LCCP 189, para 7.9.

3.2.2 *General principles under insurance law which relate to the illegality defence in tort*

(a) The narrow and wider rule in insurance law

When dealing with insurance cases which involve the claimant's conduct having been tainted by illegality in tort, courts mainly reach the same result as the illegality cases in tort. As has been discussed above, there are three main rules indicated by former cases and it is not appropriate to apply any of these rules individually. The duty of care test has clearly come under criticism in English law and it is still uncertain whether it has the same effect as in Australian law; the public conscience test which was widely used has been overruled by the House of Lords; and even though the reliance principle is one of the oldest principles in English law, it is clear that its rigid character requires this principle to be applied in conjunction with several restrictions. Therefore, it is clear that none of these three principles suitably apply when dealing with insurance cases individually. Furthermore, the consequences of illegality when applying these rules is quite unclear.

Thus, compared with former tests, the narrow and wider rules cited in the *Gray* case have clearly taken different kinds of restrictions into account and are more suitable for general application. Therefore, the assured cannot be compensated under an insurance contract with regard to losses caused by his own criminal act under wider rules or the fines and punishment imposed on him under narrow rules. However, it seems that the narrow rules will rarely be applied since fines or punishment does not constitute a proper adventure for an insurance policy to cover.

Thus, when applying the narrow and wide rule, it is clear that the insurance policy which covers the claimant's loss and the claimant's fine and punishment is unrecoverable under insurance law. For instance, in the case *Hardy v Motor Insurers' Bureau*, the judge held that the guilty driver could not force the insurance policy to release compensation because of his intention to commit a criminal act, even though this does not mean that the innocent third party is not left uncovered. This was also the case in *Marcel Beller v Hayden*, where the assured was killed in a road accident because of his own drinking and driving a vehicle at a speed which was dangerous to the public, both of which acts were contrary to statute and therefore illegal. By deciding this, the courts finally decided that the guilty claimant could not recover losses under the insurance policy.

However, it seems that applying the narrow rule in insurance law is not always the same as in tort, because there are more factors to consider because of the character of insurance law; therefore, it is not in every case in which the assured has committed a crime that the insurance policy is unrecoverable.

However, there are three exceptions that need to be considered when applying the narrow and wider rule: firstly, whether the illegal conduct is committed intentionally, which is mainly the case with motor insurance cases; secondly, the function of the Forfeiture Act 1982; thirdly, the claimant's compensation will not be barred if the cause of his illegality is the negligence of the insurer or third party.

As to the first exception, it seems both the mind of the claimant when committing such illegality and the causation link between the illegality and the loss should be considered. With regard to considering the claimant's mind, this is a matter of deciding whether the claimant committed the illegal act deliberately. This is very clear in the judgment of *Gray v Barr*, when both Lord Denning and Salmon LJ consented that if the claimant had committed the illegality intentionally he was barred from recovering damages under the insurance policy since such illegality amounted to an exception in the terms of the insurance policy; this kind of action clearly did not amount to accident under insurance law.

Furthermore, whether the illegal conduct of the claimant is intentional or not also relates to whether public policy should have an effect on the illegality issue. This is another of the inconsistencies between illegality in insurance law and tort law if the narrow rule is applied in insurance cases. The inconsistency lies in motor insurance and suggests that in motor insurance cases, although conduct which is clearly illegal under tort law will bar the defendant from recovering from the insurer, it will not bar an innocent third party from recovering damages under the insurance policy.

In the case *Tinline v White Cross Insurance Association*, the claimant with the insurance policy committed the serious crime of manslaughter, causing two people to die by driving a motor car negligently. When the claimant claimed indemnity under the insurance policy, the insurer used the illegality as a defence since the insurance is contrary to public policy if the claimant is entitled to be indemnified against his criminal act. By overruling the insurer's argument, the learned judge raised two main points, the first of which is that, by construing the words and intentions of the insurance policy, the judge held that the intention of such insurance is to cover such an accident caused by the negligence of the assured and without such cover there is no need for the existence of such an insurance policy. Therefore, the claimant's illegal conduct fell within the scope of accident in the policy. The second point is that, although generally speaking it is true that "it is against public policy to indemnify a man against the consequences of a crime which he knowingly commits",[105] if the claimant commits such a crime purely because of negligence rather than intentionally, then the difference may be drawn between intentional illegality and negligent illegality, and intentional illegality clearly should not be covered.[106]

Another case dealing with illegality in motor insurance is *Marles v Philip Trant & Sons Ltd*.[107] It was decided in this case that "a motorist can rely on his policy of insurance to indemnify him in respect of his liability for any injuries which he has caused otherwise than on purpose".[108] Thus, at least in motor insurance cases when the intention of the claimant is considered, the narrow rule is not applicable.

Another exception exists in the Forfeiture Act 1982, s 2, which deals with the discretion of the court when dealing with such cases. Section 2 of this Act authorises the court to make an order under this section modifying the effect of the rule of forfeiture when dealing with illegal killing other than murder cases. A typical example of this discretion is the case *Dunbar v Plant*. In this case, both the

---

105 *Tinline v White Cross Insurance Association Limited* [1921] 3 K.B. 327 at 331.
106 Ibid at 332.
107 *Marles v Philip Trant & Sons Ltd* [1954] 1 Q.B. 29.
108 *Gray v Barr* [1971] 2 Q.B. 554 at 582.

defendant and her fiancé agreed to commit suicide together but the defendant failed and her fiancé succeeded; the defendant, who had been found guilty of aiding and abetting her fiancé's suicide, claimed ownership of their shared house, their joint bank account and especially two insurance policies: "one on the deceased's life for the benefit of the defendant and the other charged to the building society which held the mortgage of the house".[109] On the first judgment, the judge deprived the defendant's right to ownership of the house and the insurance policy for it, but denied her right to the life insurance policy. On the second judgment, the learned judge found that the exercise of discretion of court should be based on the conduct of the offender and the material circumstances rather than on reaching justice between the two parties. Since the defendant had intended to commit suicide with her fiancé rather than kill him and the defendant had no intention of benefitting from the insurance and the suicide, and since it was also the deceased's family's will not to oppose the defendant's right to obtain ownership of the house and the money of the insurance, the court finally exercised the discretion to grant the defendant full relief from the forfeiture and the right to be compensated under the life insurance policy. However, an exception of this kind has limited use in insurance cases, except for those cases in which the claimant has no intention of causing the death of the defendant and has no intention of benefiting from the death. Since Lord Denning in *Gray v Barr* ruled that: "In manslaughter of every kind there must be a guilty mind. Without it, the accused must be acquitted",[110] cases for which such an exception can be applied should be very rare.

The third kind of exception of the wider rule in insurance cases is that if the loss or fine upon an assured is simply because of the insurer's negligence which has caused the assured to commit a strict liability criminal offence under the circumstances, then the narrow rule will not bar the claimant assured from claiming indemnity against the insurer defendant. In the case *Osman v J Ralph Moss Ltd*, the plaintiff assured was fined for driving without insurance which the defendant broker had failed to obtain for him; the plaintiff sued the defendant for compensation of the fine and his claim was allowed since in this case the claimant was not in himself guilty of gross negligence, unlike in the *Askey* case. However, this exception is largely because of the principles in tort law, since when sustaining the illegality defence, there is a requirement for causation and the turpitude of the claimant's conduct. Therefore, it is clear that, when dealing with insurance cases which relate to illegality under tort law, there is also a requirement for causation.

(b) The benefit principle in insurance: whether this is the proper rationale when illegality relates to tort

The benefit principle is a fundamental principle in insurance law, although the word "benefit" is not always correct, as indicated by Malcolm Clarke, since it is difficult to measure whether the guilty assured benefits from the illegality or not.[111] Therefore, this principle is sometimes explained thus: "a person (or those that stand

---

109 *Dunbar v Plant* [1998] Ch. 412.
110 *Gray v Barr* [1971] 2 Q.B. 554 at 568.
111 Malcolm A Clarke, *Law of Insurance Contracts* (4th edn), para 24–5A3.

in the shoes of such a person) may not stand to gain an advantage arising from the consequences of his own iniquity".[112] This is not one of the fundamental principles which constitute the illegality rule in tort law, although there is one rationale that states that no man can rely on his own criminal act. The claimant's situation in tort law is always that, rather than seeking to profit from his own criminal act, the claimants always claim for compensation from the defendant. However, the principle that no man shall profit from his own wrong is a long established rule in insurance contracts, and this principle has been applied in illegality cases which relate to tort.

In *Cleaver v Mutual Reserve Fund Life Association*, a husband was poisoned to death by his wife, but the husband had taken out an insurance contract to the benefit of his wife. When dealing with whether the executor of the husband was eligible to claim under the insurance policy or not, Lord Esher stated: "That the person who commits murder, or any person claiming under him or her, should be allowed to benefit by his or her criminal act, would no doubt be contrary to public policy".[113] However, the court finally cited that the executor of the insurance policy maintained an action on the insurance policy notwithstanding the illegality of the wife. This no-benefit principle was also recognised in the *Beresford* case; in this case, as mentioned above, the court held that the insurance contract which promised the assured to pay his executor and assignee the full amount of money insured, even if the assured killed himself in full possession of his senses, was void since, quoting the judgment of *Cleaver*: "It appears to me that no system of jurisprudence can with reason include amongst the rights which it enforces rights directly resulting to the person asserting them from the crime of that person".[114]

However, there are some exceptions to this principle. Firstly, this no-benefit rule only restrains the guilty claimant from seeking compensation from the insurance policy and does not extend to the innocent third party involved in this. Therefore, in the *Cleaver* case, the illegality of the wife did not bar the right of the executor of the husband to enforce the insurance policy even though this was for her benefit, as concluded by Fry LJ: "In a word, it appears to me that the crime of one person may prevent that person from the assertion of what would otherwise be a right, and may accelerate or beneficially affect the rights of third persons, but can never prejudice or injuriously affect those rights".[115] This exception is widely applied in motor insurance cases. In the motor insurance case *Gardner v Moore* for example, the guilty first defendant injured the claimant intentionally by driving an uninsured car; however, when the innocent claimant claimed compensation against the MIB, the House of Lords contended that the wrongdoer's illegality would not bar the innocent third party from claiming under the insurance policy and the no-profit principle should have no effect on innocent third parties, even though the defendant had not paid the compensation he should have paid, which could be seen as a profit for the defendant.

---

112 *Gardner v Moore* [1984] A.C. 548 at 558.
113 *Cleaver v Mutual Reserve Fund Life Association* [1892] 1 Q.B. 147 at 152.
114 Ibid at 156.
115 *Cleaver v Mutual Reserve Fund Life Association* [1892] 1 Q.B. 147.

Secondly, it is clear that in common law, there needs to be some connection between the illegality committed by the assured and the insurance. This used to be a controversial topic since the connection is difficult to define; however, since the judgment of *Tinsley v Milligan*, it is now clear that recovery is precluded only if the claimant must rely upon his own criminal act.

(c) How the other rationales apply in insurance
The third issue concerns how other rationales for dealing with illegality in tort law are applied in insurance illegality issues; and whether such applications are suitable for resolving the illegality issue in insurance law.

As has been discussed above, the connection principle is clearly adopted by English courts when dealing with illegality tort cases, which is to say that if the injury or loss suffered is unrelated to the criminal act then the *ex turpi causa* defence is not applicable. However, whether this rule should be applied in insurance cases dealing with illegality is controversial; that is to say, whether the insurance is still enforceable if the assured's illegality has no connection with the loss incurred. In other fields of insurance law, it seems that English courts incline towards establishing some connection between the loss and the assured's act. For example, when dealing with insurance warranties, English courts are inclined to contend that for the breach of warranty to be sustained, there should be some connection between the breach and the loss which the assured suffered.

However, compared with the connection rule in tort and the law in other fields of insurance, English courts seem to adopt another method when dealing with insurance policies which involve illegality. In the latest Court of Appeal case of *Delaney v Pickett*,[116] which dealt with a road traffic accident, the claimant who was injured by the first defendant's car because of a collision sought to recover from both the uninsured first defendant and the second defendant, the Motor Insurer's Bureau (MIB). In its first judgment, the claims against both the first defendant and the second defendant were denied since a package containing herbal cannabis, which was clearly illegal, was found concealed in the claimant's jacket. By appealing to the Court of Appeal, the claimant's claim against the first defendant was allowed since "the injury suffered by the claimant had been caused not by his criminal activity but by the tortious act of the first defendant in the negligent way in which he had driven the car".[117] However, the claimant's appeal against the MIB was dismissed since the judge found that "the vehicle was being used in the . . . furtherance of a crime, if not also in the course . . . of a crime", which fell in exclusion clause 6(1)(e)(iii) of the 1999 Agreement. From the second judgment, it is clear that there is inconsistency between the tort law decision and the insurance decision and it seems that the wide rule which has been used in tort cases cannot be applied in insurance law, since in tort cases, as analysed above, for the wide rule to be applied not only should the illegality be in connection with the loss but it should also be serious enough for judicial intervention. However, with regard to the facts in this case, neither of the two requirements were fulfilled; therefore,

---

116 *Delaney v Pickett* [2012] 1 W.L.R. 2149.
117 Ibid.

from the tort law's position, the claimant's illegality should not prevent him from claiming damages from the MIB. The main obstacle to the tort rule being applied in this case may be that there is an express exception in the agreement and for this exception to be applied there is no requirement for a causal link between the damage the claimant suffered and the illegality he committed. Therefore, since the first defendant was not insured, this particular scenario falls into this exception. However, there is a mere reference on this issue, since it is clear that, in this case, the injury which the claimant suffered was caused purely by the negligent driving of the defendant. Because of the vague language of this clause, as the judge found, there is no requirement for the seriousness of the illegality and the causation link between the illegality and loss for this exception to be applied; illegal conduct is sufficient. It seems that if the causation principle can be fully applied in insurance law, then the Agreement which the court relied upon should be ignored, even though it has been argued that if the defendant has been insured then the consequence will be different.

However, there are some obstacles to the causation principle being applied in insurance cases. Firstly, even though the illegal conduct may not cause the loss directly, it will cause the aggravation of risk and the insurer clearly has an interest in risk management and loss prevention. For example, in the *Delaney* case, even though the carrying of herbal cannabis was not the direct cause of the loss, it was difficult for the court or the insurer to ascertain the influence of the illegality on the negligence of the driving. It is probable that the defendant and the claimant were eager to trade the drugs with someone or it is probable that the judgment of the defendant had been influenced by earlier consumption of the drugs, both of which circumstances clearly create an aggravation of the risk.

Secondly, even though the illegality may not directly cause aggravation of the risk, it may enable the insurer to assess what sort of people the insurer is dealing with and moral hazards.[118] However, it is clear that, as a result of the Road Traffic Act 1981, as long as the driver is insured, the illegality will not influence his insurance claim against the third party.

Thus, these two reasons have resulted in the exclusion clause in an insurance policy possibly expressly excluding the application of the causation principle. For example, the exclusion clause in *Marcel Beller Ltd v Hayden* excludes the insurer's liability if "directly or indirectly resulting from . . . deliberate exposure to exceptional danger . . . or the insured person's own criminal act".[119]

When applying the seriousness of illegality exception in insurance cases, it seems that there is no such rule in insurance law that states that if the illegality committed by the assured is trivial, then the assured can be indemnified. When dealing with insurance illegality cases, courts tend to pay more attention to the mind of the assured. Thus, it is clear that no public policy may prevent a man from insuring his negligence and if the loss is caused by the negligence of the assured, even

---

118 Malcolm Clarke, "Aggravation of risk during the insurance period" (2004) *Lloyd's Maritime and Commercial Law Quarterly* 109 at 112.
119 *Marcel Beller Ltd v Hayden* [1978] Q.B. 694.

though such illegality may have caused serious injury, the insurance policy is still enforceable. This is especially the case with motor insurance.

Furthermore, it is clear that, when dealing with the seriousness issue in insurance law, the knowledge and the intention of the assured when committing the illegal conduct are still key factors. Therefore, if the assured commits a crime intentionally then even if the crime may not have severe consequences or lead to an unintentional loss, the insurance contract is still unenforceable since such conduct contradicts the basic principle of insurance.[120] Therefore, it is clear that the seriousness of the illegality factor only will not affect the validity of the insurance policy.

However, an exception can be found in the case *Marcel Beller v Hayden*.[121] In this case, the claimant died because he was drunk when driving. Although the judge decided that the claimant did not cause the crash deliberately or intentionally, he concluded that the dangerous driving of the claimant was still a matter of culpability or turpitude and was sufficient to be a criminal act.

The proportionality principle in tort law is not the same as the proportionality principle in insurance law. As discussed previously, the proportionality principle in tort is firstly a comparison between the claimant's illegal conduct and the seriousness of consequence he will suffer if his claim is refused because of such conduct; and secondly, comparison between the illegal conduct of the defendant and the illegal conduct of the claimant. Compared with illegality cases in tort law, where it seems that if the assured is induced into an insurance policy because of the illegality of the insurer such as if the insurer is not eligible to issue insurance in the UK, then the assured is able to be fully compensated; if the assured on the other hand has committed a crime or tort because of the illegality of the insurer, such as with life insurance, if the assured commits suicide because of the inducement of the insurer, it is clear that the court will not weigh the illegality between the assured and insurer and that, since the inducement is less serious than the suicide then the insurer can deny his liability. Therefore, the second kind of tort proportionality principle in insurance law is not applicable.

As opposed to tort law, the proportionality principle adopted in insurance law can be construed like this: "The court has to weigh the gravity of the anti-social act and the extent to which it will be encouraged by enforcing the right sought to be asserted against the social harm which will be caused if the right is not enforceable".[122] This is one of the *dictums* adopted in the case *Hardy*. In other words, "enforcement of a contract should not be refused unless the potential benefit in deterring misconduct or avoiding a misuse of the judicial process outweighs the factors favoring enforceability".[123] Therefore, unlike in tort law, in the circumstance where both the defendant and the claimant shall be blamed, the court will not refuse to enforce the insurance simply because of the illegality which has been committed by the assured; the court will weigh the illegality of the claimant against the effect on public policy if the claimant's insurance is enforced in spite of such

---

120 *Gray v Barr* [1971] 2 Q.B. 554.
121 *Marcel Beller v Hayden* [1978] Q.B. 694.
122 Malcolm A Clarke, *Law of Insurance Contracts* (4th edn), para 24–5A3.
123 *Town of Newton v Rumery*, 480 US 386 (1987).

illegality. The most typical example is in motoring cases, as indicated above; the claimant's motor insurance is enforceable either because the claimant has caused injury to the third party negligently or intentionally, as in *Gardner v Moore*. Therefore, in insurance cases, the court seems to consider more the intention of statutes and the construction of the policy, as well as the effect of enforcement.

However, the issue of whether the court will consider the seriousness of the assured's illegality and the seriousness of the loss the assured will incur if the enforcement of the insurance policy is disallowed is not clear. At least one point which relates to this issue is clear, which is that if the enforcement of the insurance relates to the compensation of an innocent third party, then the court will consider the disallowed effect. If, on the other hand, the insurance being enforceable or not will not influence the compensation to the third party, will the court then enforce the insurance policy despite the trivial illegality of the assured? It seems that if the illegality committed by the assured is slight, negligent and has no connection with the loss, then the insurance policy is still enforceable unless the illegal act is not covered by the insurance policy. It may seem that compared with the illegal act which has been committed by the assured, the refusal to grant the insurance is far more severe.

It is clear from the authorities that, if the illegality is committed deliberately by the assured, then even though such illegality may be trivial, the insurance will not cover such conduct and accordingly, the proportionality rule will not be applied.

The last exception which exists in tort law is to examine the intention of the statute. This is also an exception in insurance cases although it is only used occasionally. In *Hardy*, when dealing with whether the motor insurance policy covered the intentional criminal act, Lord Denning held that: "The policy of insurance which a motorist is required by statute to take out must cover any liability which may be incurred by him arising out of the use of the vehicle by him".[124] This argument was further affirmed by the House of Lords in *Gardener*. Therefore, the third party in this circumstance is entitled to recover damages in spite of the assured's illegality, for this is the statute's requirement.

This exception also exists in other insurance cases; if the intention of parliament does not preclude such recovery, then the illegality should not be an obstacle.

It is quite clear from the above that when dealing with insurance cases which are tainted by the claimant assured's illegality, the English court tends to adopt an approach which is different from that in tort cases. It seems that more severe consequences for the assured may emerge when dealing with such cases.

This may be the case firstly because, as stated before, society and insurers have an interest in loss prevention and risk management and therefore the insurer tends to manage the risk as small as possible, since illegal conduct of the assured, no matter of which kind, may significantly result in aggravation of the risk, which means that this conduct has changed the character of the subject matter insured.

Secondly, the illegal conduct of the assured, no matter how trivial, always falls into the exception clause of the insurance policy; therefore, even in cases where

---

124 *Hardy v Motor Insurers' Bureau* [1964] 2 Q.B. 745 at 760.

there is no causal link or the denial of the assured's claim is disproportionate, the court has to follow the words of the insurance policy. For example, in *Charlton v Fisher*[125] the injury to the claimant happened in a car park: even though the driver had been insured according to the Road Traffic Act 1988, and it had been established that the defendant had no intention of injuring the claimant, his recovery against the MIB under the insurance policy was denied, as was the claimant's request under the insurance policy. The only reason was that the accident happened in a car park rather than on a road regulated by the Act and therefore the accident was not covered by the insurance policy, which was clearly unfair to the innocent third party.

Thirdly, the assured's criminal act could not be considered as a risk in insurance law. It is clear that the insurance policy only covers risks and no more, and therefore whether the criminal activity performed by the assured is an accident that falls within the cover offered in an insurance policy is not clear, especially when this conduct is executed by the assured intentionally. It has always been decided by the authorities that the intentional illegal conduct of the assured is not an accident under the insurance policy, as in *Gray v Barr*.[126] According to the judgment of this case, the deliberate act of holding a gun and going upstairs was the dominant cause of the loss and this conduct was not covered by the wording of the insurance policy. However, a negligent act of the assured, such as the speeding cases in motor insurance, as in *Marcel Beller v Hayden*,[127] may be recognised as an accident and covered. However, if the negligent speeding is caused by some intentional act which the assured should have foreseen would cause the danger and injury to life, then this conduct would not be treated as an accident either. Just as Rix LJ cited in *Charlton v Fisher*: "A distinction should be drawn between damage caused by a deliberate criminal act and damage intentionally caused".[128] However, this judgment is still subject to public policy.

(d) What is the proper way of dealing with tort illegality in insurance law?

Based on the former analysis, it can be concluded that, when dealing with insurance cases in which tort illegality has been involved, it is improper to apply the narrow and wider rules in *Gray v Thames* commonly and that the other rationales which underlie the illegality defence in tort have limitations as well since the circumstances in insurance law are far more complex than in tort law. Instead of using one or two general rules in all circumstances concerning illegality, different rules or different factors should be considered with different modes of illegality.

Based on former common law cases, there are basically four kinds of illegality mode in tort law and each illegality mode may include a corresponding insurance illegality mode. The first mode of illegality in tort law is the simplest one, namely that A has done nothing wrong and B is the tortfeasor; therefore, any loss which B

---

125 *Charlton v Fisher* [2002] Q.B. 578.
126 *Gray v Barr* [1971] 2 Q.B. 554.
127 *Marcel Beller v Hayden* [1978] Q.B. 694. It has been established that as long as the loss is caused by the assured's negligence and not by a deliberate act, such loss can still be seen as accidental injury.
128 *Charlton v Fisher* [2002] Q.B. 578 at 579.

suffers during or after the illegal conduct cannot be recovered from A. With regard to the insurance policy, if B has insured against such behaviour, this means that B cannot recover any losses or compensation for any punishment from his insurer. Under these circumstances, both the narrow and wider rules can be applied. One typical example of this mode is *Gray v Barr*. However, one exception may exist in motor insurance: A can recover the loss suffered from B's insurer as long as the loss is covered by the insurance policy.

The second illegality mode in tort law is when C suffers loss as a result of B's illegal conduct which is caused by or contributed to by A's former tortious act. In other words, but for A's former tortious act, B would not be a tortfeasor to C, which was the situation in *Gray v Thames* and *Clunis v Camden*. Based on the court's decision it seems that, as long as B does not rely on his own criminal act in a claim for compensation, his loss prior to his criminal act should be covered by A; therefore, in this circumstance, if B is insured by D against any loss to the third party caused by B then this insurance will be unenforceable because of the wider rule and any insurance which covers B's punishment will also be unenforceable if there is any insurance of this kind, since any insurance which insured against B's criminal act will be void from the beginning. However, if A is insured under these circumstances, can A recover from his insurer against B's loss prior to his criminal act? It seems that as long as it can be decided that the loss was caused by A's negligence rather than intention, then the loss can be recovered and the recovery will not be tainted by B's later illegality since such illegality has no causal link with A's former tortious conduct and B can even bring a claim against A's insurer directly. Therefore, in these circumstances, the court should take the exceptions in narrow and wider rules into consideration and should not deny B's interest under insurance rigidly; however, if the situation falls into the exclusion clause, then B's interest will be excluded.

The third illegality mode in tort law is that A suffers loss caused by B's illegal conduct as a result of A's former threat or tortious conduct. In other words, the situation is that B overreacts to A's tortious conduct and commits a crime or causes significant loss to A, which is greater than that A caused to B. A similar case can be found in *Revill v Newbery* where the defendant shot a suspicious trespasser and in this case the plaintiff was not debarred from claiming damages from the defendant. However, the trespassing case is a special one, because the Act intends to protect the right of the intruder, and thus, according to *Revill*, "by enacting section 1 of the Act of 1984, Parliament has decided that an occupier cannot treat a burglar as an outlaw".[129] Thus, if the intruder has been insured against such injury then the insurance policy shall be enforceable. However, except for this particular situation, it seems that in other similar circumstances both A and B cannot be covered by their insurers. Since firstly, according to the current causation rule in insurance law, the reason for A's loss is purely his tortious conduct at the beginning, A cannot rely on his own illegal act to plead this claim. In B's situation, though, B's illegal act is caused by A's tortious conduct, his conduct is also illegal and is also

---

129 *Revill v Newbery* [1996] Q.B. 567 at 577.

precluded by common law. Thus, both the narrow rule and the wider rule will be applied in this situation.

The fourth illegality mode is that A and B commit a crime or engage in tortious conduct together and cause loss to C or to A and B. If A and B have caused loss to C, then it is clear that both A and B cannot recover losses under the insurance policy as long as the crime was committed intentionally. However, the difficult question is whether, if A and B have caused damages to themselves, A/B can recover losses: (1) under respective insurance policies; or (2) against the other's insurance policy. As long as the first scenario is considered, neither A nor B can recover losses under their insurance policy provided that both of them are involved in the illegality irrespective of whether the illegality has a connection with the loss which they suffered. However, if B is innocent and the damage which B suffers is purely because of A's negligence or intention, then will B's rights under the insurance policy survive? For example, in a road accident case, if B sits on a motorcycle which is driven by drunk A and suffers loss, will this loss be covered by B's insurer? It seems that B cannot recover his insurance policy either, since the insurer will argue that if B was aware that A has drunk and is willing to get on his motorcycle, then he willingly takes this risk and this clearly results in the aggravation of the risk, as has been discussed previously. This is the difference between the insurance law and tort law; in tort law as long as there is no connection between the illegality and the loss, the claimant can still recover from the defendant, as in the case of *NCB v England*.

However, the consequence will be quite different if the second scenario is considered. In the road accident example, if A is insured according to the Road Traffic Act 1988 then even though B cannot recover under his own insurance, he can clearly recover against A's insurer. Even if A is not insured, so long as certain conditions are fulfilled, B can still recover from MIB provided that B is not involved in A's illegality.

(e) The specificity of the illegality issue in motor insurance
The situation with motor insurance is quite different from other kinds of liability insurance since motor insurance against the third party is compulsory because of statute. In light of the decision in *Hardy*, the specificity of illegality rules in motor insurance can be summarised in two points: firstly, "The policy of insurance which a motorist is required by statute to take out must cover any liability which may be incurred by him arising out of the use of the vehicle by him. It must, I think, be wide enough to cover, in general terms, any use by him of the vehicle, be it an innocent use or a criminal use, or be it a murderous use or a playful use";[130] and secondly: "But if he does not pay the damages, then the injured third party can recover against the insurers under section 207 of the Road Traffic Act 1960; for it is a liability which the motorist, under the statute, is required to cover".[131] Other than the requirements of the Road Traffic Act and the insurance policy, there are two rationales which are behind the exception of motor insurance: the first one,

---

130 *Hardy v Motor Insurers' Bureau* [1964] 2 Q.B. 745 at 760.
131 Ibid at 761.

according to the judgment of *Charlton v Fisher*, is ". . . the principle of statute, that innocent third parties should be protected so far as money can do it from the harm – sometimes fatal – that may be inflicted by careless, dangerous and criminal drivers on the public roads: a protection not sufficiently given by the private law of insurance";[132] and the second one is that the aim of the exception is to protect the potential victim rather than compensate the guilty assured.

The exceptional rules for motor insurance clearly contradict general illegality rules both in contract and in tort law. Therefore, two questions may arise: firstly, what is the boundary of the exception – are there any elements which will limit this exceptional rule? Secondly, can the mode of motor insurance be applied in other areas of liability insurance?

So far as the first question is concerned, there are several elements which clearly limit the application of motor insurance rules. It is clear from the authorities that the causation link between the loss and the vehicle and the words and the coverage of policies will all be considered when the courts are dealing with motor insurance cases.

The first limitation is that, if there is an expressed exception in statute then the motor insurance rule will not be applied. One typical example of this limitation can be seen in the case of *Delaney v Pickett*, which was discussed before; the only obstacle which prevented the claimant from recovering from the second defendant, the MIB, was the exclusion clause in the 1999 Agreement. Therefore, even though the illegality did not bar the claimant from recovering against the first defendant, it barred the claimant from recovering against the MIB. Compared with the *Hardy* case, both the vehicles were uninsured and both the defendants used the vehicle to commit a crime intentionally; the sole difference between the two cases is the exclusion clause in the 1999 Agreement. However, it should be noted that, if the defendant in this case had been insured, then the consequence would have been totally different.

The second limitation is that, for the claim against the MIB to be successful, the risk needs to be covered under the Road Traffic Act 1988. In *Charlton v Fisher*, Kennedy LJ admitted the authorities in the *Hardy* case; the only obstacle in *Charlton* was that the accident did not happen on a road defined in the Road Traffic Act 1988 (RTA 1988), ss 143(1) and 145(3); and since "the incident in fact occurred off the road, the claimant has no such redress".[133] Another example of this kind is the case *AXN v John Worboys and Inceptum Insurance Co Ltd*.[134] In this case, a taxi driver raped several women in his car, and ten of his victims brought a claim against him and his insurer since his car had been insured. A preliminary issue when deciding this case is whether the "law goes as far as to require insurance under section 145(3)(a) RTA 1988 not for deliberate and intentional dangerous driving, but for the acts of administering substances as well as for actual and attempted sexual assaults".[135] However, since the injuries suffered by the claimants were not

---

132 *Charlton v Fisher* [2002] Q.B. 578 at 592.
133 *Charlton v Fisher* [2002] Q.B. 578 at 591.
134 *AXN v John Worboys and Inceptum Insurance Co Ltd* [2012] EWHC 1730 (QB).
135 Ibid at para 79.

arising out of the use of a vehicle, the judge decided that there was neither an expressed nor an implied requirement in the Act that sexual assaults should be covered, and therefore the claim failed.

The third limitation that exists in English law is that there is a requirement for a causal link between the loss that the claimant suffered and the use of the insured or uninsured vehicle, since it is the requirement of the RTA 1988 that ". . . to any person or damage to property *caused by, or arising out of*, the use of the vehicle on a road [or other public place] in Great Britain".[136] This issue was also considered in the *AXN v John Worboys* case since the court needed to consider whether the loss arose out of the use of the vehicle or not. Silber J examined both the English law authorities and the Commonwealth authorities and concluded that the true meaning of section 145(3)(a) of the RTA 1988 is that: firstly: "The term 'arising out of' encompasses more remote consequences than those envisaged by the words 'caused by'",[137] and does not mean a proximate cause or effective cause. Secondly, the words "arising out of" describe the relationship between the injuries suffered and the use of the vehicle when the injuries were suffered. Thirdly: "The application of the words 'bodily injury . . . arising out of the use of a vehicle' entails considering all the material circumstances".[138] And fourthly, "the purpose of the user of the motor vehicle is relevant in deciding whether what occurred and in particular the bodily injuries arose out of the use of his motor car".[139] These rules can be concluded as the causal link requirement in motor insurance cases, and with the application of these rules, Silber J concluded that the sexual assaults were not causally connected with the use of the vehicle on the road and therefore the claimants' claim was defeated.

Thus, so far as the first question of this section is concerned, there are limitations related to motor insurance illegality rules. However, whether or not these limitations are applied does not change the position that, so long as the statutory and common law requirements are fulfilled, there is no obstacle to an innocent third party claiming damages from the guilty assured's insurer.

Thus, the next question which relates to this issue is whether the mode of compensation in motor insurance should be applied in other kinds of liability insurance against injury to a third party; that is, whether an innocent third party in every type of liability insurance has the right to claim damages against the defendant's insurer no matter how severe the crime of the defendant is.

3.3 Conclusion

In this chapter the illegality issue under common law which relates to tort claims has been discussed. It can be seen that illegality in tort does not automatically render the claimant without protection. The key point which should be remembered is that for the illegality defence to be sustained the mere fact of illegality

---

136 Road Traffic Act 1988, s 145(3)(a).
137 *AXN v John Worboys and Inceptum Insurance Co Ltd* [2012] EWHC 1730 (QB) at para 58.
138 Ibid.
139 Ibid.

is not enough; several other factors, particularly the causal link between the loss and illegal conduct, should be considered. The last part of this chapter shows how tort law rules can be applied to motor insurance cases, and this analysis can be of great value to the extent to which section 41 in marine insurance law could be reformed.

CHAPTER 4

The illegality defence in contract law and its application in insurance contracts

4.1 Introduction

In the previous chapter, the illegality defence in tort law was considered and it is clear that the application of this defence in insurance law is closely connected to common law rationales, and that the illegality rules in tort law have been modified in order to cope with the speciality of insurance law. In this chapter, the illegality defence in contract law will be examined. Unlike the illegality defence in tort law, the illegality issue in contract law is far more complex, since in tort circumstances only the performance of the contract can be included, but when dealing with the illegality issue in contract law, both the construction and performance of the contract are involved and both statutory illegality and common law illegality are considered. This chapter will consider the origins of the illegality defence under contract law and both statutory and common law illegality. Furthermore, reasons for the differences between statutory illegality and common law illegality and the impact of the division on insurance law will also be examined, since it is obvious that the factors considered by the courts may be different when dealing with different kinds of illegalities.

4.2 Contracts rendered illegal by statute

Besides the illegality defence in tort law, there are also several illegality rules in contract law. There are basically two kinds of illegality in contract law: firstly, a contract may be expressly or implicitly prohibited by statute; and secondly, a contract may be forbidden because it violates common law and public policy.

Statutes may influence the legality of a contract in two ways, with regard to either the formation of the contract or to the performance of the contract. In the first category, statutes may expressly or implicitly state the requirements of the formation of a contract and if such requirements have not been complied with, then the contract is illegal. For example, a licence of Parliament was needed in the early nineteenth century in order to carry out trade with another country and an insurer had to be authorised before carrying out any business in the UK. With regard to the second category, if statutes have expressly or implicitly stated how to perform a contract then these regulations should be complied with. Thus, if a statute requires the seller to give the buyer a specific invoice, then if there is no invoice, the contract has been executed illegally. Similarly, if a transport vehicle is over-loaded and this is prohibited by the statute, then the transport contract becomes illegal. The difference between the two kinds of illegality is that, in the first category, the courts intend to render the contract unenforceable and in the second category there is debate as to whether what has been forbidden by statute should influence the enforceability of the contract.

When deciding whether a contract is illegal or not, it is easier if the statute provided clear instructions and stated the consequences of a violation. For example, section 2 of the Insurance Companies Act 1974 regulates that: "(1) No person shall carry on in Great Britain insurance business of a class relevant for the purposes of this Part of this Act, other than industrial assurance business"; and section 11 regulates that: "(1) A person who carries on business in contravention of this Part of this Act shall be guilty of an offence . . . (3) A person guilty of an offence under this section shall be liable – (a) . . . (b) . . .".[1] Section 83 of this Act also regulates that the ambit of the insurance business regulated by the act involves "the business of effecting and carrying out contracts of insurance".[2] Therefore, if the insurer is not entitled to write an insurance policy and he has done so negligently, then not surprisingly, even though this Act is intended to protect the assured's interest, the insurance contract is void and unenforceable.

However, difficulties exist in circumstances where statutes ignore this point or there is no clear instruction regarding the consequences of a violation. When dealing with cases like this, courts have considered both the purpose of the legislation and all the relevant facts. Therefore, it is clear that not every violation of statute renders a contract void and unenforceable.

The purpose of the legislation is for the court to examine the terms of the legislation and meaning of words in the legislation and to examine what is implicitly forbidden by the statute and whether the contract or the performance of contract falls within the ambit of the legislation. The most significant case on this subject is *Archbolds Ltd v S Spanglett Ltd*.[3] In this case, the plaintiff used the defendant's unlicensed vehicle to transfer goods, the goods were stolen during the journey and the plaintiff claimed damages against the defendant. When refusing to compensate, the defendant alleged that the contract was illegal since the vehicle used for transporting was unlicensed, according to the Road Traffic Act 1933. After examining the facts of this case and the language of the legislation, the court decided that there was no illegality with regard to the performance of the plaintiff according to the Act since, firstly, the performance of the plaintiff did not constitute the definition of "use" of the vehicle under the Act, and furthermore, the object of the Act was to control the person who provided the transport service rather than to interfere with the owner of the goods. Besides examination of the specific words of an Act to decide whether the act of the party falls within the statute's ambit, another, more simple, method is to decide what the statute aims to protect. In *Victorian Daylesford Syndicate v Dott*, after a financial transaction between the defendant and the plaintiff, the plaintiff alleged that the whole transaction was illegal since the

---

1 Insurance Companies Act 1974, s 11.
2 Ibid, s 83.
3 *Archbolds Ltd v S Spanglett Ltd* [1961] 1 Q.B. 374.

defendant had not registered himself according to the Money-Lender's Act 1900 and thus had not made the loan of money in his registered name, as required by the Act. When deciding whether the Act was so worded that the contract of loan was to be rendered illegal because of the illegality of the defendant, Buckley J decided that "statutes may be grouped under two headings – those in which a penalty is imposed against doing an act for the purposes only of the protection of the revenue, and those in which a penalty is imposed upon an act not merely for revenue purposes, but also for the protection of the public".[4] Therefore, if a statute is there to protect the interests of the public, then a violation of this Act will render the contract illegal and unenforceable and the defendant would not be able to sue under the terms of the contract.

In addition, if the Act, instead of clearly stating whether the contract is void or not, imposes a penalty on the illegal party, this regulation does not necessarily mean that the contract is not unenforceable under the Act. For instance, if the Act aims to protect the public interest, then contracts of this kind can still be construed as unenforceable and prohibited by the statute.[5] Furthermore, deciding whether an act is prohibited by the statute or not means seeing ". . . whether the penalty in the Act is imposed once and for all, or whether it is a recurrent penalty imposed as often as the act is done".[6] This means that there is a difference between statutes which are intended to penalise specific commercial activity and those which are intended to penalise the contracts in relation to illegal conduct. If it is the latter case, then such acts will be prohibited.

Besides the examination of the intention and the word of the statute, the nature of the contract may also influence the consequences of illegality in implied prohibition circumstances. Therefore, for instance, if a contract requires the performance of only one party and the other party has no involvement in the illegality, then the prohibition of statutes falls on the guilty party only and the innocent third party can be protected. For example, in a carriage of goods contract in a case such as the *Archbolds*, the absence of a licence made the carrier a guilty party who could not recover under the terms of the illegal contract, but the owner of the goods, who had no involvement in the illegality, could. However, on the other hand, if the performance of the contract needs the involvement of both parties, then both parties are under the restriction of the implied obligation and a violation of the obligation may result in the contract being unenforceable.[7]

However, there are some exceptions in statutory illegality circumstances. The first is the possibility of evasion of statutes and the second is a waiver of statutory rights. As far as the first exception is concerned, in the case *Director of Public Prosecutions v Bhagwan*[8] a commonwealth citizen from India tried to commit an

---

4 *Victorian Daylesford Syndicate v Dott* [1905] 2 Ch. 624 at 629.
5 *Cope v Rowlands* 150 E.R. 707.
6 *Victorian Daylesford Syndicate v Dott* [1905] 2 Ch. 624 at 630.
7 As to the impact of the *Archbolds* case on the implicit prohibition by statute please see M.P. Furmston, "Illegality – The Limit of a Statute" (1961) *Modern Law Review*, vol 24, no 3 at 394; and also see R.A. Buckley, "Implied Statutory Prohibition of Contracts" (1975) *Modern Law Review* vol 38, Issue 5 at 535.
8 *Director of Public Prosecutions v Bhagwan* [1972] A.C. 60.

evasion at immigration control and when deciding whether the respondent had committed an offence under the Commonwealth Immigration Act 1962, the House of Lords stated that, so far as the Act was concerned: firstly, there were no restrictions on Commonwealth citizens coming into Britain; secondly: "The appellant's entry into the United Kingdom could not have been regarded as injurious to the public interest before, or apart from, the Act of 1962, and it was not prohibited by that Act";[9] and thirdly, the intention of the Act of 1962 was not to control the immigration of Commonwealth citizens into Britain but to treat Commonwealth citizens far less rigidly than aliens. Therefore: "It is no offence under the law of England to do or to agree with others to do acts which, though not prohibited by legislation neither criminal nor tortious at common law, are considered by a judge or by a jury to be calculated to defeat, frustrate or evade the purpose or intention of an Act of Parliament".[10] Thus, so long as the former three requirements are fulfilled, the contract cannot be said to be illegal under statute.

Except for this kind of evasion of statute, the "innocent" party of an illegal contract can also evade the consequences of the illegality if the other party has committed some kind of immoral or illegal act, unrelated to the contract, which has caused losses to the "innocent" party. In *Close v Wilson* the plaintiff and defendant had a written agreement on betting and the plaintiff paid £20,000 for betting purposes; however, this money was used for his own benefit and he alleged that it was lost because of unsuccessful betting on horses. The plaintiff required the return of the money; however, his application was barred because this kind of gaming contract was made illegal under the 1892 and 1845 Gaming Acts. The Court of Appeal upheld that the agreement between the plaintiff and defendant – that the defendant should repay the money irrespective of which was spent on betting – was illegal, since such an agreement was forbidden by the Act. However, the judges agreed that: "The unenforceable nature of the agreement itself would be no bar to the Mr Close's restitutionary claim if the money was used for a purpose extraneous to the agreement".[11] Thus, since the losses which the plaintiff suffered had no connection with the illegality of the contract, then his right to recover was still enforceable.

The second exception in statutory illegality is whether a party can waive a statutory right through a contract. It is clear that, if the contract aims to waive a statutory obligation of the parties, then the waiver will be void; and if the waiving of statutory rights would undermine the public interest, then the waiver would also be void; for example, the implied warranties in the Marine Insurance Act 1906 cannot be waived through contracts. Other than these two circumstances, the possibility of waiver will depend on whether the waiver contradicts the intention of the statute, in which case it would also be void. Since as cited by Lord Hailsham in *Johnson v Moreton*, the "whole purpose of consolidation would be defeated if they were not observed and rigidly adhered to or if endeavours were made to split the

---

9 Ibid at 66.
10 *Director of Public Prosecutions v Bhagwan* [1972] A.C. 60.
11 *Gary Close v Colin Wilson* [2011] EWCA Civ 5.

various components of the consolidation Act apart and construe them by reference to their individual histories".[12]

Except for the two exceptions which have been discussed, knowledge of the illegality of the parties also plays an important part in dealing with statutory illegality cases. The courts also consider the knowledge of both parties to decide whether one of them is innocent or both are. This test was used in *Archbolds* when deciding that: "If they were aware of the true facts they would, of course, be guilty of aiding and abetting the defendants, but if they acted in good faith they would not be guilty of any offence under the statute".[13] Therefore, in this case, since the plaintiff had no knowledge of the illegal purpose and act of the defendant he was not precluded from suing the defendant according to the contract.

However, if one of the contract parties holds the knowledge that the other party has committed an illegality or plans to perform an illegal act, or that both the parties have the same illegal intention to enter the contract or perform the contract illegally, then neither of them will be innocent under the contract. This was exactly the case in *Ashmore, Benson, Pease & Co Ltd v A.V. Dawson Ltd*.[14] In this case, both the defendant transport manager and the plaintiff's servant held the knowledge that the lorry was overloaded, which was in breach of the Road Traffic Act. During the transit, the plaintiff's goods were damaged due to the load; the plaintiff subsequently brought an action against the defendant and the defendant used the illegality defence. The court decided to sustain the illegality defence and the plaintiff was not able then to recover from the defendant, since the defendant's illegality was known to the plaintiff, who had even participated in it. However, it has long been decided in English law that an illegal act committed after the formation of the contract will not render the contract unenforceable; therefore, for the contract to be unenforceable, the parties need to enter into it with the purpose of acting unlawfully.[15]

Nevertheless, if a party has taken reasonable precautions to prevent the commission of the illegality, then he will be not guilty of aiding and abetting.[16] However, if one party to the contract has no knowledge of the illegality of the contract or the illegality of his own action, then it seems that his rights under the contract will not be entirely deprived. One exception to this concerns ignorance of the law on the part of both parties. According to the case *Waugh v Morris*, "where a contract is to do a thing which cannot be performed without a violation of the law, it is void, whether the parties knew the law or not".[17]

Thus, when the courts are deciding whether one of the parties or both parties are involved in illegality or not, both the intention of the parties when entering into the contract and the knowledge of illegality of the parties when performing the contract will be considered.

---

12 *Johnson v Moreton* [1980] A.C. 37.
13 *Archbolds Ltd v S Spanglett Ltd* [1961] 1 Q.B. 374 at 385.
14 *Ashmore, Benson, Pease & Co Ltd v A.V. Dawson Ltd* [1973] 1 W.L.R. 828.
15 *Chitty on Contracts* (31st edn), vol 1, para 16–010.
16 *Davies, Turner & Co Ltd v Brodie* [1954] 1 W.L.R. 1364.
17 *Waugh v Morris* (1872–73) L.R. 8 Q.B. 202.

There used to be an argument that "failure to comply with the statute makes the contract void if the requirement is obligatory but not if it is only directory".[18] However, the meaning of the words "obligatory" and "directory" and the criterion adopted in this sentence is not clear. It seems that the requirements of performance on the part of the contractual parties may be regulated as obligatory and the requirement for formalities in the statute seems directive, the violation of which will not render the contract void. The objective of this distinction is to relieve the harsh consequence on the guilty party. However, not every formality requirement in statutes goes to the core of a contract; if there is an obligation on the contractual party to obtain some kind of licence for the contract to become valid, then the violation of this requirement will still be viewed as a breach of an obligatory requirement, thereby making the contract void. Therefore, the fundamental issue when dealing with such cases is still the meaning and intention of the statute.

4.3 Contracts rendered illegal by common law

Another kind of illegality in contract law which differs from statutory illegality is the illegality of contract in common law and public policy. This form of illegality is more complex than statutory illegality and there are no defined rules on it. Both the relevant aspects of the origin and development of the illegality of contract in common law and the general rules which underlie the illegality defence will be discussed below.

4.3.1 The origin and development of contract illegality in common law and public policy

The origins of the fundamental rules of contractual illegality can be traced back to the eighteenth century, when the judges laid down some basic principles based on specific cases they had encountered. At that time, contracts which were injurious to the fundamental interests of society, such as a contract which is a restraint of marriage,[19] would not be tolerated. The fundamental principle in public policy, that is "*ex dolo malo non oritur action*, was founded in the case *Holman v Johnson*, which was discussed earlier: "No Court will lend its aid to a man who founds his cause of action upon an immoral or an illegal act".[20] Thus, it can be said that both the illegality rule in contract and the illegality rule in tort share the same origin.

However, the public policy cited in this case is only a vague one and cannot be applied directly in other cases, since: firstly, the general principle of public policy may vary from generation to generation and therefore, some policies which were vital in the nineteenth century, such as the licence to trade with foreign countries, are unnecessary nowadays; and secondly, the seriousness of the illegality in contract is not taken into account in this principle, a limitation which led to later developments in the illegality rule in contract law. Courts have adopted different rules

---

18 *Treitel on the Law of Contract* (13th edn), para 11–009.
19 *Lowe v Peers* (1768) 4 Burrow 2225.
20 *Holman v Johnson* 98 E.R. 1120.

when dealing with different levels of severity of illegality and the consequences of different kinds of violation of the law are clearly different.[21]

Besides the lack of clarity in public policy, the unstable character of public policy also came under criticism during the development of the illegality doctrine in contract.

Just as indicated in the case *Bennett v Bennett*,[22] the case in which illegality in the contract is criminal clearly cannot be treated in the same way as where only one provision of the contract is illegal, such as in a trade contract where only the purchase price of the goods is too low and this may have violated the competition regulation. Therefore, in the former case, the entire contract will be rendered void and unenforceable and in the latter case, only the illegal section will not be executed and the other parts are not influenced.

However, there are still some difficulties when courts distinguish the severity of the illegality. Both the conduct of the parties and the consequences of their illegality are taken into account. Thus, if their illegality has not led to any serious consequences and their conduct cannot be classified as contrary to public interest, then the illegality will be considered trivial, and normally this will not result in the entire contract being made void.

This kind of development leads to a discussion of whether the word "illegal" is properly used to describe all kinds of illegality in contract law. There is an argument that when describing this issue, the word "illegal" should be used for more serious types of illegal contract – such as a contract to commit a crime – and that contracts which involve trivial illegality should be described as void and unenforceable. There is also an argument that a contract is void and unenforceable with regard to public policy when there is only a possible rather than a probable potential for it to not be in the public interest.

4.3.2 General principles of illegality under common law

The key question when deciding illegality issues under common law is to decide whether the contract is rendered illegal or unenforceable by public policy. In contrast with illegality under statute, public policy is more unstable and flexible, and it is agreed that this characteristic has made the illegality issue of contracts under common law more complex.

According to *Chitty On Contracts*, public policy can be classified into five categories: "first, objects which are illegal by common law or by legislation; secondly, objects injurious to good government either in the field of domestic or foreign affairs; thirdly, objects which interfere with the proper working of the machinery of justice; fourthly, objects injurious to marriage and morality; and, fifthly, objects

---

21 For understanding the contracts which are illegal under public policy please see Walter Gellhorn, "Contracts and Public Policy" (1935) *Columbia Law Review*, vol 35, no 5, pp 679–696. See also Percy H. Winfield, "Public Policy in the English Common law" (1928) *Harvard Law Review*, vol 42, no 1, pp 76–102; and John Shand, "Unblinkering the Unruly Horse: Public Policy in the Law of Contract" (1972A) *Cambridge Law Journal*, vol 30, no 1, pp 144–167.
22 *Bennett v Bennett*, 208 U.S. 505 (1908).

economically against the public interest".[23] However, it is clear that not all of them relate to marine insurance law and therefore, there is no need to clarify every category of illegality. According to Law Commission reports, illegality under common law can be summarised under three headings: the first one is that the content of the contract requires the parties to commit a legal wrong; secondly, the intent of the contract is to facilitate the commission of a legal wrong; thirdly, the contract itself is legal but the legal contract has been performed illegally.[24] The following section will critically consider these three headings.

So far as the first and third categories are concerned, because of the differences between them – and because these differences may require the courts to consider different factors when deciding cases and may result in different consequences – they will be considered separately. Both the categories may involve the performance of contractual parties, the difference being that, in the first category, the conduct of the parties is not a requirement when deciding whether the contract is illegal or not – the mere agreement to commit a crime is enough; however, in the third category, the conduct of the contractual parties is a necessary condition, and the illegality is based on this conduct.

However, the first category of illegality may also involve the conduct of a contractual party, so that even though the illegality resides in the conduct of the parties, it still falls into the first category. For example, a case concerning a contract for the carriage of goods by road, where the goods can only be loaded by parking the van illegally for a while, would be regulated in the first category rather than the third one since, compared with the third one, the illegal conduct in this case is the same as an implied term in the contract, without which the contract could not be fulfilled and there is no way for the parties to choose a legal method. However, in the third category, there is no such restriction; the contract in the third category is legal and can be performed legally, and the contractual parties choose to act illegally for profit or for illegal purposes. Therefore, even though both categories may involve the performance of contracts, they should be viewed differently.

This category of illegal conduct may involve statutory illegality; for instance, if the contract requires the parties to commit a crime like murder, then it is clearly unenforceable. However, this scenario is very rare, and in most illegality cases, the legal wrong the parties perform, which is in the terms of the contract, is venial, as in the example raised before; the terms of a carriage of goods contract requires the loading of the goods which can only performed by parking illegally, and the question is whether this illegality deprives the carrier's right for freight or discharges the carrier's liability under this contract? According to the statutory illegality issue discussed earlier, it seems that if there is a clear prohibition in statute then the conduct will be rendered illegal and the consequence of the illegality will be decided according to the statutory law. That is to say that, if the illegality is not a serious crime under statute or the punishment for the illegality is minor, then the illegality may not result in the contract being unenforceable.

---

23 *Chitty On Contracts* (31st edn), para 16–005.
24 Law Commission Consultation Paper No.189 3.12.

However, if the legal wrong is not a crime which has been specified in statute then the illegality will be decided according to the criteria of common law. Although this principle may seem rigid and unfair to the contractual parties, it is based upon two powerful points: firstly, according to the judgment of *Archbolds*, discussed earlier, if both the contractual parties know the contract cannot be carried out without the commission of an illegal act then the contract will be unenforceable; secondly, as was discussed previously, the ignorance of the law on the part of the contractual parties does not make any difference.

Therefore, in this category, where the contractual parties make an agreement to commit an act which is prohibited by law, the general principle can be summarised thus: firstly, where there is an express or implied prohibition of forming the contract in statute, then the contract which contains the illegality will be unenforceable, no matter whether the parties are aware of the law or not; and secondly, where the statute only prohibits the act which the terms of the contract require to be carried out, then this requirement does not entail the contract becoming automatically unenforceable. In this situation, the validity of the contract is a question under common law, and the knowledge of parties will be considered, as was discussed above: if both parties have knowledge of the illegality, then both parties shall be denied relief from the contract; if only one party has knowledge of the illegality and the other party does not, then the innocent party should not be affected by the legal wrong; however, if both parties have no knowledge of the illegality, then the intention and interpretation of statute will be considered, and if the intention of the statute is to forbid contracts which contain such illegalities, then the contract will be unenforceable regardless of whether the parties have knowledge of the law or not. Furthermore the seriousness of the legal wrong would be considered as well.

The second category of illegal contract, as summarised in the Law Commission Report, is that where the intention of the contract is to commit a legal wrong. The first question is whether the purpose of the contract is equal to the intention of the parties? Firstly, it should be stated that if the parties enter the contract with an illegal purpose, such as an intention to defraud the insurer when entering an insurance contract, then the purpose of the contract will also be illegal and in this situation, the insurance contract will be unenforceable. However, in a situation where the purpose of the contract is illegal but the contractual parties have no knowledge of that illegality and have no intention of breaking the law, would the contract then be rendered unenforceable also? It seems that the answer is no, under such circumstance – if the parties have no intention of violating the law then even though the purpose of the contract is illegal, the contractual parties can still enforce the contract. In *Waugh v Morris*,[25] the defendant chartered the plaintiff's vessel to import hay from France to England; however, neither party was aware that it was illegal for hay from a French port to be landed in the UK. After the defendant charterer became aware of the illegality, he transferred the hay alongside the ship, which caused some demurrage; the plaintiff requested the payment of the demurrage and the defendant refused by claiming that the contract was illegal. In

---

25 *Waugh v Morris* (1872–73) L.R. 8 Q.B. 202.

this case, the purpose of the contract (to land the hay in the UK) was clearly illegal, but the court decided that the contract was not void since the parties had no knowledge of the law and therefore had no intention of acting illegally. Therefore, in circumstances in which the parties have no intention of breaking the law and have no knowledge of the illegal purpose implied in the contract, then so long as the contract can be performed legally, it is still enforceable. Under these circumstances, the intention of the parties is not equal to the purpose of the contract.

Another issue which relates to the knowledge of contractual parties is that the different knowledge of illegality of contractual parties will lead to different consequences. This principle in common law is almost the same as the principle in statutory illegality cases, discussed earlier. Where only one party has the intention of breaking the law when entering into the contract and the innocent party has no awareness of that, then the contract is only unenforceable on the guilty party. This principle was decided in *Fielding & Platt Ltd v Selim Najjar*[26] where the defendant buyer used the invoice issued by the seller to deceive the Lebanese authorities, but because the seller had no knowledge of the illegal intention, the illegality defence raised by the defendant failed. Furthermore, Lord Denning's judgment of this case made the requirements for the illegality defence workable: firstly, the seller should have knowledge of the illegality and secondly, the seller should actively participate in it. This raised the question of what amounts to participation in an illegal purpose. According to Lord Denning, mere knowledge of the other party's unlawful purpose does not amount to participation: in *Foster v Driscoll*,[27] quoted by Lord Denning, the judgment stated that: "In my view the present position of the law is that the mere fact that a vendor of goods knows that the purchaser proposes to run them into a country where they are prohibited by some revenue law is not sufficient to render the contract of sale illegal, but if beyond mere knowledge the vendor actively engages in an adventure to get the goods into such country, the Court will not assist the parties to the adventure by entertaining or settling any dispute between the parties arising out of the contract".[28] Thus the active engagement of the other party is needed.

However, how active that engagement should be so that the "innocent party" will be deprived of the contractual relief is still uncertain. It seems that this question, in fact does not require a great deal of attention. If one party of the contract knows of the other party's illegal purpose and participates to facilitate that unlawful purpose then no matter how trivial that participation is, if it can be proved that the contractual parties share the unlawful purpose during the performance of the contract, then the contract is unenforceable.

Another issue which is unclear in the Law Commission Report is the closeness between the illegal intentions of the contract or the contractual parties and the contract which the parties intend to enforce. Two cases were raised in the report

---

26 *Fielding & Platt Ltd v Selim Najjar* [1969] 1 W.L.R. 357.
27 *Foster v Driscoll* [1929] 1 K.B. 470.
28 Ibid at 518.

to demonstrate this uncertainty: *21st Century Logistic Solutions Limited v Madysen Limited*[29] and *Alexander v Rayson*.[30]

In the first case, the liquidator of 21st Century Logistic Solutions Limited sued on behalf of the company for the price of goods against the buyer, the buyer refused to pay for the goods because they have been imported illegally, since the objective of 21st Century Logistic Solutions Limited in trading was to avoid payment of VAT on imported goods and to profit from the VAT, which is clearly an illegal objective. Based on this, the buyer of the goods claimed that the contract of sale was illegal and therefore, that the contract was unenforceable; the buyer therefore refused to pay. Both the contractual parties and the judges agreed that the contract to defraud the Revenue was illegal; however, the judge contended that ". . . there must come a point when the connection with the plaintiff's intention to the contract is too remote for the contract to be held to be unenforceable. In other words, not every contract entered into with the intention of committing an illegal act is illegal and unenforceable".[31] The judge came to this conclusion based on various reasons, the most important two being that: firstly, the fraud of the HMCE intended by 21st Century was not finally carried out; and secondly, the plaintiff's illegal purpose had no connection with the contract which the defendant intended to defeat.

It seems that when deciding whether the illegal purpose is close enough to render the contract unenforceable, simply having proof of the existence of the illegal purpose is not sufficient and neither is the mere connection that the "guilty party" has the illegal intention and enters a contract with the other party. The important issue is that the illegal purpose should also have been fulfilled or nearly fulfilled by the "guilty party" and the illegal purpose should not be collaterally connected with the contract.

The second case discussed by the Law Commission report was *Alexander v Rayson*, which was decided before the *21st Century* case. The two contradictory decisions were used by the Law Commission to demonstrate the uncertainty of the closeness of the contract to the unlawful purpose. The *Alexander* case was decided in 1936 and the facts of the case are simple: the claimant rented a flat to the defendant for GBP 1,200 per year, and the claimant planned to defraud the local Assessment Committee by using two documents which stated different amounts of rent to reduce the value of the flat. However, the valuation authority was aware of this conduct and restored the original value of the flat. Later, the claimant sued for arrears of rent and the defendant used illegality as a defence. In the first trial of this case, it was decided that the illegality in this case was too remote from the rent contract itself to render it illegal and unenforceable, since the contract between the two parties had been performed lawfully and there was no evidence that the claimant had entered this contract with the intention of performing it unlawfully. However, in the second judgment, the Court of Appeal reversed this decision and decided that the contract had been tainted by illegality and was unenforceable; this decision

---

29 *21st Century Logistic Solutions Limited v Madysen Limited* [2004] EWHC 231.
30 *Alexander v Rayson* [1936] 1 K.B. 169.
31 *21st Century Logistic Solutions Limited v Madysen Limited* [2004] EWHC 231.

was based on the public policy that "the contract is unenforceable if it intended that the subject matter of the contract was to be used for an unlawful purpose".[32] This general rule was cited in *Pearce v Brooks* in which a brougham was rented to a prostitute with the purpose of facilitating illegality; it was stated that: "One who makes a contract for sale or hire with the knowledge that the other contracting party intends to apply the subject matter of the contract to an immoral purpose cannot recover upon the contract".[33] However, it was recognised by the judges of the *Alexander* case that, in this case, the two documents which had been used for illegal purposes were not the subject matter of the rent contract. However, by quoting the case *Scott v Brown, Doering, McNab & Co* the court decided that "in the present case, it was the formulation of the transaction in a particular way by means of the lease and agreement, and not the subject-matter of the transaction, of which an illegal use was to be made".[34] Therefore, it makes no difference if it is the subject matter of the contract which is intended to be used unlawfully. The court came to the conclusion that: "In the present case, however, the documents themselves were dangerous in the sense that they could be and were intended to be used for a fraudulent purpose, without alteration, and the splitting of the transaction into the two documents was an overt step in carrying out the fraud. We cannot think that the plaintiff is entitled to bring these documents into a court of justice and ask the Court to assist him in carrying them into effect".[35]

It seems that the judgments of the two cases contradict each other, since by applying the rule in the *21st Century* case, the claimant's illegal purpose, although it had been performed, had no connection with the payment of the rent and the judgment of *Alexander* seems too strict, a view implied by the judgment of the *21st Century* case when it was agreed by Professor Furmston that: "The decision is understandable but it goes near to the limit of the law",[36] and that: "The Court of Appeal disagreed but it is clear that there must come a point when the connection with the plaintiff's intention is too remote".[37]

However, in *Alexander* the court did not deny the existence of the remote principle; otherwise there would be no need to distinguish whether it is the subject matter of the contract which is intended to be used illegally. The true reason is that the court treated the two documents used by the claimant to defraud the authorities as a device which originated from the contract. Another difference between the two cases is that, in the Alexander case, the illegal purpose had been performed by the claimant for a while and the claimant might have profited from the illegality; however, in the latter case, it was found by the court that there was only illegal intention on the part of the claimant, and the illegality could not be performed until the end of the accounting year, so all the facts which the defendant raised to demonstrate the illegality of the claimant were rendered as not sufficient. Therefore, although the judgments on these two cases seemed contradictory, this is because

---

32 *Alexander v Rayson* [1936] 1 K.B. 169.
33 *Pearce v Brooks* (1865–66) L.R. 1 Ex. 213.
34 *Scott v Brown, Doering, McNab & Co* [1892] 2 Q.B. 724.
35 *Alexander v Rayson* [1936] 1 K.B. 169.
36 *21st Century Logistic Solutions Limited v Madysen Limited* [2004] EWHC 231.
37 Ibid.

of the differences in the facts of the two cases and it seems that the principle cited in the *21st Century* case was more reasonable.

Besides the closeness between illegal intention and the performance of the contractual party, there is also a requirement for knowledge on the part of the contractual party of the illegal intention, as decided recently in the case *ParkingEye Ltd v Somerfield Stores Ltd*.[38] For illegal intentions to become a factor underlying the illegality defence, the courts should be particularly concerned about whether the party was aware that the intended mode of performance was illegal and if this was not the case, then clearly such illegal intention would not vitiate claims under the contract.[39]

The third kind of illegal contract in common law is where the contract is legal and there is no intention to use the contract to commit an illegal action but the contract is performed by one or both of the contractual parties in a manner which is contrary to public policy.

This area of law is complex since there are several scenarios of this kind of illegality and the differences between the facts of each scenario and the law which has been violated will result in different consequences on the contract which has been tainted by the illegality. Similarly to statutory illegality, in this area both the knowledge and the intention of the parties play an important role. This section will begin with the origin of this test.

It has been generally agreed that an illegal action which occurs during the performance of a contract does not automatically make the contract unenforceable. This principle can be traced back to the nineteenth century. In *Wetherell v Jones*,[40] the claimant himself made an illegal delivery which was prohibited by statute; however, the contract itself was not illegal. It was decided by the court that: "irregularity of the permit, though it arises from the plaintiff's own fault, and is a violation of the law by him, does not deprive him of the right of suing upon a contract which is in itself perfectly legal; there having been no agreement, express or implied, in that contract, that the law should be violated by such improper delivery".[41] Therefore, even though there was an illegality during the performance of the contract, it was not influenced by this illegality.

The most significant case which relates to this issue is the *St John Shipping Corporation v Joseph Rank Ltd*.[42] The claimant shipowner sued the defendant English charterer for part of the freight, but the English charterer refused to pay the freight on the ground that the shipowner had overloaded the vessel during the voyage, which was prohibited by statute. However, their illegality defence was rendered failed by the court, which decided that "the infringement of a statute in the performance of a contract which was legal when made did not render the contract illegal unless the contract, as performed, was one which the statute meant to prohibit".[43] Furthermore, the performance of the contract of the

---

38 *ParkingEye Ltd v Somerfield Stores Ltd* [2013] 2 W.L.R. 939.
39 Ibid.
40 *Wetherell v Jones* 110 E.R. 82.
41 Ibid.
42 *St John Shipping Corporation v Joseph Rank Ltd* [1957] 1 Q.B. 267.
43 Ibid.

carriage of goods had no connection with the illegality of what happened during the voyage and there was no need for the plaintiff to disclose it; the plaintiff could bring the right of freight into existence without relying upon the illegality. Therefore, as long as these three requirements can be fulfilled, the contract will not be rendered unenforceable.

This judgment was confirmed in another employment case, *Coral Leisure Group Ltd v Barnett*.[44] In that case, it was also decided that by virtue of *Wetherell v Jones* and *St John Shipping Corporation v Joseph Rank Ltd*: "The fact that a party has in the course of performing a contract committed an unlawful or immoral act will not by itself prevent him from further enforcing that contract unless the contract was entered into with the purpose of doing that unlawful or immoral act or the contract itself (as opposed to the mode of his performance) is prohibited by law".[45]

Clearly, according to this judgment, there is an exception to the *St John Shipping* principle, that when the contractual parties plan to perform the contract in an unlawful way, either one of them or both of them, the whole contract should not be enforced. The illegality rules which relate to the intention of the parties were explained previously: if there is one party intending to perform the contract illegally, then the contract is unenforceable on this party as long as it can be proved that the other party had no knowledge of the illegality and had no involvement in it, whereas if both parties had knowledge of the illegality and intended to act illegally, then the contract is unenforceable on both parties. However, as was proved in the case *Waugh v Morris*, if neither party had knowledge of the change in the law and intended to perform the contract in a way which they thought was legal, but is illegal because of the law, then the validity of the contract will not be influenced.

However, there is discussion as to whether the principle that a minor illegality will result in the forfeiture of contractual remedies is appropriate. It is argued by R.A. Buckley that the origin of this problem lies in the judgment of the *St John Shipping* case. In that case, there were basically two issues which needed to be resolved by the court, the first being whether the statute expressly or impliedly prohibited the shipowner from enforcing the contract because of the illegality which had been committed, and the second being whether, if there is no prohibition in the statute the contract is unenforceable under common law because of the illegality committed during the performance of the contract. In Buckley's opinion, it seems that the court answered the first question correctly but failed to answer the second one properly, although the court came to the right decision. In the judgment which relates to the second question, the court failed to divide between statutory illegality and common law illegality, and used a statutory method to resolve a common law illegality issue, deciding that ". . . whether it is the terms of the contract or the performance of it that is called in question, the test is just the same: is the contract, as made or as performed, a contract that is prohibited by the statute?".[46] Buckley contended that, based on this logic, Devlin J came to the absurd conclusion that "any infringement of a statute, however inadvertent,

---

44 *Coral Leisure Group Ltd v Barnett* [1981] I.C.R. 503.
45 Ibid at 509.
46 *St John Shipping Corporation v Joseph Rank Ltd* [1957] 1 Q.B. 267 at 284.

committed in the course of performing a contract, rendered it unenforceable by the party responsible".[47] In other words, according to this passage, no matter whether the illegality committed is trivial or not, as long as it renders the contract as a kind which is expressly or implicitly prohibited by statute, then the contract is unenforceable on the guilty party. However, this decision overlooked common law factors and was unfair to the "guilty" party.

In Buckley's opinion, according to common law rules, when dealing with illegality committed during the performance of a contract, the decisive factor is neither the seriousness of the illegality nor the regulation of statute. He argues that all connective factors, especially the degree of knowledge and deliberation on the "guilty" party, should be taken into account in order to avoid absurd decisions. This argument has been proved in two cases. In the Australian case *Fitzgerald v F J Leonhardt Pty Ltd* where a contract was performed illegally under statute, Kirby J, when deciding whether the illegality rendered the contract unenforceable, decided that: "It would be absurd if a trivial breach of a statutory provision constituting illegality, connected in some way with a contract or contracting parties, could be held to justify the total withdrawal of the facilities of the courts. It would be doubly absurd if the courts closed their doors to a party seeking to enforce its contractual rights without having regard to the degree of that party's transgression, the deliberateness or otherwise of its breach of the law and its state of mind generally relevant to the illegality. Similarly, it would be absurd if a court were permitted, or required, to consider the refusal of relief without careful regard to the relationship between the prohibited conduct and the impugned contract".[48] Therefore, based on this case, it is clear that trivial breach of statute did not render the contract unenforceable because it was proved that the illegality had not been committed deliberately and had no connection with the contract. A similar case in English law is the case *Colen v Cebrian (UK) Ltd*,[49] when the applicants sued the defendant company for unfair dismissal, breach of contract and unlawful deduction of wages. The defendant alleged that the employment contract had been performed illegally since the company paid the wages to the applicants with the intention to defraud revenue. However, the court dismissed the company's appeal on the ground that it was intended that the contract be lawfully performed.

Another factor which needs to be considered is the knowledge of illegality. In *Cunard v Hyde* the insurance policy which covered the cargo and freight was avoided not only because the cargo that had been loaded was carried in a way which was contrary to the statute, but also because "the insured knew of the master's act, in the sense of consenting to it and wanting it to be done".[50]

Therefore, it can be concluded that the seriousness of the illegality is not the only criteria that needs to be considered when dealing with the illegal performance of contract issues; as long as a trivial illegality was not committed knowingly or deliberately, then it should not render the contract unenforceable. The function of this

---

47 R.A. Buckley, *Illegality and Public Policy* (2002), para 3.14.
48 *Fitzgerald v F J Leonhardt Pty Ltd* C.L.R.215 at 249.
49 *Colen v Cebrian (UK) Ltd* [2004] I.C.R. 568.
50 *Cunard v Hyde* 121 E.R. 1.

test is that: "The formidable task of proving the necessary degree of knowledge and deliberation should deter the majority of parties from seeking to escape from their contractual obligations by relying upon the other parties' unlawful performance".[51]

As to the knowledge of the contractual parties at this stage, it is similar to statutory illegality. There is a requirement for participation as well. This issue was decided in *Ashmore, Benson, Pease & Co Ltd v A.V. Dawson Ltd*. In this case, a carriage of goods contract was made between the plaintiff and the defendant and during the performance of the contract, the defendant's driver overloaded the lorries in a way which was illegal. The manager of the plaintiff company had watched the loading process of the goods without objection. During the transportation, one of the lorries toppled over and the goods were damaged. At the trial, the plaintiff brought an action against the defendant for the damages, but the court decided that the damages were not recoverable since Lord Denning found that: "Not only did Mr. Bulmer (the plaintiff) know of the illegality. He participated in it by sanctioning the loading of the vehicle with a load in excess of the regulations. That participation in the illegal performance of the contract debars Ashmores from suing Dawsons on it or suing Dawsons for negligence".[52]

Other than the intention and knowledge factors, it was raised in this case that more factors should be considered when dealing with the issue of "whether the common law would say that a contract has by its illegal performance been turned into an illegal contract".[53]

It was cited by Waller LJ that: "If at the date of the contract the contract was perfectly lawful and it was intended to perform it lawfully, the effect of some act of illegal performance is not automatically to render the contract unenforceable. If the contract is ultimately performed illegally and the party seeking to enforce takes part in the illegality, that may render the contract unenforceable at his instigation. But not every act of illegality in performance, even participated in by the enforcer, will have that effect. If the person seeking to enforce the contract has to rely on his illegal action in order to succeed, then the court will not assist him. But if he does not have to do so, then in my view the question is whether the method of performance chosen and the degree of participation in that illegal performance is such as to "turn the contract into an illegal contract".[54]

The third factor is the reliance principle. In the expression of this principle, a person cannot rely on his own illegality to enforce the contract; otherwise the illegal performance of the contract will not influence the validity of the contract. This principle is based on the judgment of the House of Lords in *Tinsley v Milligan*. Both Miss Tinsley and Miss Milligan contributed to the purchase of a house, but the house was registered solely in Miss Tinsley's name in order for Miss Milligan to defraud the Department of Social Society; both of them had knowledge of the illegality and participated in it. Later, Miss Milligan moved out and claimed her legal title to the house and Miss Tinsley used the illegality defence. However, the

---

51 R.A. Buckley, *Illegality and Public Policy* (2002), para 3.17.
52 *Ashmore, Benson, Pease & Co Ltd v A.V. Dawson Ltd* [1973] 1 W.L.R. 828 at 833.
53 *Colen v Cebrian (UK) Ltd* [2004] I.C.R. 568 at 578.
54 Ibid at 577.

House of Lords contended that "a claimant to an interest in property, whether based on a legal or equitable title, was entitled to recover if he was not forced to plead or rely on an illegality; even although it transpired that the title on which he relied was acquired in the course of carrying through an illegal transaction".[55] However, it was indicated by the House of Lords that this principle only applied to property claims, although not explicitly. Other than this, the scope of this principle is not clear, since in contractual illegality cases, if the parties need to enforce the contract or to get remedies from the contract, the parties will always be relying on the illegality. Therefore, it seems that the reliance principle is not a proper exception to the common law rule.

4.3.3 The rationales behind the public policy which renders the contract illegal

This section will consider the rationales which underlie contractual illegality rules and discuss whether these rationales are appropriate. The rationales are the foundation of the illegality defence and are used to demonstrate the requirement for the existence of such a law. Such rationales can also be applied in the judgments of illegality cases.

(a) The first rationale recognised by the Law Commission is that of
"furthering the purpose of the rule which the claimant's illegal
behaviour had infringed"[56]

The fundamental aim of the rationale is to protect the purpose of the law which has been infringed by disallowing the guilty party's claim; the law which has been infringed contains both statute and common law and public policy. However, the application of this rationale is complex due to the vague language of the law.

The first vague point which needs to be clarified is what the rule contains. It can be demonstrated that the "rule" in this rationale contains not only statute, but also common law. One example is the case *Cope v Rowlands* in which the plaintiff broker acted as a stockbroker who was not duly licensed, authorised, and empowered according to the statute. The court decided that: "It is perfectly settled, that where the contract which the plaintiff seeks to enforce, be it express or implied, is expressly or by implication forbidden by the common or statute law, no court will lend its assistance to give it effect".[57] Even though the statute only inflicts a penalty, this penalty shows that the objective of the statute is to prohibit such conduct, and the plaintiff's claim was declined since the court needed to protect the purpose of the statute. Another kind of violation exists in the violation of common law, as expressed in the judgment in *Cope v Rowlands*. In *Awwad v Geraghty*, this dealt with the unjust enrichment of a lawyer. In this case, the defendant's claim for *quantum meruit* was declined since the judge found that "what public policy seeks to prevent is a solicitor continuing to act for a client under a conditional normal

---

55 *Tinsley v Milligan* [1994] 1 A.C. 340.
56 Law Commission Report No 189.
57 *Cope v Rowlands* 150 E.R. 707.

fee arrangement"[58] and to allow the defendant's claim would have been contrary to the purpose of the rule.

From the judgments of the two cases, it can be seen that, when dealing with illegality cases based on this rationale, the object of the law needs to be clarified first, then as far as the true purpose of the law is concerned, if it has not been infringed or the purpose of the law is not to render the contract unenforceable, then these circumstances will be exceptions to the rationale.

The first exception is that, so far as the function of the penalty is concerned, the penalty inflicted by the statute does not necessarily mean the contract is illegal and unenforceable; the true intention of the statute needs to be considered, whether it is to forbid the contract or just to impose a fine upon it. This principle has been decided by several cases, including the *St John Shipping Corporation* case.

The second exception is when the illegality which the parties have committed is not what the law is intending to prohibit. In the case *Archbolds (Freightage) Ltd v S Spanglett Ltd*, both the defendant and the plaintiff had no knowledge that the defendant's van was not eligible to transport goods for reward. The defendant and the plaintiff's company made a contract for the carriage of goods and the goods were stolen due to the carelessness of the defendant's driver; the plaintiff claimed damages for the goods and the defendant used the illegality defence which is that, by using a vehicle which was not licensed to transport goods for reward as regulated by the statute, the contract had been tainted by such illegality and was unenforceable. In this case, although there was a clear infringement of statute, the court decided that: firstly: "The plaintiffs' part of the contract could not constitute an illegal use of the vehicle by them since they were not 'using' the vehicle"[59] (that is, the plaintiff's use of the vehicle was not covered by the contract); and secondly: "The object of the Road and Rail Traffic Act, 1933, was not (in this connection) to interfere with the owner of goods or his facilities for transport, but to control those who provided the transport, with a view to promoting its efficiency";[60] and therefore, to render the carriage contract unenforceable was not the object of the statute. Thus, neither the conduct of the defendant nor the conduct of the plaintiff could be rendered illegal based on the object of the statute.

The third exception is that, even if one or both of the contractual parties have committed an illegality, either in the formation of the contract or the performance of the contract, based on the protection of the purpose of the law, the court may reject the illegality defence. In the European Union case *Courage Ltd v Crehan*[61] the defendant tenant rented a house from the claimant, a brewery, and concluded with an agreement that all tied tenants were to be obliged to buy their beer exclusively from the claimant and at specified prices. The claimant required the recovery of a sum for unpaid deliveries of beer, but the defendant denied the claim on the ground that their agreement was contrary to the prohibition of anti-competitive agreements and practices in Article 81 EC 1 and therefore unenforceable. How-

---

58 *Awwad v Geraghty* [2001] Q.B. 570.
59 *Archbolds (Freightage) Ltd v S Spanglett Ltd* [1961] 1 Q.B. 374.
60 Ibid at 379.
61 *Courage Ltd v Crehan* [2002] Q.B. 507.

ever, the court, based on EU law, decided that: firstly: "Article 81 EC is to be interpreted as meaning that a party to a prohibited lease of a public house containing an exclusive purchase clause may rely on the nullity of that lease before the courts";[62] and secondly: "Community law precludes a rule of national law which prevents a party subject to a clause in a contract which infringes article 81 EC from recovering damages for the loss suffered by it on the sole ground that it is a party to that contract";[63] although Community law does not preclude "a rule of national law which provides that courts should not allow a person to plead and/ or rely on his own illegal actions as a necessary step to recovery of damages".[64] The rationale behind these, which seems absurd in relation to English illegality rules, is that the purpose of Article 81 is to maintain effective competition in the community and to protect "a party to the agreement where that party bears no significant responsibility for the distortion of competition"[65] and if the defendant's right was denied because of illegality then the purpose would be frustrated. However, this decision is contrary to some basic principles underlying the illegality defence which will be considered later.

(b) The second rationale concerns the consistency test
This test was explained in the chapter which relates to illegality in tort law. This test originates from tort law: in the Canadian tort case *Hall v Hebert*, it was concluded that "there is a need in the law of tort for a principle which permits judges to deny recovery to a plaintiff on the ground that to do so would undermine the integrity of the justice system. The power is a limited one. Its use is justified where allowing the plaintiff's claim would introduce inconsistency into the fabric of the law, either by permitting the plaintiff to profit from an illegal or wrongful act, or to evade a penalty prescribed by criminal law".[66]

However, this rationale is similar to the previous policy which was discussed above, and similar to the policy that maintains the integrity of the legal system, which will be discussed later. Therefore, if the contract is inconsistent with statutory requirements, then the contractual parties' rights under the contract will not be allowed, since the consistency principle applies. However, this principle cannot be applied on its own.

(c) The third principle which underlies the illegality defence is that no one can profit from his or her own illegality
This is the most fundamental principle underlying the illegality defence and was first decided in *Hall v Knight* where a woman had killed a testator in circumstances which amounted to (involuntary) manslaughter. It was decided by Swinfen Eady LJ that: "The estate of the testator must go in the same way as if there were no benefit given to Jean Baxter by the will and that she cannot in any way benefit

---

62 Ibid at 513.
63 Ibid at 515.
64 Ibid at 517.
65 Ibid at 515.
66 *Hall v Hebert* [1993] 2 SCR 159.

from the crime which she has committed. I see no reason for restricting the rule to cases of murder".⁶⁷ Therefore, it was decided in this case that whether a party can profit from his illegality or not is vital when deciding whether the illegality defence can be sustained.

This was further confirmed in *Beresford v Royal Insurance Company*.⁶⁸ This case was discussed above in the tort illegality chapter and concerned an assured who had shot himself in order to recover on his life insurance policy which he had taken out with the defendant insurer. Although the life insurance policy was not illegal, the contract had been performed illegally since suicide was a crime; therefore, the assured's claim for recovery was denied on the ground that to allow the claim would permit the assured to benefit from his suicide. As Lord Atkin concluded: "I think that the principle is that a man is not to be allowed to have recourse to a Court of Justice to claim a benefit from his crime whether under a contract or a gift"⁶⁹ and "the absolute rule is that the Courts will not recognize a benefit accruing to a criminal from his crime".⁷⁰

However, there are clear limitations to the application of this principle. In *Strongman Ltd v Sincock*, it was decided by Lord Denning that: "It is, of course, a settled principle that a man cannot recover for the consequences of his own unlawful act, but this has always been confined to cases where the doer of the act knows it to be unlawful or is himself in some way morally culpable. It does not apply when he is an entirely innocent party".⁷¹ For this principle to be applied, therefore, the claimant must be a true wrongdoer and the illegality committed should be serious enough; mere illegality is not enough for this principle to be applied.

(d) The fourth principle is to deter unlawful or immoral conduct

This principle is the one most frequently cited by the courts. It was decided in the case *Taylor v Bhail* that "it is time that a clear message was sent to the commercial community. Let it be clearly understood if a builder or a garage or other supplier agrees to provide a false estimate for work in order to enable its customer to obtain payment from his insurers to which he is not entitled, then it will be unable to recover payment from its customer and the customer will be unable to claim on his insurers even if he has paid for the work".⁷² However, the function of the principle is difficult to evaluate. Firstly, both contractual parties when entering the contract or performing the contract may not be aware of the law, so, other than in cases in which both parties intend to carry out the contract illegally, the judgment of the cases may not have an impact on the parties. Secondly, in a situation where both the contractual parties have knowledge of the illegality and enter the contract with the intention to act illegally, if the deterrence principle is applied to one party

---

67 *Hall v Knight* [1914] P. 1.
68 This is a typical case where the enforcement of a contract is forbidden by public policy but the contract itself is lawful; please see the five types of illegality concluded by M.P. Furmston in "The Analysis of Illegal Contracts" *University of Toronto Law Journal*, vol 16, no 2, pp 267–309.
69 *Beresford v Royal Insurance Company* [1938] A.C. 586 at 599.
70 Ibid at 599.
71 *Strongman Ltd v Sincock* [1955] 2 QB 525 at 535.
72 *Taylor v Bhail* [1996] CLC 377 at 383–384.

then this may result in an unmerited windfall: as Lord Lowry stated in *Tinsley v Milligan*: "I am not impressed by the argument that the wide principle acts as a deterrent to persons in A's position. In the first place, they may not be aware of the principle and are unlikely to consult a reputable solicitor. Secondly, if they commit a fraud, they will not have been deterred by the possibility of being found out and prosecuted. Furthermore, the wide principle could be a positive encouragement to B, if he is aware of the principle, because by means of his complicity, he may become not only the legal owner but the beneficial owner".[73] There is a discussion on the function of the deterrence rule in criminal law and commercial law: it used to be believed that the deterrence principle had more influence in criminal and tort cases, but it was proposed by the Law Commission that deterrence is an important policy behind the illegality doctrine.[74]

(e) The fifth principle is to maintain the integrity of the courts
The general expression of this principle can be summarised as stating that the proper rule of the court is not to provide an arena in which wrongdoers may fight over their spoils.[75] This principle was concluded in the case *Thackwell v Barclays Bank plc* and proposes that the court would refuse to assist the claimant's claim if allowing the claim would be an "affront to the public conscience if by affording him the relief sought the court was seen to be indirectly assisting or encouraging the plaintiff in his criminal act".[76] This principle was cited in three cases. In *Everet v Williams*, the plaintiff's claims were denied since the court needed to reflect on the "indignity to the court". In the second case, *Tappenden v Randall*, it was decided by judges that: "Undoubtedly there may be cases where the contract may be of a nature too grossly immoral for the Court to enter into any discussion of it; as where one man has paid money by way of hire to another to murder a third person".[77] In the third case, *Parkinson v College of Ambulance Ltd and Harrison*, it was stated that: "A person in the position of this plaintiff could claim and be awarded damages for the loss of a title or for obtaining one of a less degree than that for which he had bargained; a person in the position of these defendants could claim and be awarded damages for not receiving the promised contribution, although the title had been obtained. No Court could try such an action and allow such damages to be awarded with any propriety or decency".[78]

However, this principle can also be applied even when both contractual parties do not raise the issue. In *Re Mahmoud v Ispahani*, it was cited that: "In my view, the Court is bound, once it knows that the contract is illegal, to take objection and to refuse to enforce the contract, whether its knowledge comes from the statement of the party who was guilty of the illegality, or whether its knowledge comes from outside sources. The Court does not sit to enforce illegal contracts."[79] It was also

---

73 *Tinsley v Milligan* [1994] 1 A.C. 340 at 368.
74 Law Commission Report No 189.
75 Law Commission Report No 189, para 2.24.
76 *Thackwell v Barclays Bank plc* [1986] 1 All ER 676 at 687.
77 *Tappenden v Randall* 126 E.R. 1388.
78 *Parkinson v College of Ambulance Ltd and Harrison* [1925] 2 K.B. 1 AT 13.
79 *Re Mahmoud v Ispahani* [1921] 2 KB 716 at 729.

stated in *Birkett v Acorn Business Machines Ltd* that: "The principle behind the court's intervention of its own motion in such a case is to ensure that its process is not being abused".[80]

The merit of this principle is obvious: in circumstances where there is no clear authorisation in the transaction and it cannot be rendered illegal according to common law, then, if the transaction is morally disputative and the performance of the claimant is morally unacceptable, under such circumstances this principle can be applied by the courts.

However, the limitation of this principle is also clear. The courts will not use the principle to deny the relief of the claimant if only a trivial breach of the law has been involved. Therefore, for this principle to be applied, the illegality involved in the case should be serious enough.

(f) The sixth principle refers to punishments

This principle is seldom referred to by the courts. It has been suggested by the courts that they should "refuse a civil cause of action in cases involving illegal transactions in order to punish the plaintiff".[81] However, it is agreed that this principle has a greater function in criminal law than in civil law; the intention of civil law is not to punish wrongdoers; depriving them of their relief and contractual rights is enough. This principle was therefore considered by the Law Commission Report as not being a principle underlying the illegality doctrine. However, it was also argued that if the action of the claimant is serious enough, then the punishment should be considered by the courts.

(g) The seventh principle is the proportionate test

The proportionate test was discussed in the tort law chapter. Regarding the decision in *Jorcy v O'Brien*,[82] it seems that under tort law circumstances, the proportionate test is abolished. However, under contract law, the situation is quite different. In *ParkingEye v Somerfield* the fact was that most parts of the contract could be performed lawfully and most of the contract had indeed been performed lawfully; however, both the claimant and the defendant had participated in a minor illegality and if the contract had been rendered unlawful, then the claimant would have lost all the lawful income. In deciding this case, Sir Robin Jacob decided that the repudiation of the contract by the defendant, which depended on the illegality of the claimant, was wrongful and would lead to disproportionate results, namely that "Somerfield's wrongful repudiation of the contract left ParkingEye with no remedy for a lost income, which would have been wholly lawful".[83] The proportionate test was applied in this case and the defendant's illegality defence failed. The reasons for this judgment can be analysed: firstly, for the illegality defence to be sustained "it must find its justification firmly in one or more of the rationales". Therefore, even though under such cases there was an illegal intention and participation on

---

80 *Birkett v Acorn Business Machines Ltd* [1999] 2 All ER (Comm) 429.
81 Law Commission Report No 154, para 6.11.
82 As has been discussed in Chapter 3.
83 *ParkingEye v Somerfield* [2013] 2 W.L.R. 939.

the part of the claimant, the illegality defence could not be sustained only based on this. Secondly, although the public conscience test was rejected in *Tinsley v Milligan*, this does not mean that application of the proportionate test is a matter of judicial discretion, since: "Proportionality as I see it is something rather different. It involves the assessment of how far refusal of the remedy furthers one or more of the specific policies underlying the defence of illegality".[84] Thirdly, as has been indicated by the courts in less serious cases, where both of the contractual parties are to be blamed, denial of one party's claim on the ground of illegality will mean an unjustified benefit being given to the other.

Therefore, based on these three points, it seems that the proportionate test is more valuable in contract law circumstances.

4.4 The difference between statutory illegality and common law illegality under both tort law and contract law

Contract under English law can be rendered illegal either by statute or by common law. In the Law Commission Report No 189, the law commission agreed that this kind of distinction is helpful, However, it has not been explicitly explained why this distinction is necessary and to what extent the distinction is helpful; this is the aim of this sub-chapter. Compared with illegality in tort law, the illegality cases in contract law are far more complex.[85]

To clarify the reason for this distinction is to explain the necessity for this distinction as well.

The first reason for this distinction is that the courts may come to different conclusions when dealing with illegality because of the different kinds of law. One of the more significant differences between statutory illegality and common law illegality is that, when a court is dealing with a former case, judges will be constrained by the words of the statute, especially when there is an express prohibition in the statute. In the Gaming Acts of 1845 and 1892, for example, there is an express provision that any contract made in contravention of the Act will be void, and therefore, when courts are dealing with illegality based on a violation of statutes, in most cases the courts will come to one single conclusion. However, in illegality cases based on common law, although the courts will normally take precedents into account, they may not necessarily be constrained by the judgments of former authorities and the courts will take more factors into account, such as, for example, the intention of the parties when entering the contract and the circumstances in which the illegality happened. Therefore, by taking the unique factors of different cases into consideration, the courts will reach different conclusions.

Secondly, the factors which the courts consider when dealing with illegality cases may vary from illegality based on statute and illegality based on common law. When the courts are dealing with an illegality which originates from statutes the factors which are considered by the courts may be different. Firstly, if there is an express

---

84 Ibid.
85 The necessity to highlight the distinction between these two kinds of illegality has also been argued by B.A. Buckley in *Implied Statutory Prohibition of Contracts* (2011) *Modern Law Review* vol 38.

prohibition and the consequence of such violation is explicit in the statute, then all the courts need to consider is whether the act or the contract falls into this scope.

However, secondly, if there is only a prohibition in the statute and the consequence of the violation is not clear, then the courts will take more factors into consideration. If in the circumstance where the making of the contract is expressly prohibited by the statute, then the contract will be avoided *ab initio* as was the case with *Archbolds Ltd v S Spanglett*.[86] However, if only the actions of the parties during the performance of the contract are prohibited by statute, then the intention of the statute, namely whether the statute intends to forbid a contract of such class, the seriousness of the illegal conduct and the causal link between the loss and illegality will be considered.

The most significant difference regarding this issue between illegality in common law and illegality in statute is that, with regard to illegality in common law cases, the intention of the parties when entering into the contract will be considered as well. In circumstances in which contracts are rendered illegal by statute if the true construction of the statute is to deprive the civil rights of contractual parties, then it does not matter whether the parties are aware of the law or not or whether the parties intend to break the law or not; as was decided in *Kiriri Cotton Co Ltd v Dewani*, the contractual parties have a duty to observe the law.[87] Compared with the illegality of statute, the courts, when deciding cases related to a violation of common law, see the contractual parties' intention when entering into the contract as being of great importance. Therefore, if the parties when entering into the contract had no intention of violating the law, then the illegality existing in the contract will not render the contract unenforceable.

Compared with illegality rendered by statutes, there are basically three differences between the common law illegality and statutory illegality: firstly, the principles under common law are changeable. The common law rules which underlie public policy are not immutable and are changeable with respect to changes in circumstances. As a result of this, as will be illustrated below, an illegality principle under common law, when applied to other cases where the facts are similar, will sometimes come to different results. When dealing with such cases, the courts will keep taking different factors into consideration; secondly, under some certain circumstances, the courts can create new heads of public policy under common law rather than only applying existing doctrines. With regard to this characteristic, there is doubt over whether the courts have this kind of authority. In the judgments of earlier cases, it seems that the courts were bound by the authorities of earlier cases and merely applied them with caution, as can be seen in *Egerton v Earl Brownlow*, which dealt with the restraint of trade. It was argued by the court that ". . . we are not thereby authorized to establish as law everything which we may think for the public good, and prohibit everything which we think otherwise",[88] and a contract is only illegal if it goes against the principle of established law. The reason for this prohibition is that this will lead to great uncertainty and confusion.

---

86 *Archbolds Ltd v S Spanglett Ltd* [1961] 1 Q.B. 374.
87 *Kiriri Cotton Co Ltd v Dewani* [1960] A.C. 192.
88 *Egerton v Earl Brownlow* (1853) 4 H.l.Cas.1 149.

The method which the court has adopted when dealing with new cases is that: ". . . in a new and unprecedented case to be afraid of imitating their example. I think I am bound to look for the principles of former decisions and not to shrink from applying them with firmness and caution to any new and extraordinary case that may arise".[89] However, on the other hand, it was argued that some authorities support the construction of new public policies; in the case *Maxim Nordenfelt Guns and Ammunition Co v Nordenfelt* Bowen LJ stated that: "Rules which rest upon the foundation of public policy, not being rules which belong to the fixed or customary law, are capable, on proper occasion, of expansion or modification. Circumstances may change and make a commercial practice expedient, which formerly was mischievous to commerce".[90] However, the word "modification" in this judgment does not necessarily mean that the courts have the authority to create a new public policy and it seems that the core of the debate which relates to the authority of the courts is what the new public policy is. It is very difficult to create a completely new public policy since, firstly, the courts are not likely to interfere with the freedom of contract and secondly, the government reluctant to pursue a law reform. In most cases, a new public policy which is applied is a modification of the existing principle according to the new circumstance, and therefore, from this perspective, the debate over the authority of creation more correctly concerns the authority of modification and application. According to authorities in common law, modifications have never been prohibited. Such modification of the law clearly does not exist in statute illegality cases.

Thirdly, the common law doctrine is more flexible and therefore more suitable to the unpredictable nature of illegality in contract law; with the development of society and the incomplete natures of laws, new modes of illegality in contract can be created by contractual parties from time to time, just as discovered by Sir William Holdsworth. In order to maintain the fixed principles created previously, a body like common law should be able to suppress practices under new disguises which seek to weaken or negate them.[91] Statutes also have this kind of function; however, statutes cannot be modified with respect to every new form of illegality.

Another difference which can be drawn between illegality under statute and illegality under common law is that there is a difference between the acts which are rendered illegal by statutes and the contract itself being rendered illegal by statutes. In the former case, if the contract is entered into without the objection of committing an illegality, then such contract is still illegal under common law; however, in the latter case, the contract is clearly illegal because of its violation of statute.

4.5 The application of contract law illegality principles in insurance

In the first section of this chapter, illegality issues in contract law were considered; both the basic principles of statutory illegality and common law illegality were covered, and the rationales underlying the illegality principle and factors

---

89 Ibid.
90 *Maxim Nordenfelt Guns and Ammunition Co v Nordenfelt* [1893] 3 Ch. 122.
91 *Chitty on Contracts* (31st edn), para 16–003.

which influence the courts' judgment when dealing with illegality cases were also discussed. The second part of this chapter will explore insurance illegality cases when the laws concerning contractual illegality are applied and will consider the differences between the two scenarios.

Additionally, in this section, statutory illegality cases and illegality with regard to performance will be considered separately, since, as has been demonstrated, the principles which apply in these two kinds of illegality are quite different from each other.

4.5.1 Statutory illegality rules in insurance

The statutory illegality issues in insurance contracts will be considered first. Similarly to statutory illegality in contract law, in insurance law there are two situations where an insurance contract can be tainted by statutory illegality. In the first situation, the actual formation of the insurance policy can be illegal, either by the express prohibition of a statute or by the implied prohibition of a statute; in the second situation, it is the act which the assured plans to commit that may be illegal as it is prohibited by statute.

The first situation is where the insurance policy is expressly prohibited and rendered unenforceable or void by a statute; however, such cases existed in the past when life and fire insurance were rendered as immoral and are rare now.

There are commonly no such expressly or clearly prohibited areas in statute. In most circumstances, for example, the statute may have a requirement regarding the qualifications of the insurer or it could be that the conduct which is intended to be performed under the insurance policy could be rendered illegal by statutes but under such circumstances, since there is no express statement in the statute that such an insurance policy should be rendered void or unenforceable, then, similarly to situations in contract law, the intention of the statute should be considered. When dealing with the intention of the statute in contract law, as was discussed earlier, the courts will consider the wording of the statute first in order to decide whether the illegality which the parties have committed fell in the remit of the statute and to decide whether the illegality is what the statute intends to prohibit, as was the case in *Archbolds Ltd v S Spanglett Ltd*. Besides the word and the scope of the statute, in situations where there is a penalty for illegal conduct on the part of the contractual parties, the courts need to consider the function of the penalty and the intention of the penalty, namely, whether the penalty is imposed to punish the guilty party or to protect the public interest; if the former, then the contract may not be rendered unenforceable, but if the latter, it will be. Other than these two rules, the knowledge of the contractual parties is crucial as well; if one of the parties has no knowledge of the illegal conduct of the other party, then the contract can still be enforced by the innocent party.

However, as has been demonstrated in a number of cases, the statutory illegality rules in insurance law are not the same as they are in contract law. It seems that, in different kinds of statutory illegality situations in insurance cases, the courts will adopt different methods.

In the most straightforward situation, that is, when the insurance business is carried out by an unauthorised insurer, then the question is whether the insurance policy or contract issued by the unauthorised insurer is unenforceable or void. Section 2 of the Insurance Companies Act 1974 regulates that: "(1) No person shall carry on in Great Britain insurance business of a class relevant for the purposes of this Part of this Act, other than industrial assurance business" and "(1) A person who carries on business in contravention of this Part of this Act shall be guilty of an offence . . .".[92] With regard to this statute, there are two cases in which the judgments contradict each other.

In the first case, *Bedford Insurance Co v Instituto de Resseguros do Brasil*, the plaintiff and its agent carried out insurance business in the UK without authorisation; the plaintiff's agent issued several marine insurance policies in the plaintiff's name and reinsured these policies with the defendant reinsurer to which the plaintiff was party. An assured under the marine insurance policy made a claim against the plaintiff and the plaintiff brought an action against the defendant to claim an indemnity under the reinsurance policy; however, the defendant denied the claim on the ground that both the plaintiff and the agents were not authorised according to the statute and therefore the insurance issued by them was in contravention of the statute and the plaintiff could not rely upon this illegality to establish the cause of action under the reinsurance contract. In the judgment of the case, the court regulated that section 2(1) of the Insurance Companies Act 1974 was an express prohibition and concluded that "an express prohibition upon the making of contracts avoided *ab initio* any contract made in contravention of it; and that, accordingly, the original contracts, even if they had been made with the plaintiffs' authority, would have been avoided *ab initio* and unenforceable, so that the plaintiffs could therefore not recover in respect of them under the reinsurance".[93] Therefore, by examining the wording of the statute, the court rendered that it signified an express prohibition on the contract violating this statute. However, this decision was criticised by later cases; as Leggatt J argued: "(the judgment of the case) with the probable result that the offending insurer may keep premiums paid by an innocent insured and yet not be liable to pay claims" is clearly unfair to the assured.

In contrast, in the case *Stewart v Oriental Fire and Marine Insurance Co*,[94] the court adopted a different method when dealing with the circumstances where both the insurer and its agents had no knowledge of the unauthorised insurance business. In this case, the plaintiff reassured entered into a reinsurance contract with the defendant reinsurer to reinsure its primary insurance contract. However, the defendant and its agents had no authority to carry out insurance business in the UK and the plaintiff had no knowledge of this. The plaintiff brought an action against the defendant for the compensation of the loss of its primary insurance; the key question regarding this compensation is whether the plaintiff had lost its right to compensation since, according to the judgment in *Bedford*, the court was inclined to render the unauthorised insurance policy unenforceable and void by following the statute. The solution to this is an essential question of statutory construction, that is, whether the statute expressly or implicitly prohibits the contract

---

92 Insurance Companies Act 1974, s 2.
93 *Bedford Insurance Co v Instituto de Resseguros do Brasil* [1985] Q.B. 966.
94 *Stewart v Oriental Fire and Marine Insurance Co* [1985] Q.B. 988.

and intends to render it void and unenforceable. In the judgment, Leggatt J quoted the Australian case *Yango Pastoral Co Pty Ltd v First Chicago Australia Ltd* to explain the principle of construing statute: "it is a matter of construing the statute and in construing the statute the court will have regard not only to its language, which may or may not touch upon the question, but also to the scope and purpose of the statute from which inferences may be drawn as to the legislative intention regarding the extent and the effect of the prohibition which the statute contains".[95] By applying this principle and carefully examining the word of the statute, the court found that: "The express prohibition here is against carrying on in Great Britain insurance business of a relevant class without authorisation. There is no direct reference to contracts of insurance".[96] Therefore, the judgment clearly overruled the decision of *Bedford*. Later, Leggatt J went on to consider the possibility of the implied prohibition of the statute. By citing the Australian case, Leggatt J indicated that when deciding whether there was an implied prohibition in the statute, the court should also consider the intention of the scope of the statute and, according to Devlin J, "in default of a clear implication a court ought to be very slow to hold that a statute intends to interfere with the rights and remedies given by the ordinary law of contract".[97] According to the judgment of the case *St John Shipping Corporation*, Leggatt J also agreed that the "Authority therefore requires the court in the absence of express prohibition to look at the policy of the Act and to take account of the commercial effect of construing it in a particular way".[98] The intention of the statute, as argued by Leggatt J, "is not . . . to leave a person uninsured who has entered into an apparently valid contract of insurance of a relevant class with an insurer who turns out, unbeknown to the person seeking insurance, to have effected it without authorisation and to be similarly without authorisation to carry it out",[99] and the "Act of 1974 meant to do no more than penalise the insurer who contravenes the prohibition against carrying on business in Great Britain without authorisation: it did not intend to go further and prohibit contracts of insurance, the effecting and carrying out of which constitute the carrying on of insurance business".[100] Therefore, using a combination of these three factors, the learned judge came to the decision that: "In my judgment, as a matter of commercial practicality contracts of insurance such as these should not, except of necessity, be rendered unenforceable by an innocent insured".[101]

In the judgment of this case, it is clear that the court had adopted the principles which were introduced in contract statutory illegality cases. Both the intention of the statute and the intention and knowledge of the contractual parties were considered when dealing with the issue of whether the statute intends to forbid this kind of contract. It is clear that the mere fact of illegality cannot render the insurance contract automatically unenforceable.

---

95 *Yango Pastoral Co Pty Ltd v First Chicago Australia Ltd* (1978) 139 C.L.R. 410.
96 *Stewart v Oriental Fire and Marine Insurance Co* [1985] Q.B. 988 at 1003.
97 Ibid at 1006.
98 *Stewart v Oriental Fire and Marine Insurance Co* [1985] Q.B. 988 at 1007.
99 *Stewart v Oriental Fire and Marine Insurance Co* [1985] Q.B. 988.
100 Ibid at 1011.
101 Ibid at 1009.

However, developments have been made in the unauthorised insurance area after the 1974 Act, although such new developments do not contradict the first category of statutory illegality but are still worth being introduced here. The Insurance Company Act 1974 was repealed by the Insurance Company Act 1982 and stipulated that the insurer carrying out insurance business in the UK should be authorised. The consequence of violation of this piece of law has been expressed in section 132 of the Financial Services Act 1986, which states that "in contravention of section 2 of the Insurance Companies Act 1982 shall be unenforceable against the other party; and that party shall be entitled to recover any Companies money or other property paid or transferred by him under the contract, together with compensation for any loss sustained by him as a result of having parted with it".[102] Therefore, in cases where the insurer is not qualified to conduct insurance business in the UK, the assured can still recover his losses, which is different from early authorities. Furthermore, in the Financial Services and Markets Act 2000 there are two categories of illegal activities. In the first category, if an authorised insurer does not carry on insurance business according to permission, then as stated in section 20 of this Act, such contravention of this Act does not "(a) make a person guilty of an offence; (b) make any transaction void or unenforceable; or (c) (subject to subsection (3)) give rise to any right of action for breach of statutory duty".[103] However, if an unauthorised insurer describes himself as authorised or indicates that he is an authorised person, then such activity is a guilty offence under the Act and, according to section 24(3): "A person guilty of an offence under this section is liable on summary conviction to imprisonment for a term not exceeding six months or a fine not exceeding level 5 on the standard scale, or both".[104] Therefore, an insurance policy which is made by such a guilty party is unenforceable against the other party, but "(2) The other party is entitled to recover – (a) any money or other property paid or transferred by him under the agreement; and (b) compensation for any loss sustained by him as a result of having parted with it".[105] Therefore, even if the insurance policy is unenforceable, the assured can still recover the losses which result from entering into this contract. However, the Act also provides two circumstances where the agreement between the guilty party and the innocent party can be enforced. The first circumstance is that: "The issue is whether the person carrying on the regulated activity concerned reasonably believed that he was not contravening the general prohibition by making the agreement".[106] The second one is that: "The issue is whether the provider knew that the third party was (in carrying on the regulated activity) contravening the general prohibition".[107] Namely, the knowledge of the law and the knowledge of the illegal act will be considered by the court as has been discussed above. Therefore, as can be seen from the latest development in this area of law, the statutes are becoming more generous than before. However, the factors which

---

102 Financial Services Act 1986, s 132.
103 Financial Services and Markets Act 2000, s 20.
104 Financial Services and Markets Act 2000, s 24.
105 Ibid, s 26.
106 Financial Services and Markets Act 2000, s 28(5).
107 Ibid, s 28(6).

should be considered by the court when dealing with the unauthorised insurer issue are still identical to former authorities. Therefore, even if the statute can be repealed, the common law rules still remain stable when dealing with the first category of statutory illegality.

The second category of statutory illegality in insurance law is where an insurance contract intends to act illegally or the parties enter into the contract with the intention of acting illegally.

According to the principle in contract law, as has been explained before, there is no decisive authority on this point. It was once argued by the authority that, if there is prohibition in statute either expressly or implicitly, then the unlawful contract is rendered unenforceable, even on the innocent party. Although this judgment was found to be harsh to the innocent party in the Law Commission Report No 189, there is no clear authority which overrules such a decision. The other method adopted by the court is to divide illegality into illegality by formation and illegality by performance: if the formation of the contract is rendered illegal by statute, then the contract will be unenforceable and void. However, if the illegality exists in the performance of the contract then the regulation and prohibition in a statute will not be a decisive factor and thus, the innocent party in this circumstance may have the right to enforce the contract.

Similarly, in insurance cases, if the assured enters into an insurance contract with the intention to rely on it to compensate his loss, which is a result of statutory illegality, or intends to use the insurance contract to commit a statutory illegality, then the insurance contract will be rendered unenforceable and void, just as the judgment in the *Redmond v Smith*: "A policy on an illegal voyage cannot be enforced; for it would be singular if, the original contract being invalid and therefore incapable to be enforced, a collateral contract found upon it could be enforced".[108] This was also the case in the *Beresford* case where the assured entered into the insurance with the intention of profiting the beneficiary by committing a crime.

However, if the insurance contract is not entered into with that intention and the illegality simply occurs during the performance of the insurance contract, then according to the authorities of both contract law and insurance law, it is unlikely that the contract will be rendered unenforceable automatically. In contract law, this principle was settled in the case *St John Shipping Corp* and it seems there is no authority in insurance law which regulates otherwise. In the circumstances where there is only one party entering into the contract with the intention of committing an illegal act, the other innocent party can sustain its rights under the contract as long as it can be proved that the innocent party has not shared the illegality purpose with the other party. Besides the principles which have been analysed above, according to the judgment in *Bird v Appleton*[109] and *Euro-Diam Ltd v Bathurst*, in insurance law, under some circumstances, there is also a requirement for the connection between the illegality and the loss to be shown and the assured needs to rely upon its own unlawfulness to plead. In *Euro-Diam Ltd*, the assured's diamonds were stolen in Germany and when the assured intended to recover under

---

108 *Redmond v Smith* (1844) 7 Man. & G. 457 at 474.
109 *Bird v Appleton* 102 E.R. 45.

the insurance contract, the insurer contended that there had been a violation of the German tax act when the diamonds were imported into Germany, and the insurer relied upon this illegality to reject the assured's application. However, the Court of Appeal contended that the illegality committed by the assured had no connection with the theft of the diamonds and that, furthermore, the assured had no need to rely upon that illegality.[110]

By analysing former authorities, it is clear that the factors which have been considered when dealing with statutory illegality in contract law also have an effect when dealing with insurance cases. There is also no implied term in insurance law that illegality can render the insurance contract unenforceable automatically. The tendency when dealing with statutory illegality cases in the area of insurance is not to render the whole contract unenforceable, at least on the part of the innocent party.

4.5.2 Insurance illegality under common law

Similarly to illegality in contract law, the insurance policy can be rendered illegal because of the assured's illegal conduct. As has been discussed before, the common rule in contract law is that it does not recognise a situation where a contract that is lawful in its inception and can be lawfully performed can become illegal as formed simply because one of the parties performs it in an unlawful way. Therefore, in most circumstances, the insurer of an insurance policy which has been performed illegally will not seek to render the insurance contract unenforceable and void, but to use the illegality issue as a defence to decline the assured's right to compensation. Therefore, this section will discuss whether the illegality rules in contract law can be applied in insurance cases and the specialities of illegal performance in insurance law.

(a) Construction of the policy
In contract law, the contract can be rendered illegal either by statute or by performance, but unlike contract law, in insurance law, the insurance policy can also be rendered illegal because of the construction of the insurance contract, this category being based on the judgment of Lord Atkin in *Beresford v Royal Insurance Co Ltd*: "On ordinary principles of insurance law an assured cannot by his own deliberate act cause the event upon which the insurance money is payable. The insurers have not agreed to pay on that happening. The fire assured cannot recover if he intentionally burns down his house, nor the marine assured if he scuttles his ship, nor the life assured if he deliberately ends his own life. This is not the result of public policy, but of the correct construction of the contract."[111] Therefore, according to this judgment, the assured can be precluded from recovery either because he has committed a crime or because his deliberate act has rendered the subject matter insured not an "accident" which the insurance policy intends to cover.

The first speciality in insurance law is that the assured's claim can be precluded by his deliberate acts, either illegal or legal. This principle can be divided into

---

110 *Euro-Diam Ltd v Bathurst* [1990] 1 Q.B. 1.
111 *Beresford v Royal Insurance Co Ltd* [1938] AC 586 at 595.

two: the first is where the assured has committed a criminal act intentionally and the second is when the deliberate act committed by the assured is not illegal but results in loss. Under both circumstances, the assured's claim can be denied. Firstly, according to the *ex turpi causa* principle (discussed above), if the assured commits a criminal act deliberately then the assured cannot recover the loss or profit from the insurer. This was discussed in the section dealing with illegality of tort and, with the exception of motor insurance cases, it seems that as long as the assured has committed a crime which results in loss, then the assured cannot recover from the insurer, even though there is a debate in Australian case law over whether an exclusion for "criminal act" could exclude negligent or unintentional criminal acts rather than only intentional criminal acts.

In the Australian case of *Australian Aviation Underwriting Pty Limited v Henry*, the assured died in a traffic accident because they failed to pay due attention and collided with a vehicle on the other side of the road. There was an exclusion clause in the insurance policy which excluded loss resulting from the assured's own criminal act and the insurer used this as a defence. However: "The Court construed the word 'criminal' as excluding acts of negligence, notwithstanding that they were also criminal. Part of the basis of the Court's reasoning was that the parties to the agreement must have contemplated that a substantial reason for the existence of the cover was an accident arising from the insured's negligence and it could not have been intended to exclude that liability by reference to criminal acts".[112]

In *Rian Lane v Dive Two Pty Ltd* Mr Todd, the director of the defendant company, was in breach of the Crimes Act 1900 (NSW) because of dangerous navigation, the plaintiff was compensated by the defendant, and when the defendant claimed compensation against his insurer, the insurer claimed that the criminal act was expressly excluded by an exclusion clause in the insurance policy. However, the court decided that, for this exclusion clause to be applied, the criminal act must have been committed intentionally and negligence should not be taken into account: "The exclusion clause does not exclude cover in the instant case because the criminal act committed by Mr Todd was not intentional".[113] In fact, in this case, the only obstacle preventing the defendant from being indemnified by his insurance policy is that the defendant's broker failed to procure a proper insurance policy which should cover private and non-business risk for the defendant assured. In a later judgment on the same case, the judge decided that as there was no such negligence on the part of the broker, the defendant should be compensated by his insurance policy, and therefore, the broker himself should be responsible for the defendant's losses.[114] Therefore, *Rian Lane v Dive Two Pty Ltd* is a typical case of constructing the words of the exclusion clause of the insurance policy to decide whether the insurance policy has been tainted by illegality or not. In the judgment of a later appeal which was raised by the broker (Horsell) in 2013, it was confirmed by the New South Wales Court of Appeal that, although the insurance failed to respond, this was not because of the assured's illegality; this was all because of the

---

112 *Australian Aviation Underwriting Pty Limited v Henry* (1988) 12 NSW LR 121.
113 *Rian Lane v Dive Two Pty Ltd* [2012] NSWSC 104.
114 *Rian Lane v Dive Two Pty Ltd (No 2)* [2012] NSWSC 209.

broker's failure to perform his duty. Therefore, the broker was still responsible for the losses suffered by the assured.[115]

In English law, a case which was similarly decided was *Patrick v Ronson International Ltd*. In this case, Mr Patrick and his friends started a fire in a mill for amusement, neither of them having the intention of destroying the mill nor of destroying the goods stored within; however, the fire destroyed the stock which belonged to Ronson International Ltd and caused loss. Mr Patrick and his friend were arrested and charged with arson but acquitted. Mr Patrick was insured by a home and house insurance policy, and the exclusion clause in the insurance policy excluded "(viii) any wilful, malicious or criminal acts . . .". Ronson International Ltd sought compensation against the insurer and the insurer denied compensation based upon this exclusion clause. At the core of this case is the correct construction of the exclusion clause, based upon a former common law decision: the court decided that: "So interpreted, as it seems to me, what is damage arising from a wilful act is damage deliberately caused, consciously intended. On the evidence in the present case it was not even suggested that Mr Patrick intended to burn down the Mill. The first ground of defence relied upon on behalf of Royal London thus fails".[116] Therefore, in English law, for the insurer to deny the assured's compensation based on the exclusion clause, the common principle needs the unlawful act to be performed intentionally as well. Therefore, except for in motor insurance law, if a criminal act has been performed by the assured negligently, the court will adopt the principle seen in the *Patrick* case and consider the intention of the assured rather than the illegality and the loss as a primary factor.

Besides the situation where it is necessary to distinguish whether the assured intends to commit a criminal/non-criminal act or not, there is also a necessity to distinguish whether the consequences caused by the assured's act are consequences which the assured intends to achieve. The reason for such difference is whether the deliberate act committed by the assured is illegal or not. Thus, if the assured commits a crime intentionally, then even though the outcome of his criminality is not what the assured has planned, his compensation under the insurance policy will be denied, as happened in the case *Gray v Barr*. However, if the deliberate act committed by the assured is not illegal, then as long as the deliberate act of the assured is not the direct cause of the loss, then the assured can be compensated by the insurer.[117]

Another difference which exists between contract law and insurance law in the performance of a contract is that, in insurance law, because of the illegal performance of the assured, the subject matter or risk insured can be transferred into a category of "accident" which the insurance policy does not intend to cover.

There is a connection between this kind of illegality and the wilful misconduct discussed above, since it is clear that, if there is no accident, then the assured will be precluded from recovery according to the terms of the insurance policy. Therefore, it is important to distinguish the circumstance which amount to no accident.

---

115 *Horsell International Pty Ltd v Divetwo Pty Ltd* [2013] NSWCA 368.
116 *Patrick v Ronson International Ltd* [2005] EWHC 1767.
117 *Tompson v Hopper* (1858) E.B. & E. 1038.

A famous case that discussed this issue is *Gray v Barr*, which was discussed in the chapter dealing with tort. In this case, when deciding whether the shooting by the defendant was an accident under insurance law, it was decided by Lord Denning that: ". . . the word 'accidents' does not include injury which is caused deliberately or intentionally.".[118] This point is agreed by Phillimore LJ, who contended that: "No doubt the word 'accident' involves something fortuitous or unexpected, but the mere fact that a wilful and culpable act – which is both reckless and unlawful – has a result which the actor did not intend surely does not, if that result was one which he ought reasonably to have anticipated, entitle him to say that it was an accident".[119]

Therefore, according to early authorities, there are two factors that should be considered when deciding whether the conduct of the assured amounts to an accident or not. Firstly, whether the conduct is intentional and secondly, whether the consequence of the intentional conduct is foreseeable. This argument is supported by the authors of *MacGillivray on Insurance Law* (11th edn) who propose that: "For injury or loss to be other than accidental . . . it suffices that he embarked upon a deliberate course of conduct where the occurrence of injury or loss was, objectively viewed, a natural and probable consequence of his actions".[120]

However, the drawback to this solution is obvious, as indicated by Rix LJ with regard to the *Charlton v Fisher* case: "if 'accident' was to be construed as excluding a deliberate act of damage or injury, then there would be a danger that a great number of situations frequently encountered in the context of driving would also have to be treated as no accident".[121] Rix LJ therefore adopted another method of deciding whether a risk is an accident or not: he contended that: "In this connection I would emphasize that it is not every deliberate criminal act, such as the deliberate decision to drive while drunk, or the deliberate decision to drive at excessive speed, or in contempt of road markings or directions or traffic lights, that would mean that any resultant loss/damage or injury would be no accident, even if, in a general way, the consequences of such conduct can be foreseen. In my opinion, such cases would still be cases of accident (see *Tinline v White Cross Insurance Association Ltd* [1921] 3 KB 327), just as deliberate but reckless conduct which results in the actor's death is not without more suicide. Thus I would for myself draw the distinction between damage caused by a deliberate criminal act (cf paragraph 36 of the judgment of Laws LJ) and damage intentionally caused. For these purposes it matters not that the actor is deliberately committing a crime but that he is deliberately causing damage".[122]

In *Tinline v White Cross Insurance Association Ltd*, which Rix LJ cited, the assured knocked down three people while driving excessively; he sought compensation from the insurer but the insurer denied liability on the ground that "the personal injury did not arise out of an accident, but that it would be against public policy to

---

118 *Gray v Barr* [1971] 2 QB 554 at 566.
119 Ibid at 586.
120 *MacGillivray on Insurance Law* (11th edn), para 25–4.
121 *Charlton v Fisher* [2002] Q.B. 578.
122 Ibid at 600.

indemnify a person against the civil consequences of his criminal act".[123] However, Bailhache J drew a distinction between loss caused by negligence, no matter how serious it is, and loss caused by intention, and said that: "It must of course be clearly understood that if this occurrence had been due to an intentional act on the part of the plaintiff, the policy would not protect him. If a man driving a motor car at an excessive speed intentionally runs into and kills a man, the result is not manslaughter but murder. Manslaughter is the result of an accident and murder is not, and it is against accident and accident only that this policy insures".[124]

Therefore, what Rix LJ tried to emphasise is that when deciding whether a risk is an accident or not, the mere fact that the assured has committed a criminal or non-criminal act intentionally is not enough; it has to be proved that the assured commits such conduct with an intention to cause loss.

As has been previously examined, besides the common law principles which underlie the illegality defence in contract law, in insurance contracts the courts have raised the construction of policy as a defence. Thus, if there is a clear exclusion clause in the insurance policy, or the insured subject has been rendered as not an accident because of the assured's performance, then the contract can be rendered unenforceable. However, for this defence to be triggered, the courts still need to consider the factors under common law.

(b) Insurance policies rendered illegal by the public policy

The public policy which underlies the illegality defence in contract law is also effective in insurance law, as the famous phrase states: "*ex dolo malo non oritur actio*". No court will lend its aid to a man who founds his cause of action upon an immoral or an illegal act. The accurate classification of public policy is not clear and there is no need to classify it, since the main object of the illegality defence is simple – that the wrongdoer cannot recover indemnity for the loss which has been caused – and various factors will be considered according to the facts of every individual case.

In the context of insurance, the methods for dealing with the illegality relating to tort claims under an insurance contract were discussed in chapter four which deals with contract circumstances. The public policy applied in insurance cases which do not relate to tort claims is almost the same as the public policy applied in contract law. There is also a requirement for the intention and knowledge of the illegality on the assured's part; the causation between the illegality and the loss and the seriousness of the illegality; the assured should not rely on or benefit from his own illegality. There is no need to discuss these principles any further since they have been examined in an earlier chapter and there is no difference between the contract law and insurance law rules on this point. The essence of these principles to apply is that the intention and knowledge of the assured is of great importance, and this is the first fact which needs to be clarified by the courts, since in its absence, under most circumstances, the illegality defence will be denied except for a situation where there is an express prohibition under statute. The

---

123 *Charlton v Fisher* [2002] Q.B. 578 at 599.
124 *Tinline v White Cross Insurance Association Ltd* [1921] 3 K.B. 327 at 332.

tendency of the courts when dealing with illegality issues in insurance contracts under common law is not to render the whole policy unenforceable, except when all the requirements have been fulfilled, since the harsh consequence of this is to leave the innocent party uncovered.

4.6 The difference between tort illegality and contract illegality

This part will be divided into two sections: the first will explore the differences between contract law and tort law when dealing with the illegality defence issue; and the second will discuss the reasons for these differences.

4.6.1 The differences between contract law and tort law when dealing with the illegality defence

The first and most significant difference between the contract illegality defence and the tort illegality defence is that the objective and consequence of the defence are different.

Under tort law circumstances, the objective of the illegality defence is to leave the claimant (maybe a tortfeasor) without protection, and to bar the unlawful party from claiming loss or compensation from the other party, which may be an innocent third party like an insurer or a joint illegality conductor. There is no contractual privity between the defendant and the claimant before the tort conduct happens and the objective of the defence is clear and specified. However, under contract law, the objective of the defence is to render the contract unenforceable because of the illegality which exists in the formation of the contract or in the performance of the contract. The differences in the objectives results in differences in the consequences of these two illegality defences. In the tort situation, the illegal party only loses the right of compensation; however, if a contract is rendered unenforceable, the illegal parties will lose every remedy and contractual right under the contract, the right to compensation being only one of them. This is very harsh for the illegal party especially in the circumstance where the formation of the contract is rendered illegal or the party has committed an illegality which is expressly prohibited by statute.

The second difference is that the factors which the courts consider when dealing with the illegality issues are different.

For example, the intention and knowledge of the illegality are considered a significant factor in contract law when determining whether the illegality defence should be sustained. However, in tort law, as was concluded, the intention and knowledge of the illegal party is not as important as in contract law; if a tort action has been performed, the courts will pay more attention to the causation link between the tort conduct and the loss; even if the illegality is not intentionally performed by the claimant, the mere causation link between the conduct and the loss is enough for the defence to sustain. This has been demonstrated in numerous cases especially after the narrow and wide rule.

Other differences exist in the rationales which underlie the illegality defence. For example, with regard to the causal principle, when the courts deal with tort cases they will pay more attention to the issue of whether the tort conduct is the main causation of the loss, whereas in contract law circumstances the courts will consider whether the illegality of the contractual parties has a connection with the content of the contract. When dealing with statutory illegality, in tort law the courts will consider whether the statute intends to forbid the tort action, whilst in contract law the courts will consider whether the statutes which forbid such illegal conduct are intended to render the whole contract unenforceable.

The third difference is that the formation of illegality and the conduct which triggers the defence is different under contract law and tort law. It is clear that under tort law, there is only one kind of illegality – illegal performance. Under contract law, however, the formation of the contract, such as when the insurance contract is entered with an unauthorised insurer or the aim of the contract is to perform some illegal wrong, can be illegal as well.

In spite of this difference, there are more actions which trigger the illegality defence under contract law than under tort law. In a contract situation, not only might the tort or criminal act committed during the performance of the contract trigger the illegality, but so too might illegal acts which are not that severe, such as illegal parking or illegal transfer.

In conclusion, besides the difference between the formation and objectives of illegality, when dealing with illegality issues under contract law the courts are more cautious than in tort law and take more factors into consideration.

4.6.2 The reason for these differences

This section will explore the reasons which underlie the differences. As can be seen from the previous two chapters, both the tort and contract illegality defences originate from the same case, namely *Holman v Johnson*, and there should be a reason why the defence has been applied differently.

The first reason is that under most circumstances, tort conduct can be seen as a special performance of contract and the illegality defence under tort law only protects the defendant from the consequences caused by the claimant's illegal act. However, under contract law, the illegality, such as, for example, the illegal intention of the contractual parties when entering into the contract, may exist before the formation of the contract or prior to the performance of the contract and therefore the illegality defence under contract law may have the function of preventing further illegality, for instance, rendering a sale of gun contract unenforceable and possibly preventing the criminal from firing the gun.

However, this difference is also the reason why the courts, when dealing with contract illegality, have adopted a more careful method than in tort cases and view the intention and knowledge of the contractual parties as vital. The function of the illegality defence here is to prevent any further illegality, and if the contractual parties enter into the contract without the intention to commit a legal wrong or without the knowledge of such a legal wrong, then this is clearly not fair to the contractual parties.

The second reason for the differences is because of the severe consequences under contract law. As has been demonstrated by the authorities, if a contract is rendered illegal, then the guilty party or both of the contractual parties cannot enforce the contract if both of the parties need to be blamed; if a contract is illegal in its formation and the contract can be determined as void, this means that the contract has not existed before. Under some circumstances, this consequence may leave the innocent party or the third party without cover.

The third reason for the difference is that the relationship between the contractual parties under contract and the relationship between the victim and the tortfeasor are different. Therefore, under contract law, the reason why the courts deal with the illegality defence with caution is in order to avoid the non-guilty party failing to perform their contractual obligation or gaining a windfall benefit under insurance circumstance by keeping the premium and refusing to indemnify the assured. However, under tort law, there is no such concern; because the tort action has been performed, most of the liabilities of the tortfeasor to the victim are regulated by statute.

4.7 Conclusion

The illegality issue in contract law is far more complex than it is in tort law. Under contract law circumstances, not only are the performances of the contractual parties considered, but the intention and knowledge of the parties are also taken into account. Unlike illegality in tort, the illegality issue in contract has closer connections with insurance contracts, as was discussed; when rendering an insurance contract unenforceable because of illegality, the mere fact of illegal conduct is clearly not enough, and both the intention and knowledge of the illegality as well as the construction of the insurance policy should be considered. There is clearly no implied term of legality under contract law.

PART 3

COMMON LAW RULES IN MARINE INSURANCE

A necessary reform or a supplementary instrument?

In Part 1, the development of the warranty of legality in marine insurance was discussed. In Part 2, the principles of the illegality defence in both contract law and tort law and the rationales which underlie it were introduced, as were the situations under insurance law. It can be seen from these two parts that there is a big difference between common law illegality defence and the warranty of legality in marine insurance law.

In this third part, this thesis will concentrate not only on the proper method for dealing with the illegality issue under marine insurance law, and whether common law illegality principles can be properly applied to marine insurance issues, but will also introduce and clarify the issues of foreign law illegality and the pending draft Bill for insurance contract law. After this, every aspect of the issue of the warranty of legality in marine insurance law will be examined, and a way to reform marine insurance law will be proposed.

This part consists of five chapters. The first chapter will explore the differences between the illegality defence and the warranty of legality and the reasons behind these differences. The second chapter will consider a special aspect of the warranty of legality, that is, the illegality issue under foreign law. The third chapter will consider the law regarding the issue of marine insurance legality in other Commonwealth jurisdictions, especially in Australia. The fourth chapter will introduce and analyse Law Commission Report No 353 and the new Insurance Act 2016 in detail, paying particular attention to their impact on the warranty of legality in marine insurance law. Finally, the fifth chapter will propose reasonable methods for reforming section 41 of the Marine Insurance Act 1906, even though a reform has already been proposed by the Law Commission.

CHAPTER 5

The differences between the illegality defence in common law and the warranty of legality in marine insurance and the reasons for the differences

This chapter acts as a conclusion to the research covered in the first two parts of this book. The aim of the chapter is to compare the illegality defence and the warranty of legality in marine insurance and to give a clear picture of the differences between them. By analysing these differences, this chapter will try to highlight the insufficiency of warranty of legality from the common law perspective and then attempt to explore why the English courts have adopted another method in marine insurance cases and whether these reasons still function nowadays to prevent marine insurance law from adopting the illegality defence in common law. This work will form the basis of the chapter on the reform of marine insurance law. The chapter contains three parts: the first deals with the nature of section 41; the second examines the differences between section 41 and the illegality defence in common law; and the third part considers the reasons underlying these differences.

5.1 The nature of section 41

This section considers the nature of section 41 of the Marine Insurance Act 1906 and assesses the nature of a violation of this section, in order to see whether the violation can be rendered as a statutory illegality or a common law illegality.

This issue is important firstly because, as has been discussed, under English law the factors considered by the courts when dealing with illegality issues vary according to whether it is a statutory illegality or a common law illegality; and secondly, because the consequences of a statutory illegality and a common law illegality will also be different. Furthermore, the reform proposal will also be based to a large extent on the nature of section 41. If a violation of section 41 is a statutory illegality then, as will be discussed later, an appropriate reform proposal would be its abolition, since, as was discussed in the previous chapter, statutory illegality requires more strict compliance and the defences for the unlawful doer are very limited, which is very different to common law illegality.

To answer this question, this section will first consider early marine insurance cases in order to clarify the intention of the construction of this warranty and the early application of it. The early application of section 41 in certain marine insurance cases will then be compared with the illegality rules under common law to decide whether the warranty of legality is a statutory illegality or a common law illegality.

Besides this question, other aspects of the nature of the warranty of legality will also be considered. One of these aspects concerns whether the warranty of legality is a pre-contractual or a post-contractual requirement. If the warranty is a pre-contractual one, then the proper consequence of it being breached is to make it void; if, however, the warranty is a post-contractual one, then there can only be a termination of the contract from that point, and this termination should have no influence on the remedy of parties under the contract. In either circumstance, there should be no single rule or punishment for each individual situation.

By analysing these two questions, it will be easier to come to a conclusion as to whether the warranty of legality should be rendered as a warranty in marine insurance law any longer.

5.1.1 Is violation of section 41 a statutory illegality?

The first question which needs to be clarified is whether a violation of section 41 is a statutory illegality. It is clear that the Marine Insurance Act 1906 is a statute under English law; however, the mere fact of this is not enough to render a violation of section 41 a statutory illegality.

Based on the previous two chapters, the features of statutory illegality under common law are clear: the statutory illegality may exist in the circumstances of the formation of the contract, the adventure of the insurance contract which needs to be covered and the performance of the contract. As to the consequence of the statutory illegality, besides very limited exceptions, in most situations, especially when the contract is formed illegally, the contract is rendered as void from the beginning and the factors the courts will consider when deciding such a consequence are basically the intention and words of the statute.

In the context of marine insurance, in the analysis of the intention and words of section 41 cases prior to 1906 shall be analysed since the Act is a codification of marine insurance cases before 1906. A conclusion will then be reached as to whether Sir Mackenzie Dalzell Chalmers intended section 41 to be a statutory illegality or not.

This question will be considered in two parts because of the distinct two parts of section 41. As to the first section, which requires the adventure to be a lawful one, it is clear that the violation of such a requirement is a statutory illegality. This is because firstly, cases prior to 1906 required strict compliance with statutes related to shipping and an adventure can be rendered unlawful in violation of any statute, including the King's or Council's order or the Merchant Shipping Act.[1] Secondly, the consequence of such a violation is harsh and there are very limited defences for the assured. Under most such circumstances, the adventure is rendered illegal and the insurance policy upon it is made void, except in the situation where there is no possibility of the assured having information of the illegality. Thirdly, the words and the intention of the orders and statutes are the only two factors which have to be taken into consideration by the courts[2] when deciding whether an adventure was unlawful or not. Therefore, the violation of the first part of section 41 is clearly a statutory illegality.

---

1 *Farmer v Legg* 101 E.R. 926.
2 Ibid.

However, the situation becomes more complex in the context of the performance of adventure. The complication is that this requirement is codified in the 1906 Act, but based on former authorities, unlawful performance during a marine adventure should not be rendered as the commission of a statutory illegality for three reasons.

Firstly, not every illegal performance is a violation of statute; it is impossible for statutes to cover every kind of illegal performance and sometimes a performance can be illegal because of a violation of common law or public policy such as in *Potts v Bell*.[3] Secondly, assureds clearly have more defences in illegal performance cases than in cases where adventures are illegal from the beginning. This is why the phrase "so far as the assured can control the matter" is used, and all the defences which have been mentioned in Chapter 2 have clearly exceeded the boundary of defences for statutory illegality. For example, in cases of a violation of statute during performance, not only is the intention of the statute considered, but so too is the intention and knowledge of the assured, which is clearly different to what happens with a statutory illegality. The third reason is that, unlike in the illegal adventure part where the courts are normally limited to certain statutes and patterns and always reach the conclusion that the warranty is breached, judgments of illegal performance are unconstrained and the courts can reach different conclusions based on the factors which the courts take into account.[4]

Therefore, based on the above analysis, it is clear that section 41 should not be considered as a whole. The first part of this section requires that the adventure is a lawful one, breach of which should be viewed as a statutory illegality, especially in the circumstances of the formation of the insurance contract and before the attachment of the adventure; breach of the second part of this section, however, should be regulated as a common law illegality, in spite of the fact that it has been enacted by the 1906 Act. However, under current marine insurance law, the whole of section 41 has been viewed as a statutory requirement.

5.1.2 Section 41 – a pre-contractual or a post-contractual requirement?

The next question is whether the legality requirement is a pre-contractual duty or a post-contractual duty? This question is of great importance since in marine insurance law, the difference between the violation of a pre-contractual duty and a post-contractual one is significant. For instance, in cases of the violation of utmost good faith, if the assured breaches the pre-contractual duty of utmost good faith, for instance, through non-disclosure, then the insurer is entitled to avoid the contract.[5] However, if the assured breaches a post-contractual duty, through fraud, for example, then under such circumstances the insurer cannot void the contract, but only entitle damages under it. However, this is not the case with section 41, since there is no difference between the consequences of a violation of the legality requirement; under both pre-contractual and post-contractual circumstances, the insurer is entitled to discharge liability, which is clearly inappropriate.

---

3 *Potts v Bell* (1800) 8 T.R. 561.
4 As with the exceptions discussed in Chapter 2.
5 Marine Insurance Act 1906, s 17.

However, according to cases prior to section 41, it seems that there was a difference between them; that is, before the conception of the contract, if the assured had the knowledge that the voyage was illegal and intended to perform it, then the insurance policy was void. However, if during the performance of the voyage, an illegal act happened, then the courts would take the assured's intention, knowledge and the connection between the illegality and the loss into consideration, even though under most circumstances the assured was only entitled to the return of the premium, rather than to compensation from the insurer.

Based on the above, it is clear that the legality duty upon the assured is a continuing one and that there is no distinction between the pre-contractual and post-contractual issue in this section. The law requires the adventure to be lawful from the beginning until the end of the adventure and the performance of the assured shall be lawful throughout the adventure as well. Although, as in those cases introduced in Chapter 2, the assured will have no excuse for his illegal performance before the beginning of the adventure. All the defences which the assured can use are only available after the start of adventure.

5.2 The differences between the common law illegality defence and the warranty of legality in marine insurance

The aim of this second part of the chapter is to discuss the differences between the warranty of legality in marine insurance and the illegality defence in common law. After analysing these differences, the reasons for them will be discussed in turn.

The objective of the comparison between the common law illegality defence and the warranty of legality in marine insurance law is to clarify the defects of the warranty of legality.

5.2.1 The nature of these two defences is different

There are two main differences in the nature of the two defences. The first one is that a violation of the implied warranty is a statutory illegality and a violation of the illegality defence in some circumstances is a common law illegality. Since, as has been demonstrated, when the courts deal with statutory illegality issues the factors which they can take into consideration are quite limited; only the intention of the statute and the meaning of the words of the statute are considered. This is partly the reason why the consequences of a violation of section 41 is more severe than it would be in common law. For this reason, the origin and true scope of section 41 needed to be explored in Chapter 2 first, an exploration that revealed that, based on a true interpretation of the intention and the words of this piece of law, a violation of this regulation should not entitle the insurer to discharge their liability automatically in every circumstance. It is true that it is not appropriate to regulate such a requirement as an implied warranty in marine insurance law. Furthermore, as stated in Section 5.1, it is also inappropriate that a violation of section 41 should be dealt with as a statutory illegality.

The second aspect is that the character of the illegality defence in common law and that of the warranty of legality is different. It is clear that in common law, the legality defence is not rendered as a fixed contractual term and therefore the character and function of the illegality defence in common law is changeable. In some circumstances, for example, if the construction of the contract is illegal, then the illegality is a condition and the contractual parties can avoid the contract or claim damages under it.[6] However, if an illegal act is committed during the contract, then this conduct only entitles the other party to claim damages or to deny payment under the terms of the contract. Thus, the illegality defence clearly cannot be regulated as one single type of term in contract law; the important factors which may influence the character of the illegality defence include the time when the illegality is committed or the seriousness of the illegality.

However, under marine insurance law, the illegality is rendered as an implied warranty, the function of which is quite obvious and unchangeable. It can only be altered by abolishing the implied warranty in marine insurance.

5.2.2 The consequences of a breach of the law are different

The second difference between section 41 and common law illegality rules exists in the consequences of a breach of the law.

It is commonly understood that, with regard to the consequences of illegality on contractual rights, there is a distinction between contracts that are illegal as formed (which includes circumstances where entry into or performance of a contract need to involve an illegal act) and contracts which are capable of being performed legally (with one or both of the parties intending to perform the contract illegally or for an illegal purpose or when the subject matter of the contract is for the use of an illegal design).

The situation is clear in the first category of illegality, that is, if the contract itself is illegality or with illegal attention, and then such contract will be treated as void as if it had not been made at all, and neither party can claim contractual rights under such a contract. However, under some circumstances, if one of the parties is induced to enter into the contract, and is entirely innocent, then this party is entitled to claim damages from the other party.[7] This principle was applied in *Strongman LD v Sincock*.[8] In this case, a builder was assured by an architect that all the licences required by the Defence Regulation to carry out building work had been acquired but later, when the builder intended to claim the balance of the price over the licensed amount and other damages, the court held that the builder could not recover under the contract, since the contract was clearly forbidden by the Act. However, the builder could still recover damages against the architect unless the builders had themselves been morally to blame or culpably negligent, since the oral promise of the architect amounted to a warranty and breaching that promise was a breach of warranty.[9]

---

6 For example, if construction of contract is forbidden by statute, as can be seen in Chapter 4.

7 For example, in cases where assured is induced to enter an insurance contract, as can be seen in Chapter 4.

8 *Strongman LD v Sincock* [1955] 2 Q.B. 525.

9 *Strongman LD v Sincock* [1955] 2 Q.B. 525.

However, the rules which relate to the second kind of illegality are more complex. If both the contractual parties have knowledge of the illegal performance and intend to perform the contract unlawfully or for an unlawful purpose, then the contract is unenforceable, as in the first category; however, if one of the contractual parties has no knowledge of the other party's illegal act and illegal purpose, then the contract is still enforceable on the innocent party, and the innocent party can clearly claim damages under the contract.

Under common law circumstances, the consequence of such a violation is clear. Under most circumstances, if one of the contractual parties has committed an illegal act, and the other party has no relation to it, then the contract is unenforceable on the guilty party. However, if both the contractual parties have committed the illegal act, then the contract is unenforceable on both sides.

Compared with the illegality defence in contract law, in tort, if during the performance of the insurance contract, the loss is caused by the assured's own tort act, then under both circumstances, the assured will be denied payment; however, unless the adventure which is insured is unlawful, the insurer will still cover the losses which occur before the commission of the illegality.

However, the consequence of breaching the warranty of legality is the most severe one. In marine insurance cases, according to the Marine Insurance Act, since the illegality defence is regulated as a warranty, then the insurer is discharged from liability from the date the illegality was committed, even though, according to cases prior to the Act, this was not always the case. In cases where the adventure is unlawful, such as trading with an enemy or sailing in a prohibited area, the marine insurance policy is normally voided and the insurer can retain the premium.

5.2.3 The rationales underlying the common law illegality defence are more persuasive

The common law illegality defence rules are more specific than section 41 and the rationales behind them are more reasonable. For example, with regard to the *ex turpi causa* principle in tort law, and the reliance and no-profit principle in contract law, there are several factors which the courts should consider when dealing with similar cases. Even though this may result in complexity and instability in the law, it still provides clear and sufficient defences for the guilty party. The warranty of legality, on the other hand, is far more ambiguous: the rule is general, the meanings of the words in this section are unclear and there is no convincing rationale for the section. Although the judgment in *Redmond v Smith* is always considered as the origin of the section, it requires that the adventure must be lawful but fails to explain why this requirement must be an implied warranty. This general rule results in the defences for the assured being insufficient and ambiguous. There is only the "so far as the assured can control" defence for the assured, but the factors which may influence the judgment have never been clarified by the courts.

THE DIFFERENCES BETWEEN THE ILLEGALITY DEFENCE

The consequence of this difference is that it is more difficult for the illegality defence to be sustained in common law than in marine insurance law. For example, as was demonstrated previously,[10] only if it can be proved that the guilty party has knowledge of the illegality and intends to perform it, or if, in contract law, the construction of the contract itself is illegal or it is intended for the contract to be performed illegally, then the guilty party will lose every defence and either the contract is made unenforceable or the guilty party loses the right to claim compensation; otherwise, the illegality defence is not sustained automatically. In marine insurance law however, if there is an illegality during the adventure or the adventure itself is illegal, then the insurer's liability is discharged from the beginning of the illegality, and there is no need to prove that there is a causal link between the loss and the illegality – the assured loses all cover and is not entitled to a return of the premium.

5.2.4 Factors and exceptions are different

The fourth difference between section 41 and common law illegality rules is that the implied warranty of legality is an absolute defence for the insurer as long as the insurer can prove the illegal act of the assured; however, in common law, for the defence to be sustained, the courts need to consider more factors than in marine insurance law, as has been explained. This difference may lead to an increase in the possibility of a breach of section 41 being abused by the insurer, in circumstances where the courts fail to explore the true scope of section 41; the assured may then face an unfair judgment and strict consequences.

Examining cases prior to the 1906 Act, in some circumstances, the courts adopted the identical logic to that applied in common law. In cases where the assured's illegal conduct renders the adventure illegal, if the assured entered into the contract without the intent to perform it unlawfully, or is unaware of the illegality, such as in cases dealing with trading with enemies,[11] the insurance policy is not void and the insurer may need to return the premium.

The first factor which considered differently is the knowledge of the assured. In the circumstances where the adventure which is insured is an unlawful one and the assured or both the assured and the insurer have knowledge of such illegality, then the insurance policy is void in both marine insurance law and non-marine insurance law. If the adventure which is to be insured is illegal, and the assured has no knowledge of it, then according to former authorities, this policy would also be void in marine insurance law. However, in common law, if it can be proved that the assured has no knowledge of such illegal intention, and does not intend to perform the contract illegally, then even though the contract may still be unenforceable, the assured can recover the loss which relates to the contract. This

---

10 As can be seen in Section 4.2 above.
11 Such as *Parkin v Dick* (1809) 11 East 502 along with other cases which have been discussed in Chapter 2.

is also the case if the assured intends to perform the adventure illegally from the inception of the risk; if both the insurer and the assured have the knowledge that the adventure will be performed illegally, then it is clear that the insurer is unable to use the warranty as a defence, since its application would make the insurer profit from his own illegality for not performing his contractual responsibility.

In the circumstances where the illegality is committed during the performance of the adventure, the 1906 Act regulates that this is also an implied warranty, although only in circumstances where the assured can control the matter, the concept of which is unclear. Exploring the authorities prior to the Act, it is clear that there were some exceptions which would not render the insurance contract unenforceable; however, these exceptions were not covered by the 1906 Act.

In the cases prior to 1906, there are basically two exceptions: one is the intention of the assured and the other is the knowledge of illegality of the assured. In *Ingham v Agnew*,[12] it was decided that, if the parties had no intention of obeying the law or had the intention of breaking the law, then the insurance contract was void. A similar case was that of *Atkinson v Abbott*.[13] In this case, which concerned trading with the enemy, the court decided that, even though the assured's vessel was captured because of trading in a battle area, there was no intention of the assured and his agent to violate the law which forbade trading with the enemy and the assured was entitled to be compensated. With regard to the knowledge of the assured, in *Oom v Bruce*,[14] a case also dealing with trading with the enemy, the court decided that, since the assured and his agent had no knowledge of the breakout of war between the two nations, and the illegality of carrying out business between the two nations, then, even though the insurance policy was void, the assured was entitled to the return of the premium.

However, with reference to common law cases, the difference is clear; in common law, not only have the intention and knowledge of the assured been considered, but the following two questions will be considered as well: whether the assured needs to rely on his own illegality to plead and whether the assured intends to profit from his illegality. Besides these two important factors, another significant factor is whether there is a casual link between the loss and the assured's illegality, a factor which the Law Commission refuses to consider even in the new Insurance Act 2016.

5.2.5 The specificity of section 41 in marine insurance law

Fifthly, the implied warranty of legality is only applied in marine insurance law; there is no such implied warranty in common law. However, there is no restriction on the application of the illegality defence in common law in marine insurance cases. And the question of how to apply this rule in marine insurance cases is the next question which needs to be discussed.

---

12 *Ingham v Agnew* 104 E.R. 939.
13 *Atkinson v Abbott* 170 E.R. 1048.
14 *Oom v Bruce* 104 E.R. 87.

5.2.6 Conclusion

The main contradictions between the illegality defence in common law and in marine insurance law are that: firstly, the illegality defence has been considered as an implied warranty under marine insurance law; secondly, there are differences between the consequences of a breach of warranty under common contract law and under marine insurance law; thirdly, the factors considered by the courts when dealing with illegality under contract cases and marine insurance cases are different; and fourthly, under the 1906 Act there is no difference between the pre-contractual duty and post-contractual duty of the assured. Another difference between marine insurance law and common law is that, in marine insurance scenarios, the illegality issue has been rendered as a statutory illegality, as discussed previously; when the courts decide whether a statutory illegality sustains, they will consider the intention of the law and the words of the statute. However, when the courts adopt this method, the law is still harsh for the assured, since the words of this piece of law are clear – the illegality is an implied warranty and the contract shall be void *ab initio*, which means that the assured loses every defence he may have. This is the reason why section 41 should be abolished, since it is unfair and causes confusion.

5.3 Why the courts adopt another method when dealing with illegality in marine insurance cases

It has been shown that before 1906, when the courts were dealing with illegality issues in marine insurance cases, the courts adopted a method other than the illegality rules in common law. Therefore the question arises as to why the court abandoned the illegality rules settled in *Holman v Johnson*[15] and sought to use another more severe method in maritime scenarios? This question has not been seriously considered yet, and it is difficult to give an accurate answer since it is difficult to understand the judges' thoughts when dealing with this issue. However, there are a number of possible explanations, as will be discussed below.

The first reason may be that non-marine insurance does not in general constitute insurance on an adventure but on property, whereas marine insurance is on an adventure at any rate in the case of goods if not also of a ship.[16] Therefore, when the courts deal with marine cases, the dangerousness of the adventure is the most important factor the courts need to consider. In earlier times, the carriage of goods by sea was quite a dangerous industry. The risks of sea transportation were quite high and, unlike the insured subject in non-marine insurance policies, such as property insurance or health insurance, once the vessel was out of the port, the insurers were unable to contact the vessel effectively or to control the risks of the adventure, which is a basic responsibility of the insurer. Therefore, in order to encourage insurers to engage in this high risk industry, the courts needed to

---

15 *Holman v Johnson* 98 E.R. 1120.
16 *The Bamburi* [1982] 1 Lloyd's Rep. 312 at 318.

provide effective defences for the insurer and to set strict liabilities on the assured because of the lack of supervision by the insurer during the adventure.

The second reason is that, because of the lack of supervision discussed above, it was possible for the assured to commit an illegality at any time. The assured, normally a shipowner or a cargo owner, always sought to gain high profits from this high risk industry, and this may therefore sometimes have led to a shortage of seamen, smuggling, taking short course and trading with enemies. It was not possible for the courts or the insurers to know accurately the time the illegality was committed, and the categories of illegality which could be committed by the assured were also unpredictable. Therefore, for the convenience of commercial activities, the courts needed to establish a piece of law which was not accurate but which covered a wide range of situations which should be distinguished.

Another reason why the English courts adopted a method other than the common law illegality defence in marine insurance law was that, when dealing with marine insurance cases, given the special circumstances involved, the courts tended to apply insurance principles rather than common law rules. For instance, in *Furtado v Rogers*, the judge contended that: "I forbear to enter into the argument suggested at the bar in favour of the Defendant that the law will not enforce a contract founded on a transaction detrimental to the public policy of the state. The ground upon which we decide this case is, that when a British subject insures against captures, the law infers that the contract contains an exception of captures made by the government of his own country".[17]

Fourthly, there were various kinds of statutes or orders that regulated the shipping industry and that forbade any kind of shipping activity in contradiction of the regulations. The courts' decisions were clearly constrained and they had very limited choice except to adopt a severe approach.

Finally, there should be a fine line between an unlawful act and an unlawful act which entitles the parties to abolish the contract. However, in early judgments, since the regulation of the shipping industry required the severe punishment of actions which violated the statute, then the courts ignored this difference and settled most of the marine insurance policies which included illegality unenforceable or void. As can be seen in the *Redmond* case, the foundation of a marine insurance policy is adventure, and if the adventure is illegal, the contract upon it is illegal as well. However, there are numerous factors which can amount to an illegal adventure. In earlier times, it was always the duty of the statute to give clear guidelines regarding which kinds of adventures were and were not illegal, but the courts ignored the scenarios in which the act of an assured could render an original legal adventure illegal, and this is a possible reason for the differences between common law and marine insurance law.

As a result, the English courts adopted a more severe method when dealing with illegality issues in marine insurance cases and the main reason was the particularities of the shipping industry in early times.

---

17 *Furtado v Rogers* 127 E.R. 105.

5.4 Conclusion

In this chapter, based on the former three chapters, the nature and character of the warranty of legality in marine insurance law has been examined from a comparative perspective with the illegality defence in common law, and a clear picture of the defects of section 41 have been given, along with the reasons which underlie it. As was introduced at the beginning of this chapter, the purpose of this chapter is to provide the foundation for the proposal for the reform of section 41; this will be discussed in Chapter 9.

CHAPTER 6

Foreign law illegality in marine insurance law

This chapter will consider a very special and controversial area of section 41, that is, whether the English courts recognise or *should* recognise foreign law illegality in marine insurance. Based on former authorities, it is implied in section 41 that the English courts do not recognise a breach of foreign law as a breach of the warranty of legality. However, in other areas of common law, when dealing with whether foreign law illegality should be recognised, the English courts have adopted another approach. Therefore, what are the differences between these two approaches and should this area of section 41 be reformed as well if common law rules were applied in marine insurance cases?

This chapter will begin with the origins of the rules on dealing with foreign law illegality in common law and in marine insurance law and then will introduce the current position of these two approaches; by comparing the differences between them, this chapter will consider whether this part of section 41 should also be reformed.

6.1 The English legal position on foreign law illegality in common law

The principle that English law does not recognise foreign law illegality derived from the cases which have been introduced in Chapter 2 and has been developed in both common law and marine insurance law since then. However, the effect of foreign law on the English legal system when dealing with common law illegality has never been settled. There are several cases which need to be discussed in relation to this issue.

The earliest and most straightforward judgment on this issue is found in *Planche v Fletcher*. In this case, it was decided by Lord Mansfield that the courts in this country do not take notice of foreign revenue laws.[1] However, this is not the sole case; the English law has been developed in detail in this area, and not every foreign law is unenforceable in England.

However, with the exception of *Planche*, based on the following cases which will be discussed, it seems that, in English law, the issue of whether the law that

---

1 *Planche v Fletcher* (1779) 1 Dougl 251.

parties breach is foreign or not has never become an important factor which would influence the decision of the English courts.

One, more recent, and clear authority on the foreign law illegality point is *Ralli Brothers v Compañia Naviera Sota Y Aznar*. In this case, the key question is whether to pay more freight for imported jute at more than 875 Pesetas per ton which is illegal under Spanish Law would also be illegal when such a case was decided in English court. The court came to the judgment based on two reasons. Firstly, the clause of the contract required the place of payment to be Spain. Secondly, payment in cash was due on delivery in Spain, the simultaneous acts of delivery and payment were both to be performed in Spain, and the shipowners were a Spanish company. Therefore, even though the whole charterparty should be governed by English law, the part which related to payment should be governed by Spanish law and the English courts should respect the Spanish law. Therefore, the English court was clearly unable to give effect to this contract under common law, and "that part of the contract which required the payment of freight in excess of 875 pesetas per ton was invalid and could not be enforced against the charterers".[2]

In *Foster v Driscoll*, five people sought to sell whiskey from England in the United States, when the sale of alcohol was illegal, Scrutton LJ delivered the judgment: "I have no doubt that if seller and buyer agreed to ship the whisky into the United States contrary to the laws of that country the contract would not be enforced here".[3] When deciding this, he also considered former authorities and explored the differences between them. The first case he referred to was also decided by Lord Mansfield; in *Holman v Johnson*, even though the seller knew the buyer intended to smuggle the goods into England, Lord Mansfield declined to give effect to the laws of his own country. In *Clugas v Penaluna*[4] the violation of foreign law was given effect in English courts, when the seller not only had the knowledge that the buyer intended to smuggle goods, but had also assisted in this illegality. It can therefore be seen that, when the English courts deal with illegality based on a violation of foreign law, the key factor is whether the parties have been involved in the illegality. In this case, Lawrence LJ also contended that: "On principle, however, I am clearly of opinion that a partnership formed for the main purpose of deriving profit from the commission of a criminal offence in a foreign and friendly country is illegal, even although the parties have not succeeded in carrying out their enterprise, and no such criminal offence has in fact been committed; and none the less so because the parties may have contemplated that if they could not successfully arrange to commit the offence themselves they would instigate or aid and abet some other person to commit it".[5] Lawrence LJ in this case set a more restricted rule than Scrutton LJ, stating that it is only the actual intention of the parties to perform the contract in a way that is illegal under a foreign law, even if the action has not been carried out, that can render the contract void. This rule was adopted by the House of Lords in the case *Regazzoni v K.C. Sethia*.

---

2 *Ralli Brothers v Compañia Naviera Sota Y Aznar* [1920] 2 K.B. 287.
3 *Foster v Driscoll* [1929] 1 K.B. 470.
4 *Clugas v Penaluna* 100 E.R. 1122.
5 *Foster v Driscoll* [1929] 1 K.B. 470.

Regazzoni v K.C. Sethia, which concerned the smuggling of goods from India to South Africa in contravention of Indian law, is significant. On the face of it, the contract could have been performed without violating any countries' law, but the buyer had hidden his intention to commit this illegality. It was decided in this case that, "whether or not the proper law of the contract is English law, an English court will not enforce a contract, or award damages for its breach, if its performance will involve the doing of an act in a foreign and friendly State which violates the law of that State".[6] Lord Reid delivered the leading judgment of this case, and by quoting Scrutton LJ's judgment in *Foster*, he agreed that, when dealing with an illegality issue involving a violation of foreign law, the English courts should base their judgment on the public policy of the international comity. He also cited *Dicey's Conflict of Laws*: "It must, however, be noted that if a contract is an English contract, it will only be held invalid on account of illegality if it actually necessitates the performance in a foreign and friendly country of some act which is illegal by the law of such country".[7] It is clear from the above that the English courts can take foreign law illegality into account. However, at the end of Lord Reid's judgment, he discussed the limits of this application, and said that the English courts would not enforce a law which is "a foreign law involving persecution of such a character that we would regard an agreement to break it as meritorious".[8] However, this is a vague definition,[9] as Denning LJ said when he delivered the Court of Appeal judgment of this case: "these courts do not sit to collect taxes for another country or to inflict punishments for it".[10] It is clear that contractual relationships between private persons are not of this kind.

However, Lord Mansfield and Denning LJJ's judgments do not automatically apply in all circumstances; under some circumstances the English courts can also take the foreign state's revenue laws into account. In *Re Emery's Investments Trusts* it was decided that the husband's act to register the common stock in American securities in his wife's name was in order to avoid payment of American Federal tax, which was clearly illegal and the English court would not grant relief in respect of a transaction carried out in contravention of a law, albeit a foreign revenue law.[11] Even though this was a case in which both the parties were American, and it took place in America, using American dollars, the judgment of this case complies with the rules set in *Euro-Diam Limited*, which will be introduced later, and Lord Mansfield's decision in *Planche v Fletcher* was clearly now out of date.

This case also provided the reason why English courts will not enforce a contract which is carried out in a foreign territory and which violates foreign law. As Lord Reid stated, once a contract is tainted, the English courts will not assist either party to enforce it.

---

6 *Regazzoni v K.C. Sethia* [1958] A.C. 301.
7 *Dicey's Conflict of Laws* (4th edn), p 620.
8 *Regazzoni v K.C. Sethia* [1958] A.C. 301.
9 Please also see the analysis of this case by F.A. Mann LL.D in "Illegality and the Conflict of Laws" *Modern Law Review* vol 21, Issue 2, pp 130–137.
10 *Regazzoni v K.C. Sethia* [1956] 2 Q.B. 490.
11 *Re Emery's Investments Trusts* [1959] Ch. 410.

In the latter case of *Royal Boskalis Westminster v Mountain*, the English courts enlarged the boundaries of this rule. This was a case in which five Dutch companies sought to recover expenses paid to the Iraqi Government in order to secure the demobilisation of their fleet and the repatriation of their employees under the sue and labour clause in their insurance policy, after they had waived all their claims under the construction contract which was a violation of an international sanction. Both the Iraqis and the five Dutch companies took this action according to a finalisation agreement between them which was legal under Iraqi law; the situation in this case was that there was no violation of the applicable law. However, when the issue of whether the transfer of the money was illegal or not was pleaded in an English court, Pill LJ and Stuart-Smith LJ contended that the *Regazzoni* rule should also apply to contracts governed by their proper law: if the contracts are illegal according to English law, then the English courts clearly cannot give effect to such contracts, even if the contract is legal under its proper law.[12]

Based on the judgments of the cases above, it can be seen that the current position of English law on foreign law illegality is that, firstly, the adventure cannot be rendered illegal under either common law or marine insurance law purely according to foreign law; secondly, for foreign law to be effective under English law, several requirements need to be fulfilled, and such requirements differ from case to case. For example, the clearest category is when the activity of the assured is also illegal under English law, in which case the defence will be triggered. Also, foreign law must not contradict with the English law, as decided in the case *Re Claim by Helbert Wagg & Co Ltd:* "this court must be entitled to consider whether, looking at all the circumstances, the law is so far-reaching in its scope and effect as really to offend against considerations of public policy of this country".[13] It also requires that there is a connection between the illegality which the assured committed and the foreign law; and certainly that the application of foreign law will need to fulfil the requirements of the Rome I Regulation.

For English courts to decide whether a violation of foreign law is illegal in England, the detail of the foreign law is not relevant; the English courts only need to decide the intention of the parties when entering into the contract and the connection between the parties and the illegality, which is purely an English common law method as has been explained before, unless the foreign law which has been violated contradicts English law.

For example, in the circumstances of the United Nations sanctions, the Member States were required to give effect to them in their own domestic law and any violation of the sanctions should be viewed as an illegal act in English law as well.

Moving the focus from the rules in ordinary contract law to the insurance contract law and the question arises whether the rules will still work in insurance contracts, since there are always differences between contract law and insurance contract law.

---

12 *Royal Boskalis Westminster v Mountain* [1999] Q.B. 674.
13 *Re Claim by Helbert Wagg & Co Ltd* [1956] 2 W.L.R. 183.

The leading case in insurance law which relates to this point is *Euro-Diam Limited v Bathurst*.[14] The fact of this case is that the assured seller insured the amount of diamonds which had been sold to the buyer but, in assisting the buyer to deceive the German customs authorities, the seller issued a false invoice for the buyer. The diamonds were stolen after this and the seller claimed losses under the insurance policy. One of the insurer's defences was that by issuing a fake invoice to deceive the custom authorities, the insurance contract has been tainted by this illegality. One of the points of dispute was whether the English court should recognise the illegality under German law. In the judgment of this case, it was clear that there is no implied term in insurance law that the adventure would not be illegal under foreign law. The judge recognised the rule of foreign law but found it of no assistance since: "Performance of the contract of insurance would take place wholly in England". Therefore, a new pattern developed by the judge was that: "The question is therefore whether it has that degree of connection with illegal acts in Germany which would render it tainted and therefore unenforceable here. One can divide this question into two parts. First, if the acts concerned had been illegal by English law, would the contract of insurance have been enforceable? Secondly, if so, do the rules of conflict of laws justify reference to German law, and so produce the same result in this case?"[15]

The judge delivered the judgment based on the *Bowmakers* and *Beresford* rules which have been discussed in Chapter 4; the illegality defence was not sustained in this case and the second question was not triggered. However, in the event that it had been triggered, then there are three factors which would have been considered regarding the judgment: "First, what is the legal topic with which the case is concerned? Secondly, what is the connecting factor prescribed by the rules of conflict of laws for assigning cases on that topic to a particular system of law? Thirdly, what system of law does the connecting factor point to in the case before the court?"[16]

The significance of this case was that, except for the deception of the German customs authorities, there was no single connection between this contract and German law: the forum was English; the proper law of the insurance contract was English law; the place of performance of the contract was England. Therefore, strictly speaking, this is not a case which involved a foreign law illegality, as did the former cases; it seems that, in this case, the court adopted a more complex approach. However, it is clear that Staughton J still agreed to the rules which have been developed by *Regazzoni v K.C. Sethia*[17] and also examined the case according to English law criteria to decide whether it was illegal or not. It seems that, on this point, there is no clear difference between common contract law and insurance contract law.

---

14 *Euro-Diam Limited v Bathurst* [1990] 1 Q.B. 1.
15 Ibid at 15.
16 Ibid at 17.
17 *Regazzoni v K.C. Sethia* [1958] A.C. 301.

6.2 The English legal position on foreign law illegality in marine insurance

The next point this chapter will discuss concerns the position of marine insurance law on foreign law illegality. According to authorities, it seems that there are still no defined rules on this due to the specificity of section 41. The position of section 41 on this point has been discussed in three cases – *Euro-Diam Limited v Bathurst*, *Royal Boskalis Westminster v Mountain* and most recently, *The Nancy* – and although the former two cases do not relate to marine insurance, section 41 was raised and considered in both of the judgments. The following section examines the judgments of the three cases and attempt to explore the courts' position on this particular issue.

In *Euro-Diam Limited v Bathurst* section 41 was raised as a supportive argument in the insurer's defence – that there was an implied term in the contract of insurance that "in so far as the defendant (which must have been intended to mean the plaintiffs) could control the matter, the adventure would be carried out in a lawful manner".[18] Staughton LJ rejected this argument, but went on to consider the question of whether, if there was an implied term in the contract, such as section 41 in marine insurance, then would section 41 embrace foreign law illegality as well as illegality under English law? Based on two old cases, *Parkin v Dick* and *Planche v Fletcher*, Staughton LJ came to the conclusion that: "There is nothing in that case to suggest that illegality by a foreign law would have the same result; or, for that matter, that it would be a breach of any implied warranty".[19] However, the key point is that there was also nothing in those two cases to suggest that illegality by a foreign law would not have the same result; therefore, his final decision that "an implied term so far as concerns compliance with English law, I would have considerable doubt whether it extended to foreign law",[20] based on lack of evidence, although it is an inconclusive decision.

This issue was then further considered by Rix J in the case *Royal Boskalis Westminster v Mountain*. In this case, section 41 was one of the three defences which the defendant raised under the Marine Insurance Act 1906, and the plaintiff submitted that, in any event, section 41 did not apply to foreign illegality. Rix J carefully examined the former authorities, especially the judgment in the case *Euro-Diam*, and came to the conclusion that: "No case has been drawn to my attention in which the unlawfulness of an adventure or the manner of its performance under foreign law had resulted in the failure of a policy or a claim under one prior to the Act".[21] And although *Foster* was rightly decided, the rules in that case "would be so as a matter of common law", irrespective of the Marine Insurance Act.

Besides the reasons given in the *Euro-Diam* case, Rix J also gave two reasons why section 41 does not cover foreign law illegality. The first one was that, "the warranty contained in s. 41, if it applied to foreign law would be extremely wide"[22] and the assured would easily be unknown to foreign law or would ignore foreign law; the

---

18 Marine Insurance Act 1906, s 41.
19 *Euro-Diam Limited v Bathurst* [1990] 1 Q.B. 15.
20 Ibid at 18.
21 *Royal Boskalis Westminster v Mountain* [1997] Lloyd's Reinsurance LR 523 at 589.
22 Ibid.

remaining two factors were the severe consequences of a breach of warranty and the lack of previously clear authorities, as pointed to by Rix J: "It seems to me to be odd to imply by way of a term with the strength of a warranty to a situation not reflected in cases before the Act or even to the common law relating to foreign illegality as it has now developed".[23] Rix J therefore concluded that section 41 only applies to English law and the consequences for a policy of marine insurance of unlawfulness under foreign law are therefore a matter for common law.

This was the first time that the application of section 41 had been confined to illegality under English law only and not under foreign law; although there was still no final view on this point, it seems it had been rightly decided. In the most recent case *Sea Glory Maritime Co, Swedish Management Co SA v AL Sagr National Insurance Co*, the judge found that he should follow the judgment of Rix J.[24]

Based on the former authorities, it seems the rules which they developed were appropriate. As has been criticised above, section 41 is an implied warranty and no causal link is required; therefore, if section 41 can embrace foreign law illegality, it will be clearly unjust to the assured.

Section 41 of the Marine Insurance Act 1906 is not mentioned in *Dicey & Morris, The Conflict of Laws* (10th edn), although that may be because, if it does embrace foreign law, it is not a conflict rule but a rule of construction.

As to the question of whether the English courts recognise foreign law, it seems that the English courts only apply the English illegality rules when dealing with such cases; as long as the English courts have the jurisdiction, the illegality issue is not changeable.

6.3 A criticism of current marine insurance law with regards to foreign law illegality

It has been made clear that, under section 41, English law does not recognise the illegality in foreign law; the only category of illegality which can trigger this implied warranty is illegality under English law.

However, the issue of whether the English law should recognise foreign law illegality never ceases to be a controversial topic: firstly, from the English law point of view, it seems there is no need to modify this area of the law, because English law is still the dominant law of the marine market, and most sea transportation activities choose English law as their governing law. Furthermore, major international trade countries have developed their own maritime laws and regulations with reference to English law. Another point in support of not changing the current law is that it is not the English courts' responsibility to be familiar with foreign law and apply it in English courts since such application may result in deviation from the original law, and in circumstances where both parties have already chosen English law as the governing law, the raising of the illegality issue in foreign law by one party is not fair to the other party and naturally the English court should ignore this.

---

23 Ibid at 590.
24 *Sea Glory Maritime Co, Swedish Management Co SA v AL Sagr National Insurance Co* [2013] EWHC 2116 at 295.

However, from the non-English law point of view, this rigid and limited responsibility on the parties and the English court imposed by section 41 should be modified. Firstly, the modern marine insurance market is becoming a global one, and even though most countries have developed their respective regulations based on fundamental principles in English law, they have also developed their own particularities – for example, in Australian law, section 54 is very different to the English principles – and in this global market, it is impossible not to respect the positions on illegality issues in other jurisdictions.

Secondly, marine insurance and the maritime industry are not two isolated fields, and both parties to a contract are required to comply with both maritime law and marine insurance law. According to section 41, the adventure can be an unlawful one if it has been carried out in an unlawful way. If the assured locates in a foreign country and carries out the adventure in an unlawful way according to the law of that country, it would be absurd if the English court did not recognise the illegality and enforce the insurance.

Thirdly, the lack of recognition of foreign law illegality can result in contradictory judgments on the same issue. For example, if the assured receives a punishment under the domestic law of his country, he may also get compensation under English law.

Fourthly, although Rix J proposed the difficulties of recognising foreign law illegality in marine insurance, it seems from his point of view that he must have been aware of the harsh consequence imposed by section 41 on the assured and that he sought to lighten the assured's liability by confining the boundaries of foreign law illegality in marine insurance. However, the harsh consequences for the assured are not caused by foreign law illegality and this restriction may result in a situation in which cases which involve both a foreign assured and a British insurer, and in which foreign law illegality is not recognised, can cause losses to British insurers.

6.4 Possible methods for dealing with foreign law illegality in marine insurance

Thus, the pattern which English law should adopt is that, when dealing with foreign law illegality in marine insurance cases, it is the common law rules rather than section 41 which should be considered by English courts.

Besides this approach, the English courts should also allow parties to choose their own governing law and jurisdiction, and the English court should respect this choice. In the case *Mackender v Feldia A.G*, it was decided by Lord Denning MR that: "It all comes to this: the English courts have discretion whether or not to give leave to serve this writ out of the jurisdiction. Seeing that the underwriters have agreed to a foreign jurisdiction clause which gives exclusive jurisdiction to the Belgian courts, I think we should allow these disputes to be decided in the courts of Belgium".[25]

Furthermore, English courts should also allow the parties to contract out section 41 in their insurance policy: As was pointed out in the judgment of *Euro-Diam*

---

25 *Mackender v Feldia A.G* [1967] 2 Q.B. 590 at 599.

Limited: "For an implied term which the parties cannot contract out of is, so far as I am aware, a creature unknown to the common law".[26]

The most significant feature of common law when dealing with foreign illegality in English courts is that English courts may not apply the foreign law; however, the English courts will analyse whether they can find corresponding points in English law or whether the English law shares the same spirit as the foreign law. If this is not the case, then clearly the English courts will not adopt the foreign law in English courts. However, in marine cases which involve carriage of goods, international trade or admiralty, which are mostly covered by international treaties or law which originate from English authorities, it is unlikely that the English courts will adopt an approach which opposes international conventions. Therefore, with regard to this point, the meaning of the phrase "foreign law" in section 41 should be precisely defined. The foreign law which the English courts should not consider when dealing with foreign law illegality in section 41 should be confined into the following categories: (1) a law which contradicts with English law or practice; (2) a law which has no common ground with English law either in spirit or practice, meaning that the English law has no common/similar intention, no common/similar regulation and no common/similar practice as the foreign law; (3) in circumstances where there is a violation of international treaties, for the treaties to be ineffective, the treaties should not have been integrated into English law or the English law should not have similar domestic regulations and should have no intention of joining the treaties; (4) when the foreign law is not the foundation of the insurance policy or is immaterial to the policy and does not concern either of the parties, otherwise, English courts should also consider the foreign law. An example is the situation in the case *Bell v Carstairs*[27] – even though in this case, the assured was in violation of a treaty between the USA and France, since this treaty was the foundation for deciding whether the risk was illegal or not, and since it concerned an English underwriter, the foreign law was also considered. Therefore, these four categories are the circumstances where section 41 should not be applied. Besides these four circumstances, the violation of foreign law should be recognised by English courts and as has been suggested in this chapter, the common law rules should be applied accordingly.

6.5 Conclusion

Based on the analysis above, it is clear that, either in common law or in marine insurance law, foreign law never ceases to be effective. The approach adopted in common law cases is clearly fairer to both parties. In marine insurance cases, although there are concerns (as raised by Rix J), if illegality is still confined to a violation of domestic law, it will be unfair to the insurer, especially in such a closely connected commercial world. Therefore, the foreign law which cannot be applied should be confined as was suggested in Section 6.4 above. However, a major precondition for this is that the harsh consequences of section 41 should be reformed first.

---

26 *Euro-Diam Limited v Bathurst* [1990] 1 Q.B. 1.
27 *Bell v Carstairs* (1811) 14 East 374.

CHAPTER 7

The marine insurance legality issue in Australia and other common law jurisdictions

This chapter will consider the warranty of legality in Australia and two other common law jurisdictions, New Zealand and Canada. These three countries have warranties of legality in their own marine insurance law and although these derived from English law, they have been developed according to the circumstances of each individual country.

The aim of this chapter is to assess the current position of the warranty of legality in these three countries in order to provide supportive evidence for the need to reform section 41 from a foreign law perspective.

This chapter will have three sections: the first will provide a detailed analysis of the warranty of legality in Australian law; the second part will give a brief assessment of this warranty in New Zealand and Canada; and, finally, the third section will conclude the development of the warranties of legality in these countries and analyse the valuable experience they provide for developing English law.

7.1 The Australian legal approach to the illegality issue

As well as the UK, other Commonwealth countries have adopted the same approach as the Marine Insurance Act 1906 (MIA 1906). In the Australian Marine Insurance Act 1909, for example, there is also an implied warranty of legality that shares the identical words as the MIA 1906 Act. Section 47 of this Act provides that:

> 47. There is an implied warranty that the adventure insured is a lawful one, and that, so far as the assured can control the matter, the adventure shall be carried out in a lawful manner.[1]

The warranty of legality in Australian law raises similar concerns to those in English law; that is, that section 47 is so broad, given the numerous regulations and statutes and other kinds of rules which regulate the shipping industry, that it is very easy for an assured to violate one or two of the rules and the insurer is entitled to discharge his liability under many circumstances. Besides this, there is no difference between the consequences of breaching the lawful adventure and those of breaching the lawful performance of the adventure.

---

1 Marine Insurance Act 1909, s 47.

There are two significant cases which relate to this issue in Australia. In *Doak v Weekes*[2] it is clear that there are various regulations which regulate the navigation of a vessel, such as that it has sufficient and qualified crew. In this case the owner knowingly sent the vessel without prudent and qualified crew to sea, then there was a breach of the warranty, even though the statute only required penalties for the breach. In a later and similar case, *Switzerland Insurance Australia Ltd v Mowie Fisheries Pty Ltd*,[3] there were two express warranties in the insurance policy which provided: "(1) That the vessel is in survey and will remain in survey with the appropriate governmental authority of the State of registration at all times during the currency of the policy. (2) That the vessel will be skippered, manned, crewed, operated and licensed in accordance with the regulations and by-laws and all other applicable laws of the appropriate governmental authorities of the State of registration at all times during the currency of the policy".[4] In this case, the vessel was lost during its voyage from Eden in New South Wales to Portland in Victoria and the insurer denied his liability on the ground that there had been a breach of express warranty as well as a breach of implied warranty, since there was no qualified crew on board, as required by the Marine Act, when the loss happened. In the first judgment of this case, based upon the construction of the statute, Tamberlin J found there had been no breach of express or implied warranty since the issue here did not fall into the scope of the statute.[5] In the appeal judgment, even though Beaumont J agreed with the judgment in the *Doak* case, since the Marine Act 1976 (Tasmania) had no jurisdiction on this vessel, there was no breach of implied warranty in this case. Therefore, when dealing with the illegality issue, whether there has been a violation of the law is not a simple question; there must be a careful construction of the wording of the statute in the statutory illegality scenario and the intention of the parties in the violation of common law cases.

These two judgments bring to mind the *St John Shipping Corp* case in English law. According to the view of some authorities,[6] it seems that Australia and the UK have adopted different ways of dealing with similar issues; that is to say that, even though all three statutes that the three cases violated only led to an imposition of penalties on the assureds, in English law the judge did not recognise the illegality issue but in Australian law the court did, especially in *Doak v Weekes*. However, it seems that there is little difference between these two jurisdictions, since the scenarios of the *St John Shipping* and the *Doak* cases are different. Firstly, *St John Shipping* was not a marine insurance case, and it was the freight under a charterparty contract rather than the insurance that the claimant sought to recover, and since there is no implied warranty of legality in contract law it is impossible for the court to judge this in the same way. Secondly, in *St John Shipping* there were no losses and the shipowner did not need to rely on the issue of overloading to recover their freight under the contract, whereas in *Doak* there was a loss, the

---

2 *Doak v Weekes* (1986) 82 FLR 334.
3 *Switzerland Insurance Australia Ltd v Mowie Fisheries Pty Ltd* [1997] FCA 231.
4 Ibid.
5 Ibid.
6 Baris Soyer, *Warranties in Marine Insurance* (2nd edn), p 126.

adventure had been performed in an unlawful manner and the assured needed to rely on the illegality to claim the insurance. The third difference is that, in the Australian case, the assured had knowledge of the illegality and intentionally sent the vessel, whereas in *St John Shipping* neither the owner nor the captain had such knowledge. Therefore, from these perspectives, it seems that the Australian judgments on these two cases are reasonable, and it cannot be said that the Australia courts should adopt a stricter approach to dealing with illegality issues in marine insurance.

As far as Australian law is concerned, it seems that the warranty of legality issue is more commonly raised under Australian law than English law and the method Australian law adopts now is different to the English one, although the Australian courts are very cautious when dealing with this warranty. In *Solway v Lumley General Insurance Ltd* where the court went on to decide whether the non-registration of a vessel, which is a violation of the Transport Operations (Marine Safety) Act 1994, constituted a breach of implied warranty and the insurer would be able to deny liability because of it, it was decided that there was a reasonable excuse for the assured since the assured had already registered according to other similar Acts: "In other words, prima facie there was an arguable representation that the owner of the vessel had complied with all the relevant requirements of the Queensland Act".[7] Therefore, there was no breach of the warranty and the insurer's appeal was set aside. If a similar case was to be decided under English law, then the reliance principle and the causation principle could be applied since the assured clearly did not need to rely on the illegality to plead his claim.

Identical English common law factors have also been considered by the Australian courts. For example, in the case *Norwest Refrigeration Services Pty Ltd v Bain Dawes*, the insurance policy excluded the liability of the insurer in the case of a vessel which did not have a current Certificate of Survey issued pursuant to Western Australian legislation. However, both the agent of the assured and the broker failed to inform the assured of this exclusion clause; the vessel failed to obtain the certificate and was subsequently lost in a fire. In the second trial of this case, the agent of the assured sought to rely on the implied warranty of legality to discharge its liability. However, the judge decided that, if the assured had been informed of the clause, he would have obtained a certificate, and that because the assured had no such knowledge nor the intention to violate the law, there was no breach of warranty.[8]

In addition, in the Western Australian Supreme Court case *Mercantile Mutual Insurance (Ltd) v Gibbs*, the third party in this case was injured because of the negligent navigation of the assured. However, the court decided that there had been a breach of the warranty of legality since the Certificate of Survey for the assured's boat had run out, and even though there was no link between the illegality and the loss, by navigating the uncertified boat, the assured had rendered the adventure illegal. In this case, there were no defences for the assured like those in

---

7 *Solway v Lumley General Insurance Ltd* [2003] QCA 136.
8 *Norwest Refrigeration Services Pty Ltd v Bain Dawes* (1984) 157 CLR 149.

the former two cases, since the assured had full knowledge of this and there was no reasonable excuse.[9]

Based on the judgments of these two cases, it is clear that, in circumstances in which Australian courts apply the warranty of legality in marine insurance cases, factors such as knowledge of the assured and a connection between the illegality of the assured and the loss are still required.

In circumstances where there is an express warranty in the policy which requires that the insurance shall be carried out according to local law and regulations, then it seems that the implied warranty does not take priority.[10]

Another area of Australian law which concerns cases that deal with the insurance policies which cover fines and penalties is the same as English law. In these circumstances, moral culpability is still the most important factor which needs to be considered, and if there is a lack of culpability, then especially with motor insurance, the assured or the third party can recover under the insurance.

However, even though Australian courts have adopted a reasonable approach when dealing with illegality issues in marine insurance, section 47 is still an obstacle in Australian law, and therefore, in order to avoid problems, the Australian Law Reform Commission proposed the following options for reform:

> "1. Amending the MIA to provide that an insurer may not avoid a contract of marine insurance by reason of a breach of a warranty if the insured proves the loss was not caused or contributed to by the breach of warranty.
> 2. Redrafting the MIA to distinguish between technical, non-material breaches of regulations and other illegality which substantially affects the risks involved in the adventure. As noted above, the wording of s 47 of the MIA distinguishes between adventures having a lawful purpose and being carried out in a lawful manner, but the consequences of a breach are the same in each case.
> 3. Restricting the circumstances in which the insurer is entitled to deny liability under the contract for breach of the warranty of legality to situations where the insured knew or should have known of the illegality".[11]

Furthermore, the Law Commission suggested that:

> "1. The MIA should continue to provide that an insurer may avoid a contract of marine insurance by reason of a breach of the implied warranty that the adventures have a lawful purpose.
> 2. The MIA should be amended to provide that an insurer may not avoid a contract of marine insurance by reason of a breach of the implied warranty that the adventure be carried out in a lawful manner if (i) the loss in respect of which the insurer seeks to be indemnified was not caused or contributed to by the breach of warranty and (ii) the insured neither knew

---

9 *Mercantile Mutual Insurance (Ltd) v Gibbs* [2001] WASCA 271.
10 *Allison Pty Ltd Tans Pibara Marine Port Service v Lumley General Insurance Ltd* [2006] WASC 104.
11 Review of the Marine Insurance Act 1909.

nor ought to have known about the illegality at any time that it would have been possible for the insured to intervene".[12]

The Law Commission also proposed the abolition of the implied warranty and that the insurer and the assured should insert the terms which express this function into the insurance contract; that is, to transfer the implied warranty into an express contract term and express the function of this term and the consequences for breaching it. For example:

> "So far as the insured can control the matter, the insured adventure shall have no unlawful purpose. If there is a breach of such a term, the insurer is automatically discharged from all liability under the policy".
>
> "So far as the insured can control the matter, the insured adventure shall be carried out in a lawful manner. If there is a breach of such a term, the insurer is not liable to indemnify the insured for any loss that is attributable to the breach".[13]

From the previous discussion, it can be seen that in marine insurance cases Australia seems to have adopted the same method as in England, and the proposals which have been raised by the Law Commission in Australia are also suitable for application in England. However, it is commonly argued that the express term solution proposed by the Australian Law Commission should be adopted by English law. In the English law system, although there is still no official reform proposal from the Law Commission, it is commonly agreed that the illegality defence in common law should be applied in marine insurance cases, as demonstrated by the recent case the *Sea Glory*.

When section 54(2) of the Insurance Contract Act 1984 is considered the situation may be seen as confusing. In this section, the insurer may not refuse to pay the claim if the assured can prove that the loss which gives rise to the claim is not caused by the assured's act, or that part of the loss which gives rise to the claim is not caused by the assured's act.[14] The aim of this section is to insert a causation link between the loss and the act of the assured and to restrain the insurer's power to exclude their liability. However, setting aside the discussion and chaos this section caused to Australian insurance law, section 54 was found to be little help to the illegality issue in insurance law or marine insurance law. Firstly, this Act does not apply to marine insurance, and secondly, in ordinary insurance law, the causation link should not be viewed as the only factor which needs to be considered when dealing with illegality issues. If, for example, a motor has been used to transfer drugs and is involved in an accident which is caused by another car, it is difficult to argue that the assured of the motor can recover under his insurance policy, especially when the assured has the knowledge that this motor was being used to transfer drugs; if this insurance was allowed, this would be a typical example of a lack of consistency between the criminal judgment and the commercial judgment.

Based on these points, it is hard to believe that the model of section 54 is helpful to English law on illegality issues, and it is clear that, based on limited cases,

---

12 Ibid.
13 Ibid.
14 Insurance Contract Act 1984, s 54(2).

apart from the reform proposal raised by the Law Commission of Australia, the Australian system adopts almost the same approach as the English legal system. That is, it does not rely on the implied warranty of legality and does take the factors which have been considered in common law, such as knowledge and intention, into account.

Compared to the reform proposal in Australia, the status in England is more shocking and conservative. In English Law Commission Consultation Paper No 204, when considering whether the implied warranty needed to be reformed or not, the Law Commission contended that there was no need to reform the current implied warranties since firstly, according to the International Group of P&I Clubs: "If they were not implied they would need to be expressed in the policy. The effect of these sections is well-known to marine insured and their intermediaries."[15] And secondly, the LMA were not aware of any significant discontent on the part of the insurance buying community or their representatives.[16] In the Law Commission's summary of responses to the third consultation paper, 66% of the consultees agreed to retain the implied warranties and make no change to them, and 78% of the consultees agreed that the implied warranty should operate exactly the same way as in express warranties conditions.[17]

Furthermore, if it is true that the warranty of legality in English law is to be reformed rather than abolished, then English law needs to at least distinguish the consequences of a violation of an adventure which shall have a lawful purpose, and those of a violation of an adventure which shall be carried out lawfully.

7.2 The warranty of legality issue in New Zealand and Canada

In New Zealand and Canada, there are also sections which require a warranty of legality in marine insurance; however, in both of the countries, the piece of law equivalent to section 41 in English law has been reformed.

In New Zealand, when dealing with the illegality issue in marine insurance cases, pieces of legislation are of great importance. The first one is section 42 of the Marine Insurance Act, which adopts the same wording as section 41 in English law, and the second Act is section 11 of the Insurance Law Reform Act 1977 which provides that:

    (a) By the provisions of a contract of insurance the circumstances in which the insurer is bound to indemnify the insured against loss are so defined as to exclude or limit the liability of the insurer to indemnify the insured on the happening of certain events or on the existence of certain circumstances, and

    (b) In the view of the Court or arbitrator determining the claim of the insured the liability of the insurer has been so defined because the happening of such events or the existence of such circumstances was in the view of the

---

15 Law Commission Consultation Paper No 204.
16 Ibid.
17 Ibid.

insurer likely to increase the risk of such loss occurring, the insured shall not be disentitled to be indemnified by the insurer by reason only of such provisions of the contract of insurance if the insured proves on the balance of probability that the loss in respect of which the insured seeks to be indemnified was not caused or contributed to by the happening of such events or the existence of such circumstances.[18]

It was further provided that no provision in the 1908 Act shall override section 11 because of section 14 of this Act. Therefore, it is clear that, when New Zealand courts decide illegality cases in marine insurance, the causation link between the illegality and the losses is of great importance.

There are very limited cases which relate to this issue, but two typical cases will be looked at below.

The first case is *Harbour Inn Seafoods v Switzerland General Insurance Ltd*.[19] In this case, a fishing vessel drifted onto a reef while "laying to" (i.e. drifting at sea at night with no watch, the engine turned off and all the crew asleep) which is a common practice when vessels sail overnight. However, during the night the vessel struck rocks and was later abandoned. The assured claimed losses against the insurer. The insurer denied coverage on the basis of a clause in the policy which provided that the vessel was to be operated "in accordance with the regulations and bylaws and all other applicable laws", and also that this practice was a breach of the implied warranty of legality. In the judgment, the court found that this practice, although common, was a serious violation of Collision Regulations, and that the adventure had clearly been carried out in an unlawful manner in terms of section 42, and that furthermore, the ship owner had knowledge and would have been able to prevent the losses caused by the "laying to" but did not do so. Therefore, this was clearly a violation of section 42.

Another case which is important is *Womersley v Peacock*.[20] In this case, the assured's vessel did not obtain the certificate required by law and caused losses. When dealing with whether there had been a breach of the warranty of legality, the judge concluded that: "The real question is whether the illegality, the absence of a certificate of survey, caused or contributed to the capsize".[21] Therefore, in this case, since there had been no such causation link between the breach and the losses, the breach of section 42 was not sustained.

Based on these cases, it is clear that, when dealing with whether there is a breach of the warranty of legality, the causal connection is clearly a vital factor which needs to be considered by New Zealand courts. However, one exception which has been noticed by judgments of these two cases is whether section 11 of the Insurance Law Reform Act can override a statutory warranty is still doubtful. However, New Zealand law inclines to the position that, where the assured can establish an absence of causal connection, it is likely that section 11 can still be applied.[22]

---

18 Insurance Law Reform Act 1977, s 11.
19 *Harbour Inn Seafoods v Switzerland General Insurance Ltd* (1991) 6 ANZIns 61,048.
20 *Womersley v Peacock* (Unreported, High Court of NZ).
21 Ibid.
22 *Womersley v Peacock* (Unreported, High Court of NZ).

In Canadian law, there is a similar warranty in both the British Columbia Marine Insurance Act and the Marine Insurance Act 1993.[23]

The first important case is *James Yachts Ltd v Thames and Mersey Marine Insurance Co*[24] which involved a boat builder who stored boats in his yard contrary to municipal by-laws. A fire destroyed the boats and equipment so stored. The British Columbia Supreme Court agreed with the insurer that the assured's behaviour was a breach of the implied warranty of legality and that the insurer was therefore discharged from liability. In this case, it was also possible to establish that there was a causal connection between the fire caused by the illegality of the assured and the losses, that the breach was a violation of statute, and that the assured also had the knowledge of the illegality.

Another case involving the breach of this warranty is that of *Federal Business Development Bank v Reinsurance and Excess Managers Ltd*.[25] That case involved a tugboat that sank while towing a jet boat loaded with cedar shingles that had been illegally taken from a cutting site without being scaled. The court declined to find that this technical breach of the Forestry Act discharged the insurer from liability as the assured was not deliberately acting in an unlawful manner and the failure to have the shingles scaled did not bear a direct relationship to the cause of the loss.

7.3 Conclusion

From the Acts and the judgments of these three jurisdictions, two points are clear. Firstly, the requirement for a causal connection between the assured's illegality and the losses is of great importance and has been established either by common law or statute in all three jurisdictions; although this approach has caused confusion at some points (such as in New Zealand law), the merits of such a rule are clear and it is clearly fairer to the assured in circumstances where only technical rules have been breached. Secondly, the knowledge and intention of the assured is another vital factor which needs to be considered; in circumstances where the assured had no intention to commit an illegality, this policy should not be compromised.

Therefore, the most significant points that English law should absorb from other common law jurisdictions are to adopt common law rules, as in Australian law, or to adopt a causal connection test when dealing with issues concerning breaches of the warranty of legality. If English law does not do this, it is clear that it will be outdated.

---

23 Section 43 of the British Columbia Act and s 35 of the Marine Insurance Act 1993 both adopt the same words as in English law.

24 *James Yachts Ltd v Thames and Mersey Marine Insurance Co* [1977] Lloyd's Rep vol 1 at 206.

25 *Federal Business Development Bank v Reinsurance and Excess Managers Ltd* (1979) 13 BCLR 376.

CHAPTER 8

Warranty of legality from the perspective of the Insurance Act 2015

It is unfair to say that the English courts have not achieved any progress on the illegality issue in marine insurance, and the status of the current law in England is fast-changing. In Law Commission Report No 353, the Law Commission proposed reform of various controversial areas in insurance law, including the areas of good faith, fraudulent claims and warranties. The Insurance Contract Law Bill 2014 (now the Insurance Act 2015) was drafted according to this reform report, in Part 3 of which the warranty issue was considered, with section 9 being concerned with warranties and representations and section 10 with breach of warranty.

On 12 February 2015 the Insurance Act 2015 received Royal Assent and will come into force in August 2016. This is viewed as the most major change in both marine and non-marine insurance law since the introduction of the 1906 Act. However, it is worth noting that the Marine Insurance Act 1906 will only be partially repealed. Also, it is not entirely accurate to view the aim of this new Act as to protect the interests of the assureds. This Act aims to bring transparency to both parties. For example, as can be seen from sections 4 and 5 of Part 2, which deal with the knowledge of the assured and the insurer in their duty of fair presentation, it is clear that there are no changes to the obligation of the assured to disclose his knowledge of the insured subject. What has been changed in these sections are the concepts which are vague in the 1906 Act but are now more transparent.[1]

This chapter will first provide a clear introduction to the reforms proposed by the Law Commission and the new Act generally, and will then consider the impact of these on the issue of the warranty of legality in marine insurance law, considering whether the new Bill contains useful methods for dealing with this issue.

8.1 Reform recommendations of the Law Commission

As can be seen from the introduction of current warranty rules in Chapter 1, the current rules are questionable and have come under criticism for years. Therefore a reform has been urgently required by assureds and also respondents of the Law

---

1 To understand this part of new Act more specifically please see: "Knowledge of the assured in the context of the pre-contractual duty of disclosure: A new approach under English law and prospective reform" *Chinese law Insurance Law Journal* vol 27/06–27013.

Commission.² After a long consultation procedure which can be traced back to 2006 when the first consultation report which solely deals with the warranty issue was published, four issue or consultation papers have been published by the Law Commission.³ Since this is part of a reform programme which was launched by the Law Commission in 2006 changes in some key areas have been codified and warranty is one of them. Since the Insurance Act 2015 is largely based upon Law Commission Report No 353 recommendations and the reasons which underlie these recommended reforms will be introduced first.

The warranty issue, as noted by the Law Commission, needs to be reformed. On one hand this is because of the severe consequence of breaching. On the other hand the inconsistency between warranty as a term in contract law and insurance law also requires the Law Commission's endeavours to reform this issue.⁴ Furthermore, this area of law still lacks transparency on some issues which has resulted in it being the third most common ground for claims disputes. Finally, from the prospect of international law, the current regime of warranty in English law has been abolished in other major Commonwealth countries such as Australia and New Zealand. Such controversy seldom exists in Scandinavian countries.⁵

In chapter 13, the Law Commission gives a brief introduction to the current law of warranty in insurance and marine insurance law: since the legal position on warranty has not been changed in the last two issue papers published by the Law Commission, and because this law has been discussed before, this chapter will not re-introduce it here.

The most significant problems identified by the Law Commission are that the consequences of breach of warranty in insurance law are harsh, the assureds are normally not familiar with the content of the insurance policy and contractual terms and, particularly, the fact that: "With the law as it currently stands, policyholders are at the mercy of their insurer as to which approach is taken, and insurers are increasingly accepting that this situation is unfair".⁶

The Law Commission then provides an important reason why the arguments opposing reform should not stand: "The reality is that people and organisations are fallible, and that insurance is often purchased to protect against human error. If only perfect businesses were able to buy insurance, the market for insurance would be a small one".⁷

---

2 "Insurance Contract Law: Business Disclosure; Warranties; Insurers' Remedies for Fraudulent Claims; And Late Payment" Law Com No 353 at p 154.

3 "Issues Paper 2: Warranties (November 2006); Misrepresentation, Non-Disclosure and Breach of Warranty by the Insured" (June 2007) Law Commission Consultation Paper No 182; "Consumer Insurance Law: Pre-Contract Disclosure and Misrepresentation" (December 2009) Law Com No 319; "The Business Insured's Duty of Disclosure and the Law of Warranties" (June 2012) Law Commission Consultation Paper No 204.

4 "Insurance Contract Law: Business Disclosure; Warranties; Insurers' Remedies For Fraudulent Claims; And Late Payment" Law Com No 353 at 14.2.

5 Ibid at 14.7.

6 "Insurance Contract Law: Business Disclosure; Warranties; Insurers' Remedies For Fraudulent Claims; And Late Payment" Law Com No 353 at 14.3.

7 "Insurance Contract Law: Business Disclosure; Warranties; Insurers' Remedies For Fraudulent Claims; And Late Payment" Law Com No 353, p 169 at 14.20.

The Law Commission thus agreed that the law of warranty in marine insurance should be reformed and since the warranty is codified in the Marine Insurance Act 1906, the reform would constitute a statutory reform. The details of the reform can be summarised as follows.

This first reform which is proposed by the Law Commission is to abolish the basis of contract clause. This is a kind of clause which allows the insurer to deny the assured's whole policy when representations by the assured turn out to be untrue no matter how minor it is. However, from the legality prospect, this can hardly be a problem since this is an express clause on a proposal form which the assured needs to sign for its effectiveness. Therefore, there is obviously no need for an express clause to reaffirm the requirement of legality. Naturally, the abolishment of the basis of contract clause will not affect the existence of warranty of legality.

Secondly, the insurer should ensure that the consequences of a breach are set out fully in the contract, and should take sufficient steps to draw the insured's attention to them. With regard to the warranty of legality, if the insurer requires that some specific law needs to be strictly complied with, the insurer should put the name of the statute or other legal document into the insurance contract, and specify the consequences of a breach, this should be done in a way which will draw the attention of the assured.

The most significant recommendation in the Law Commission's report is the abolition of the automatic discharge of the insurer's liability in a situation where there has been a breach of warranty. The effect of this recommendation on warranty of legality will be discussed further below.

Another recommendation which is of great importance to the warranty in insurance law is that "the insurer's liability should be suspended rather than discharged in the event of breach, and that liability could be restored if the breach of warranty is remedied. Where the breach is remedied before a loss, the insurer should pay the claim. Where loss occurs, or is attributable to something happening, after a breach but before remedy, the insurer should not be liable for that loss".[8]

Finally, a factor which the Law Commission found significant when deciding the warranty issue is whether the wording of the contract is material to the risk of loss or whether the suspensory provision has been carried out before the deadline.

However, the limits of the law of warranty of legality remain unclear. This is primarily because the implied warranty was not considered separately in the Law Commission's reform since the implied warranty sections were considered better if untouched.[9]

However, the proposal for the requirement of a causation link to trigger a breach of warranty was abolished by the Law Commission for the following reasons: increased investigation costs, complex litigation, uncertain outcomes and difficulties of proof. Furthermore, it was felt that a causation test would not be appropriate

---

8 "Insurance Contract Law: Business Disclosure; Warranties; Insurers' Remedies For Fraudulent Claims; And Late Payment" Law Com No 353 at ch 16.
9 Ibid at p 191.

for all warranties since some warranties may be relevant to the loss without having a causal connection with it – for example facts which are critical to the insurer during the period of the acceptance of the risk, such as the age of the driver and the criminal record of an employee. Therefore, it is unlikely that the causation principle adopted in common law will be applied here. One uncertainty may lie in section 11 of the Act which implies that breach of term which is not relevant to the actual loss may not entitle the insurer to deny his liability. However, such regulation is still subject to several conditions which will be analysed in the second part of this chapter.

8.2 Warranties in the Insurance Act 2015

Based on the recommendations of the Law Commission, sections dealing with law of warranty in Insurance Act 2015 have been formed thus:

10 Breach of warranty

(1) Any rule of law that breach of a warranty (express or implied) in a contract of insurance results in the discharge of the insurer's liability under the contract is abolished.

(2) An insurer has no liability under a contract of insurance in respect of any loss occurring, or attributable to something happening, after a warranty (express or implied) in the contract has been breached but before the breach has been remedied.

(3) But subsection (2) does not apply if –
   (a) Because of a change of circumstances, the warranty ceases to be applicable to the circumstances of the contract,
   (b) Compliance with the warranty is rendered unlawful by any subsequent law, or
   (c) The insurer waives the breach of warranty.

(4) Subsection (2) does not affect the liability of the insurer in respect of losses occurring, or attributable to something happening –
   (a) Before the breach of warranty, or
   (b) If the breach can be remedied, after it has been remedied.

(5) For the purposes of this section, a breach of warranty is to be taken as remedied –
   (a) In a case falling within subsection (6), if the risk to which the warranty relates later becomes essentially the same as that originally contemplated by the parties,
   (b) In any other case, if the insured ceases to be in breach of the warranty.

(6) A case falls within this subsection if –
   (a) The warranty in question requires that by an ascertainable time something is to be done (or not done), or a condition is to be fulfilled, or something is (or is not) to be the case, and
   (b) That requirement is not complied with.

(7) In the Marine Insurance Act 1906—
  (a) In section 33 (nature of warranty), in subsection (3), the second sentence is omitted,
  (b) Section 34 (when breach of warranty excused) is omitted.[10]

For the convenience of readers and analysis the main section in Part III has been illustrated above. Section 9 states that the representations made by the assured in a non-consumer insurance proposal form cannot be converted to warranty by the insurer by using a contract term or other device, either on the proposal form or in the policy document. Namely, the basis of contract clause in proposal form has been abolished. However, since warranty of legality is an implied warranty, therefore, this section is of little importance to it and will not be discussed further here.

The most fundamental changes on warranty lie in section 10. Section 10(1) and (2) reflect the major recommendation of the Law Commission that the automatic discharge rule should be abolished and the insurer only has no liability after the breach of warranty and before the remedy of it.

Not surprisingly such regulation is subject to conditions. Section 10(2) is of great importance since it illustrates two circumstances where the assured's liability to the assured will be discharged: the first scenario is clear – when loss happens during the breach of warranty, the insurer will be discharged from liability; the second category – that something happening during the breach of warranty does not result in losses immediately, but will potentially lead to losses after the breach of warranty has been "remedied" – is not quite so straightforward and needs to be analysed. One possible example set out by the Law Commission is that a box of fine wine requiring storage in a cool place was stored in a warm house, and even though it was transferred to a cool warehouse later, the high temperature during the breach may have already spoiled the wine. In this situation, even though the warranty was remedied, something happened during the breach that attributed to the loss.

In clause 10(5), two different modes of remedy for a breach of warranty are listed: firstly, in clause 10(5)(b) it is stated that a breach of warranty is generally to be taken as remedied when the insured "ceases to be in breach of the warranty". The essence of this is the question of whether the risk the insurer agreed to insure has been altered after a remedy of breach. Thus, as in the example given by the Law Commission, the insurer is still liable if a vessel which deviated from an approved course for a while and came back to it later got lost as a result of encountering a storm on the approved course, since the risk of encountering a storm is the same whether or not the vessel had deviated from the approved course and no new character has been added.

Unless the assured ceases to be in breach of warranty there is another kind of remedy. A warranty can be seen as remedied if the risk to which the warranty relates later becomes essentially the same. However, according to section 10(6)(a) this principle can only be applied to three kinds of warranties. However, the meaning of "essentially the same" in section 10(5)(a) has not been specified in the Act.

---

10 Insurance Act 2015, s 10.

According to the Law Commission a warranty of this kind can be seen as remedied "when the risk is restored to the state it would have been in had the breach not taken place".[11] Therefore, even if the risk has been raised during the breach, as long as the warranty is restored according to the contract later, the insurer will again be liable. A typical case of this principle is that a vessel which is short of crew during a period of a voyage only discharges the insurer's liability during this period.

In addition to restoring the risk according to the words of contract, the nature of the subject matter insured should also not to be changed after the remedy. For example, if a container of frozen meat has not been stored according to the agreed temperature and results in decay then such breach cannot be remedied by turning down the temperature, since the subject matter insured has been compromised. Therefore, as long as the purpose to insert a warranty has not been frustrated after the remedy, then such warranty should be seen as remedied.[12]

Under section 10(3) non-compliance with warranty can be excused in three circumstances which are quite clear and will not be discussed further here.

The imminent revised Insurance Act 2015 can also be applied to the marine insurance implied warranty, as stated by the Law Commission: "clause 10 applies to all warranties in all contracts of insurance. Many of the existing warranties provisions in the 1906 Act are deleted or amended by our draft Bill. The new regime is designed to also apply to warranties in contracts of marine insurance."[13]

According to the Law Commission Report, implied warranties should be retained; there were no strong arguments in favour of their removal, and the Report stated that "we do not recommend any changes to the implied marine warranties."[14] Because there is no distinction between implied marine warranties and other warranties of this kind, clause 10 therefore applies to all warranties, express and implied.

Based on the imminent changes to the law of marine insurance warranty discussed above, it can be seen that the major changes to the law are: firstly, the insurer's liability for breach of warranty will be suspended rather than automatically discharged; secondly, the breach of warranty can be remedied after a breach except in circumstances where a breach of warranty has altered the risks; thirdly, the insurer can only suspend those liabilities caused by the breach of a warranty, and not the insurer's other liabilities.

8.3 Causal link and section 11

As has been mentioned at the end of Section 8.1, the causal link proposal was once again denied by the Law Commission for reasons which seem to be persuasive. However, the Law Commission added another instrument which aims to narrow

---

11 "Insurance Contract Law: Business Disclosure; Warranties; Insurers' Remedies For Fraudulent Claims; And Late Payment" Law Com No 353 at 17.43.

12 The other two kinds of breaches which cannot be remedied are leak of confidential materials and the inaccurate representation of past or present facts: "Insurance Contract Law: Business Disclosure; Warranties; Insurers' Remedies For Fraudulent Claims; And Late Payment" Law Com No 353 at 17.50.

13 Ibid at 17.77.

14 Ibid at 17.78.

the categories of breach which can result in the discharge of insurer's liabilities. This section reads:

11. Terms not relevant to the actual loss

(1) This section applies to a term (express or implied) of a contract of insurance, other than a term defining the risk as a whole, if compliance with it would tend to reduce the risk of one or more of the following – (a) Loss of a particular kind, (b) Loss at a particular location, (c) Loss at a particular time.

(2) If a loss occurs, and the term has not been complied with, the insurer may not rely on the non-compliance to exclude, limit or discharge its liability under the contract for the loss if the insured satisfies subsection (3).

(3) The insured satisfies this subsection if it shows that the non-compliance with the term could not have increased the risk of the loss which actually occurred in the circumstances in which it occurred.

(4) This section may apply in addition to section 10.

As noticed by scholars[15] when dealing with the issue of warranty there are two terms which should be considered, terms related to the risk and terms related to the loss. In the Law Commission's Report terms related to the risk have not been considered, and the current situation that warranty can be seen as a condition precedent in some cases remains untouched.[16] Therefore, based on the introduction of current law in Chapter 1, it is perfectly clear that a breach of warranty of this kind can defeat a perfectly good claim. It is really a missed opportunity that the Law Commission did not follow the precedents which had been set by New Zealand and Australia.[17]

There are several issues which need to be noted and discussed in detail. The first one is that the term if complied with would reduce the risk. This is an objective test. Therefore, a term which only aims to limit the insurer's liability is not enough.[18] A policy on a building which requires a fire alarm tends to reduce the risk of loss by fire. However, if it is stated as the insurer will not be liable without an installation of a fire alarm then such term as implied by the Law Commission Report may not fall within section 11(1).

The second spotlight of section 11(1) is that this section cannot be applied on a term which defines the risk as a whole. This is again a vague explanation, since it is extremely easy to transmit a term which aims to reduce a risk into a term which defines a risk. For instance, in the example above, if the policy states under the title of risk definition that: "This policy can only be applied on buildings with fire alarms". Then section 11 cannot be applied here.

---

15 Rob Merkin and Ozlem Gurses, "The Insurance Act 2015: Rebalancing the Interests of Insurer and Assured" (2015) *Modern Law Review* vol 78, Issue 6, pp 1004–1027 at 1019.
16 Ibid.
17 Insurance Law Reform Act 1977, s 9 (New Zealand) and Insurance Contract Act 1984, s 54(1) (Australia) both of which require that the insurer's interests must be prejudiced by the assured's breach.
18 No 353 at 18.13.

The third issue is that the term must relate to a loss of particular kind, at a particular location or at a particular time. The parties can expressly state it in the insurance policy or the court will determine whether such warranty falls into this kind by construction.[19] However, a term which has a more general effect of defining the scope of the policy will be seen as relates to the contract generally rather than a term tending to reduce the risk of a particular kind. Therefore, section 11 cannot be applied on a breach of a warranty which forbids a yacht for commercial use since by such breach the risk which the insurer agreed to take at the beginning has been changed.[20]

The Law Commission emphasised that there is no causal connection required when applying section 11. However, it seems that the Law Commission contradicts itself on this point. The example which is raised by the Law Commission is that a term which requires an insured to maintain a particular type of lock on a door would tend, if complied with, to reduce the risk of break-in (and related events such as arson and vandalism). If the relevant lock was not fitted, the insurer's liability in respect of a break-in would be suspended until this was remedied. However, the Law Commission held the opinion that the insurer would have no liability for loss resulting from a break-in, even if the break-in was through a window rather than the relevant door. The conclusion of the Law Commission on this particular case is quite controversial since according to section 11 the loss which results from a break-in through a window clearly has no causal connection with the breach of warranty. Although it can be argued that such breach can be seen as an increase of certain risk, as according to the explanation of this piece of law addressed by the Law Commission itself: "We do not think it is fair that an insurer can refuse a claim on the basis of the policyholder's breach of warranty or other condition in circumstances where those terms are clearly irrelevant to the loss – that is, where the type of loss which occurred is not one which compliance with the warranty or condition could have had any chance of preventing".[21] And it is clear in the Law Commission's case that no matter how particular the locker can be, there is no way to prevent the thief from breaching through a window.

Therefore, as concluded by Professor Rob Merkin, although the Law Commission denied the causal link determinedly, it would be interesting to know what this statement refers to, if not causation.[22] Clearly, this section will definitely be the most controversial section of this new Act.

8.4 The application of the 2015 Act on warranty of legality

Following the discussion of the reform of warranty in Insurance Act 2015 and the summary of this new Act in the Law Commission's paper, this sub-chapter will consider the possible changes to the warranty of legality in marine insurance

---

19 *Amlin Corporate Member Limited v Oriental Assurance Corporation* [2013] EWHC 2380 (Comm) at [34].
20 No 353 at 18.21.
21 No 353 at 18.7.
22 Rob Merkin and Ozlem Gurses, "The Insurance Act 2015: Rebalancing the Interests of Insurer and Assured" (2015) *Modern Law Review* vol 78, Issue 6, pp 1004–1027 at 1022, fn 82.

law which would be initiated by the 2015 Act. It will consider how to deal with the illegality issue in marine insurance law after the 2015 Act comes into force, and will make a comparison between the impending Act and the illegality rules in common law, which, this thesis holds, form a better approach for the English courts to adopt.

The changes which could be initiated by the new Insurance Act 2015 on the warranty of legality are tremendous, especially changes to the second part of section 41. The potential changes to the two parts of section 41 will be analysed separately.

In the first part of section 41, which requires the adventure insured to be a lawful one, if the adventure is unlawful when the assured enters into the contract, and the assured intends to insure this unlawful adventure, then the warranty will be breached according to the new Act. This breach of warranty cannot be remedied, as according to section 10(2) and (5), even though the insurer's liability is still suspended rather than automatically discharged, this suspension will not cease until the assured cancels the insurance policy on the unlawful adventure and insures a lawful one. If this is the case then it cannot be said that the warranty has been remedied since the illegal insurance policy does not exist any more.

If the adventure insured is lawful at the time when the assured enters into the contract, but becomes unlawful due to a change of law or a change in circumstances which are impossible for the assured to predict or know – for example, sanctions being placed by one nation on another or a declaration of war between two nations during a voyage[23] – then based on section 10(3) this situation constitutes a change in circumstances in which the warranty ceases to be applicable; since it is impossible for the assured to know the adventure has become an unlawful one, this section of warranty shall cease to apply. Therefore, in such circumstances, the insurer's liability should not be suspended and the adventure is still under cover. It is worth noting that this is the same case if section 34(1) of the Marine Insurance Act 1906 is applied. Section 10(3)(a) and (b) extend the application to non-marine insurance contracts.

When moving to the second part of section 41 one important issue which needs to be clarified is whether a breach of the warranty of legality can be remedied. According to the new Act, a breach of warranty is irremediable where the assured has given a warranty as to past or present fact. As has been stated, this only relates to the first part of section 41 where the assured promises that the adventure is a lawful one before the attachment of the risk. Since the warranty of legality is a continuing or a promissory warranty, the breach can clearly be remedied after the adventure which is lawful in its inception has been carried out.

The second part of section 41 requires the adventure to be carried out in a lawful manner so far as the assured can control the matter, and the forthcoming Act clearly has more impact on this part than on the first part of section 41. This is the case firstly because of the three main defects discussed in the second chapter of this book: (1) the lack of clarity in the meaning of "so far as the assured can

---

23 For example, the new UN sanction on North Korea.

control the matter"; (2) the harsh consequences for the assured after a breach of the warranty; and (3) the numerous technical or non-technical rules which it is not possible for the assured to be aware of.

The application of section 10 will address these weaknesses: the insurer will not have the right to an automatic discharge of liability; the insurer's liability will be suspended only when the adventure is carried out in an unlawful manner; and as soon as the assured is aware of the illegality and corrects it properly without any possibility of causing potential loss, then the insurer will be liable again; and if the insurer intends the assured to comply with some specific technical rules or laws, the insurer shall express such requirement explicitly in the insurance policy so as to gain the attention of the assured, otherwise, there will be no such implied warranty on the assured.

However, there are still weaknesses in this section, the first one being that it requires strict compliance with the warranty, since there is still no requirement for a causal link for a breach of warranty to be sustained; any losses which occur during the breach of the warranty of legality are still not covered by the policy, whether the losses were caused by the illegality or not.

The first defect of section 10 of the 2015 Act results in the second deficiency of this section, that no matter how trivial the illegality is, under this Act the losses which may occur during the breach are still unrecoverable. These two defects have actually lessened the positive impact of this Act on the warranty of legality since in some circumstances a breach of the warranty can simply be because, for example, a loading limitation has been exceeded (such as in the *St John Shipping* case) or a payment to a company in a country under sanctions has been initiated (such as in *The Nancy* case), neither of which circumstances has any relation to the losses which the assured sought to recover. Even worse, in some situations, a breach of the warranty of legality is claimed by the insurer for illicit purposes, the aim being to discharge his liability as far as possible, regardless of whether it is possible for the assured to comply with the warranty. The insurer himself in some cases may have no idea which law he intends the assured to comply with or which law has been violated by the assured; the law may even be unknown to the insurer until he finds a violation that will sustain the breach of warranty, only as an instrument to discharge his liability.

The third problem is still caused by clause 10(2). A violation of a law or the illegal performance of the assured is sometimes committed unbeknownst to the policyholder, so unintentionally. It is clear that, based on the words of section 10 of the Act, if the illegality is unknown to the assured, it cannot be remedied, and therefore the warranty will remain breached until the assured becomes aware of the illegality and corrects it, during which time, the insurer's liability would be suspended. If such a breach existed throughout the voyage, then the assured would not be able to recover all the losses occurring during this voyage, which is what happened in the *St John Shipping* case. If this is the law that is applied in this special situation, then it is clearly not fair to the assured.

Besides the defects which the new Act may cause with regard to this implied warranty, there are also technical problems that need to be clarified when applying the Act. The first problem exists when deciding when it can be said that the breach has been remedied and whether the warranty is a general warranty or a specific warranty.

According to clause 10(5), the insurer will be back on risk as soon as the breach has been remedied. The criterion used to decide whether a breach has been remedied is based on seeing that "the risk to which the warranty relates later becomes essentially the same as that originally contemplated by the parties". As has been described before, the rule of remedy in a general warranty and in a time specified warranty is different, and the warranty of legality should be viewed as a general warranty as per the Law Commission's explanation, since it requires the adventure to be lawful and carried out lawfully during the whole period of voyage, not simply for a specified period of time. Therefore, the rule for the remedy of a breach of the warranty of legality follows the rules of a general warranty.

The pattern which has been adopted with general warranties is to ascertain whether the risk has been altered after a remedy of breach. There are two meanings of the phrase "risk has not been altered": the first one, as in the vessel deviation example given by the Law Commission, means that in the event of a random breach of warranty, if there is an equal risk of encountering a loss even without the former breach of warranty, then the breach has been remedied from the point when the assured ceases to breach. The second one is that, in the event of a planned breach of warranty, the warranty can only be remedied when the original risk has not been changed into some adventure which both parties have not contemplated in the contract, meaning that, even if, at the time of suffering loss, the warranty is not being breached, as long as it has been contained in the period of changing risk, then the warranty is still un-remedied.

Therefore, with regard to the first meaning, what has been implied by the Law Commission is that there shall be some link between the breach of warranty and the losses after the breach has been "remedied". However, since the Law Commission denied the causal link principle, which principle should be fulfilled in the event of a breach of the warranty of legality is still unclear. For example, if a vessel has been navigated illegally for a period then even though the illegality is corrected later, the loss caused by a collision sustained after the alteration cannot be covered since the breach has not actually been remedied. Another situation in which a breach of warranty cannot be said to have actually been remedied is when illegal acts have increased the risk of suffering losses even if after the illegal act has been corrected.

Furthermore, according to the second meaning of remedy, a breach of the warranty of legality cannot be said to be remedied in the event where, for example, a vessel has constantly been secretly used to smuggle goods into one country and loss happens because of a tornado during the period of mooring in that country when no smuggling is actually taking place; then it cannot be said that the breach of warranty has been remedied simply because the unlawful act has ceased. In a situation where an adventure has been carried out unlawfully, for example where the crew requirements of the navigation code have not been met, then when the vessel seeks to supply enough seamen when mooring in a port and suffers losses because of the weather, then even if there are enough seamen on board when these losses are suffered, as per the meaning of the Act, the breach is still un-remedied.

However, there are several points needing attention when applying this law. The first one is that, in the event of a random breach of the warranty of legality, if the insurer intends to deny that the warranty has been remedied, he should prove that the loss which the assured has suffered after the remedy of the breach is not a loss which could equally have happened had the warranty not been breached; so, there should be a connection between the breach and the loss. The second issue which needs attention is that the time when the warranty seems to have been "remedied" needs to be part of the planned breach of warranty or that the intention of parties by that time is still to carry on the breach of warranty. Otherwise, the breach would be remedied.

The next problem is about ascertaining the time of the breach of warranty and the time of the remedy. Especially in circumstances which involve the transfer of money, when can it be said that the breach has been remedied? There is no official regulation on this issue and when the new Act comes into force, this regulation will cause problems.

It can be seen that the reform that will be implemented by the impending Act will have a limited impact on the current law of the warranty of legality. Despite the automatic discharge of liability being abandoned, the lack of a requirement for a causation link is still reserved and the words "any losses" in clause 10(2) are clearly unfair to the assured. Furthermore, even though the breach of warranty is able to be remedied now, there is no clear restriction on when the insurer can argue that the breach has been remedied or that it is incapable of being remedied.

Thus, the new Act still favours the insurer on the warranty of legality issue.

Based on this analysis, it can be seen that, when dealing with a breach of the warranty of legality in marine insurance law, clause 10 is still not the best method to adopt. The essence of this reform is that it abolishes the automatic discharge of liability which prevents the former failing of a mere illegality rendering the whole adventure void. However, problems such as a causation link, foreign law illegality, moral hazard of the assured and circumstances which are outside the control of the assured have not been considered. These are the really controversial issues. The following section will give a brief comparison of the Act and common law rules and clarify the reasons why common law rules should be applied first, despite the Act coming into force in the near future.

The most significant difference between the Act and common law rules is that common law rules require a causal link between the loss and the assured's illegal act. The position of clause 10 and common law rules on the unlawful point is the same: if the adventure is unlawful from the beginning, then the warranty is breached and the insurer is not liable. The differences are concentrated in the area of illegal performance. As has been discussed before, the common law which governs this sector is a combination of different factors; the illegal act itself cannot render the adventure, either the whole of it or only part of it, void. Other factors need to be taken into account. The causal link, which has not been approved by the Law Commission, states that if there is no connection between the loss and the illegal act, then the loss will be covered; this criterion will be examined first. In addition, in commercial cases, if the assured does not need to rely on the illegality for a compensation plea, then the compensation will also be granted. Furthermore, even if there is a causation link between the loss and the illegality, if it can be proved that the assured had not planned to carry out the adventure unlawfully or does not intend to profit from his illegality then the adventure will be covered as well. In common law, the insurer is only not responsible for losses which have been caused by the illegality, not losses that may have occurred during the period of the breach; this is a big difference between clause 10 and common law rules.

It can be seen from the above that the obstacles which underlie the unfairness of section 41 and the reform of section 41 still exist. As has been stated before, the main obstacles preventing section 41 from being a fair law is the different character and function of the terms of warranty in common law and in marine insurance law: the automatic discharge of liability, no causal connection test and strict compliance. In this new draft Bill and the Law Commission Report, only the automatic termination of the risk has been abolished. This seems adequate in cases involving an express warranty, since this warranty is promised by the assured to the insurer under the stipulations of an express warranty which both parties have knowledge of and which therefore clearly requires strict compliance, making the rejection of the causal connection reasonable in this situation. However, the Law Commission failed to distinguish the rules which govern an express warranty from those which govern an implied warranty of legality. The rules cannot be the same because of the unique character of section 41, and at least the causal connection test should be applied when dealing with the breach of a warranty of legality.

There are basically two reasons given by the Law Commission for rejecting the causal connection test, as has been discussed above. The first one is that warranties which are about former facts or claims that may be relevant to current losses, such as a criminal record or a former claim history in motor insurance, are crucial to the insurer when deciding whether to accept the risk; the second one is that warranties which are about objective facts (such as information of the vessel or ship route) even though their breach may not cause loss, are still crucial to the insurer when assessing risk.

However, it is clear that both these kinds of warranties are about objective facts before the attachment of the risk; they are not warranties which relate to the time of the adventure. Therefore, the two reasons provided above cannot sustain the warranty of legality, since this is not a warranty which is only about former or current objective facts before the insurer decides whether to accept the risk or not. The only part of section 41 which does not need a causal connection test is when the assured pledges to the insurer that the adventure is a lawful one, before the issue of the policy.

Based on the above analysis, until the causal connection test is applied in the warranty of legality, a better approach to dealing with illegal issues is still to apply the common law rules.

8.5 The market's reaction to the new Act

When being drafted it was recognised that the new Act might not be required in sophisticated markets, with the marine insurance sector named as one such market.

Rather, it was anticipated that some insurers would contract out of (i.e. not apply) many of the new Act's provisions.

P&I is a sophisticated insurance market, with well-established practices that benefit Members (the insured) and the P&I Club (the insurer). Eight of the Clubs in the International Group ("the IG") are affected by the new Act because their Rules are subject to English law, including the MIA 1906. Accordingly, and in the interest of continuity across the wider International Group, the consensus amongst the eight IG Clubs is to contract out of certain aspects of the new Act. Nevertheless, those eight IG Clubs recognise that some provisions of the new Act should be adopted as they clarify certain aspects of the law which are presently uncertain.

Compliance with certain warranties, e.g. maintaining a vessel's Class, is a condition precedent to cover by a Club irrespective of the type of loss suffered. Current practice and law may give Clubs a wider right to reject claims than would be possible under the new Act's remedies for breach of warranty: at present a Members' breach of a warranty will discharge the Club's liability under the insurance from the date of the breach, unless and to the extent the relevant Club's Board determines otherwise.

When considering the new Act, importance was given to the mutual nature of the risk, the availability of the relevant Club's Board's or managers' discretion in appropriate cases and also uncertainty as to how the new Act's provisions on warranties and other terms may be applied. Accordingly, it was felt best to preserve the current position. The affected IG Clubs will, insofar as permitted, maintain existing practices by contracting out of the new Act's provisions on warranties.

Under sections 9 to 11 of the Act the effect of a breach of warranty will be less severe. Any warranty breach by an insured now merely suspends (rather than entirely discharges) the insurer's liability until the breach is remedied. The insurer will have no liability for any claim arising if the policy is suspended but once the breach has been remedied then the policy resumes in full force. The Act also prevents an insurer avoiding an insurance contract if a warranty ceases to be applicable to the circumstances of the contract due to a change of circumstances or if it is rendered unlawful (e.g. by sanctions) or is waived by the insurer.

The Act also abolishes "basis of the contract" clauses in non-consumer contracts. Such clauses currently have the effect of converting all pre-contractual representations in a proposal form into warranties sometimes using wording that is not necessarily clear to the insured. This then means that the insurer can be discharged from liability if the proposal form contains any statement that is inaccurate even where that misrepresentation is immaterial to the loss and in no way induces the insurer to enter the contract. These so called "basis of the contract" clauses or any other attempt to give pre-contractual representations the status of a warranty by way of a provision in the insurance contract will not be valid when the Act comes into force. It will not be possible to contract out of this prohibition.

Section 11(1) of the Act will also apply to conditions precedent and exclusion clauses provided they relate to a particular type of loss or a loss at a particular location or time. Other types of conditions precedent and exclusion clauses appear to be unaffected.

A further, potentially very significant, amendment to the existing law under the Act arises from the Law Commission's proposal that insurers should not be entitled to avoid a claim where the insured's breach did not relate to the loss. Section 11 of the Act provides that if an insured does not comply with a warranty or other term which relates to a particular type of loss, or the risk of loss at a particular location or time, the insurer may not rely on non-compliance with that contractual term by the insured if the insured is able to show that non-compliance with the term could not have increased the risk of the loss which actually occurred. This seems complicated but essentially introduces a type of causation requirement into insurance contracts to ensure that a breach of a term of an insurance contract must be related to the particular loss in question. A direct causal link between the breach of the term or warranty and the loss is, however, not required.

The joint submission of the LMA and IUA illustrates this with an example in which a household policy contains a clause warranting that all outside doors should be locked by five-bolt locks at night. Thieves break down the locked door, which is found to have only a three-bolt lock, and rob the house. In such circumstances the assured can argue that the thieves were so well equipped/armed that whatever precautions had been taken by way of locks they would still have got in: in other words that the risk of loss would not have been affected by failure to have a five-bolt rather than a three-bolt lock.

Section 11 of the Act does not apply to terms which "define the risk as a whole". The introduction of such a requirement is entirely new to English insurance law and could introduce considerable uncertainty over the application of warranties and other terms to a particular loss, which will need to be clarified and defined by the courts.

Furthermore, the introduction of a causation requirement could open the door to extensive expert evidence to answer the questions of whether compliance with a certain warranty or term would have a tendency to reduce risk, and whether non-compliance with that warranty or term could not have increased the risk of the loss which actually occurred.

8.6 Conclusion

It seems from the above that the method of solely relying on the new Act is clearly not a good solution to the warranty of legality issue. The reform of the rigid system is of little use to this particular implied warranty and consequently, the most reasonable approach is to adopt common law rules in marine insurance, as has been suggested with regard to the foreign law illegality issue and in other jurisdictions.

CHAPTER 9

A proposal for the reform of section 41

As the last chapter of this dissertation, this part will propose ideas for the reform of section 41 based on the analysis in the former eight chapters. Despite the new report from the Law Commission, it is hoped that the recommendations from this chapter will still be valuable.

9.1 The need for reform

Even though the Law Commission revealed that the implied warranties should be retained and not changed, the warranty of legality on the other hand should be abolished or reformed, as pointed out by Professor Howard Bennett: "In my opinion, the implied warranties should be retained. Notwithstanding the views of brokers, it is hard to see an argument in favour of illegality . . .".[1] Therefore, at least from the brokers' and the assured's points of view, the warranty of legality should be changed. In Chapter 14 of the most recent Law Commission Report, the Law Commission provided clear reasons why the warranty of insurance law should be reformed, all of which are applicable to section 41.

The reasons in favour of reform can be concluded as follows: firstly, section 41 in the Marine Insurance Act has become a rigid system and one which is unusable if the illegality issue under foreign law is involved; secondly, the consequences of a violation of the warranty are too harsh and unclear, and there should be a distinction made between unlawful adventure and unlawful performance to prevent this; and thirdly, and unreasonably, there is no requirement for a causal link between the illegality committed and the losses which the assured seeks to recover.

9.2 Reform proposals

The question is: how section 41 should be reformed and how the market should deal with the illegality issue in marine insurance? The first option, as listed in the Australian Law Commission Report is that the parties could make the legality requirement and the consequences of a breach of these express terms in the insurance contract. This method is simple but may cause further problems if the construction or the wording of these express terms is disputed, which would make the issue

---

[1] "Summary of responses to third consultation paper the Business Insured's Duty of Disclosure and the law of warranties", Law Commission Ch 2: The Law of Warranties at 4.7.

more complex. Also, as suggested by the Law Commission Report: "The principle of automatic discharge of liability is subject to any express terms of the contract. It therefore represents the default position. Where there is an express provision, the effect can be that it 'waters down' section 33 by restricting the circumstances in which a warranty will bite".[2] Therefore, it seems that the most straightforward way to avoid legal disputes is for the parties to specify the boundaries of what may amount to illegal performance and breach of the warranty at the policy-drafting stage, as well as, naturally, specifying the consequences of such a breach.

The second recommendation is that the warranty of legality should be abolished and that it should not be rendered as a warranty in marine insurance law. As can be seen from the analysis in Chapter 2, the warranty character of section 41 is the main reason which causes the huge problem of the illegality issue in marine insurance.

The three reasons for this proposal are complex and are that, firstly, under current circumstances in English law the implied warranty should be abolished rather than reformed into an express warranty, since, as the law of warranty in marine insurance law is under reform itself, it does not seem beneficial to incorporate the legality issue into it. Even if the legality requirement becomes an express warranty, the consequences for the assured could still be severe, since there is still no causal link requirement under English law and the strict compliance principle has already been demonstrated to be a disaster with regard to the illegality issue.

Secondly, the Australia Law Commission proposed that the implied warranty of legality should either be abolished and replaced with the illegality defence under common law or that the implied warranty should be converted into an express warranty or express terms in the policy. The English Law Commission currently has no plans to reform this piece of law in Insurance Act 2015 or in the near future, as has been explained before, but the issue has constantly been raised in academic area,[3] and in the light of the recent judgement of *The Nancy*, it may attract more attention from the Law Commission.

The third reason is that the abolishment of section 41 will not result in the illegality issues in marine insurance law being unlegislated since common law rules could be applied in its stead.

The key fact resulting in the current problem is that, in marine insurance law, section 41 uses a statutory instrument to regulate a common law issue. This statute clearly forbids all unlawful performance and adventures, but does not stipulate what factors should be taken into account.

It is clear that, in English common law, when dealing with statutory illegality, the court will consider the words and intentions of the statute; in Chapter 2, the boundaries of section 41 have been examined and the exceptions which lie in the law have been cleared up. Therefore, it is clear that, even when dealing with statutory illegality issues in marine insurance law, section 41 is not the only authority which the courts should follow; this section should still be under the restriction on common law.

---

2 "Insurance Contract Law: Business Disclosure; Warranties; Insurers' Remedies For Fraudulent Claims; And Late Payment" Law Com No 353, p 160 at 13.19.
3 As can be seen in articles which have been raised in previous chapters.

It is a fact that, prior to the 1906 Act, when the court dealt with marine insurance illegalities, some factors which were considered in common law were considered in marine insurance as well.[4] However, there is a big difference between them. In marine insurance scenarios, only in very exceptional circumstances would the court consider the failure of the illegality defence, for example, the impossibility of supplying seamen; and the judgments commonly contradicted with each other.

There was no general rule in marine insurance law the same as rules in contract law or tort law, which required the court to consider certain factors when similar circumstances arose again. Therefore, the author of the 1906 Act only regulated all exceptional circumstances as outside the control of the assured, but since the circumstances which are out of the control of the assured during an adventure are numerous, there are actually no clear boundaries.

Furthermore, technology is far more advanced today than it was in the eighteenth and nineteenth centuries, and therefore communication between the assured and the carrier has become more effective and the assured's knowledge and control of the goods or the adventure has grown; in addition, insurance law which relates to the risk of war has been more fully developed. Because of these developments, scenarios in which the assured is not in control of the adventure rarely happen. Thus, the *so far as the assured can control the matter* defence rarely sustains either. From this perspective, marine insurance still needs the help of the common law when dealing with illegality issues.

The question is whether common law rules can be applied in marine insurance cases? It seems that there is no obstacle to do this. There is a big difference between marine insurance law and other kinds of insurance law, and not every piece of law or every rule that is functional in general insurance law can be applied in marine insurance law; the function of the warranty term, for instance, is different in insurance law and marine insurance law. The main reason behind this is that marine insurance policies should be based on marine adventures which mean exposure to maritime perils and this resulted in great uncertainty and danger for the insurer, especially in early times. This explains why marine insurance law always seems to be severe as far as the assured is concerned, and the reason why ordinary principles in contract law and insurance law cannot be applied in marine insurance cases; the application of ordinary principles would probably result in the insurer being vulnerable.

However, this is not the case when dealing with issues of illegality. Firstly, in circumstances when parties enter into an insurance policy with illegal intentions, then no matter whether it is a marine insurance policy or not, the guilty party will perform the contract illegally and therefore even applying common law principles in marine insurance cases would not result in unfairness to the assured. Secondly, illegality can exist in every aspect of a marine adventure, such as in the transaction of freight, as in *The Nancy* case; therefore, if only marine insurance law is applied, it is clearly unjust to the assured. Thirdly, the application of section 41 is too narrow; this section only recognises illegality under English law.

---

4 As according to the research in Chapter 2.

The application of common law principles has been demonstrated in the most recent case, *Sea Glory Maritime Co v Al Sagr National Insurance Co*. In this case, it can be seen not only how common law rules are applicable in marine insurance cases, but also how section 41 can be used abusively as an instrument to defend the insurer's profit. In this case, the ship *The Nancy* became constructive total loss on the Sea of Japan because of a fire on board and the assured claimed damages against the insurer. However, in order to discharge his liability the insurer claimed five defences, one of which was illegality. The insurer claimed that a payment from the bank to the assured with regard to a voyage from China to Iran was illegal under US law since the US had placed sanctions on the Iranian Government. The insurer sought to rely on section 41 to discharge his liability. However, in this case, the court decided that section 41 could not be applied since it only applies in English law. The court went on to consider common law principles in English law, including the reliance principle in the *Bowmakers* case and the no-profit principle decided in the *Beresford* case. In this case, the assured did not rely on the illegality of his former voyage to claim his indemnity in his current policy, nor had he profited from his illegality. Furthermore, when the court dealt with the illegality in connection to the former transaction, it was found that the assured had no intention to violate US law and had not known that the transaction was illegal under US law. The illegality defence was therefore not sustained.

At the end of the judgment, the court made it clear that, if at the time of entering into the policy, the claimants had intended to perform the adventure in a manner which involved a breach of US law, and then the defence may have been sustained.

It is clear from the judgment of this case that section 41 is unworkable when dealing with illegality issues, since the factors which need to be considered are unclear and only applicable in English law. However, in contrast, common law has clear rules regarding which factors should be considered and which factors are in front of the court for consideration. It seems that there is no need to apply section 41 any more. Even though this section in the 1906 Act may have had the function of reminding the contractual parties that illegality was forbidden in marine insurance, the chaos and uncertainty it causes is far greater than this function now.

The illegality issue can exist in two types of marine case. It can exist in scenarios where there is a contractual relationship between the two parties, for example, when there is a dispute over the contract or over the actual construction of the contract. In addition, the illegality issue may exist in scenarios when there is no contractual relationship between the two parties, for example, in tort cases on the sea, which may involve collision claims, salvage or towage claims. In these situations, the key question is whether, if any of the several codes or statutes regulating the collision or towage dispute have been broken, then to what extent can the illegality defence be applied, such as the collision convention and the salvage convention, and there are also so many technical rules which regulate the operation of the vessel and loading and unloading of goods and so on. Therefore, should the violation of technical rules be rendered as unlawful conduct under the concept of the Marine Insurance Act 1906, namely whether section 41 aims to cover this kind of violation. Another issue is whether the assured should be punished by Convention or by the Act. One particular area which may deserve some attention is the circumstances of tort actions such as collisions at sea, which are subject to the regulations of common law and statute. If the collision or damage to the vessel is caused by negligence, then tort law will apply, and there is no room for section 41 even if the negligence results in a violation of statute. If the collision is caused intentionally, then clearly it is subject to criminal law, and clearly the insurer is not liable for the loss. However, this cannot be seen as an application of section 41 since it is very obvious.

It seems logical that the implied warranty of legality under English law should be abolished, and that when an illegality issue arises under marine insurance law, common law principles can be applied. There may be obstacles, however, such as an underwriter being afraid of the increase of the risk on his part if there is no warranty of legality. However, it is commonly agreed that only a slight violation or alteration of the adventure or the warranty cannot be seen as creating an increased risk, and there is no implied requirement that during the period of the cover the assured would not alter the adventure so as to increase underwriters' risk as happened in the case *Hussain v Brown*. Therefore, in marine insurance law, unless the assured commits a criminal act, an illegality under technical rules is not serious enough to change the essence of the adventure, and section 41 cannot therefore be invoked.

After the abolishment of section 41, when dealing with illegality issues, the common law method should be applied, although the illegality defence in common law, as was discussed in Chapters 3 and 4, is also complex and needs to be reformed. However, by applying it, the main concerns in marine insurance law, such as the causation link and the overly severe consequences, can be addressed. The factors adopted by common law could make the current marine insurance law more flexible. Creating a consistent approach based on both common law and marine insurance law could make this area of law less complex as well. The application of common law rules in marine insurance law can be concluded as follows.

Firstly, in the first part of section 41, it is still necessary for the adventure to be a lawful one. In this section, both the intention and the knowledge of the insurer and the assured should be considered and if the assured has the knowledge that the adventure is not lawful and still insures it, then the insurance shall be void. If the assured has no knowledge that the adventure is unlawful and the insurer does have this knowledge, then the insurer should refuse to grant the insurance. In this event, if the insurer does not deny it in the beginning and then seeks not to cover it and to retain the premium later, then the insurer will lose the illegality defence under common law, and should compensate the assured's loss.[5] Moreover, if both the assured and the insurer have no knowledge that the adventure they intend to insure is unlawful, then if it is an adventure which is forbidden by statute the insurance policy is void *ab initio* as well, which is completely different to the same situation in the performance of contract. In addition, if the assured intends the subject matter insured to be used in an unlawful way or to achieve an unlawful objective, then this insurance is also void.

---

5 *Strongman (1945) Ltd v Sincock* [1955] 2 Q.B. 525.

The second part of section 41 is more complex and is in great need of reform. As can be seen from the discussion above, common law does not recognise the unenforceability of a contract which is lawful and has later been performed unlawfully. Therefore, if common law rules were to be applied in marine insurance law, it would not be possible to make the marine insurance contract unenforceable due to illegal performance. Furthermore, as has been illustrated in the *Sea Glory* case, the court still needs to consider other factors as well, such as whether the assured relied on his illegality to claim for loss and, most importantly, whether the loss was caused by the illegal act. The difficulty of applying common law rules may occur in a situation when the illegal act is committed by an agent of the assured, such as the crew, raising the question of what defence the assured should have. In this scenario, the *so far as the assured can control the matter* defence should still be the relevant law, and the assured should not be liable for losses caused by his agent's illegality, so long as the assured can prove that he has no knowledge of it. This is especially true in tort cases at sea. However, when dealing with sea tort cases, there is still a question as to what extent the illegality rules can be applied, and how the illegality rules may influence the judgement of such cases, since it is clear that there are numerous regulations in this area and the consequence of a breach vary from country to country. When encountering such scenarios, the English courts can make reference to Australian law. When there is an express warranty in the marine insurance policy which requires the assured to carry out the policy according to local regulations and lawfully, then it seems that the implied warranty will not be effective, since firstly, the express warranty is the agreement between the insurer and the assured, and the assured's responsibility shall be confined to this accordingly, and secondly, if the adventure is carried out in foreign territory water, then the implied warranty will not be triggered, since it is only recognised in English law. In this situation, if there is no implication or explicit statement in the express warranty that there is a requirement to comply with local regulations, then it should be construed that the underwriter does not want this protection.[6] For example, in *Elafonissos Fishing and Shipping Company v Aigaion Insurance Company SA*, the express warranty which required that the vessel should be laid up in the port of Mahajan GA did not mean that the regulations of this port automatically applied in the policy.[7] Therefore, in this situation, it is clear that section 41 will not be applied.

In conclusion, set out below are the methods which could be used to resolve the implied warranty issue in marine insurance law. Firstly, section 41 should be abolished and common law rules should be applied in marine insurance cases, as was proposed by the Australian Law Reform Commission and as was applied in the *Sea Glory* case. The difficulties with this are whether common law rules are too complex for the marine insurance scenario, and might make the law more unstable. Secondly, the main issue with marine insurance law, an issue which attracts

---

[6] *Elafonissos Fishing and Shipping Company v Aigaion Insurance Company SA* [2012] EWHC 1512 (Comm).
[7] Ibid.

condemnation and criticism, is that, in marine insurance law, for a violation of the implied warranty to be sustained, there is no requirement for the connection between the illegal conduct and the losses to be shown, and this is because section 33 of the Marine Insurance Act requires complete compliance. If the Law Commission could reform this aspect of the law in the marine insurance warranty then it would not be necessary to abolish section 41 at this point. Thirdly, if it is not possible to implement both the former two solutions, then according to the authorities before 1906, the court can narrowly construe the scope of the word "unlawful" and apply the rules in technical conventions and treaties rather than the Marine Insurance Act. Therefore, for instance, a violation of the Collision Convention 1989 would not be rendered unlawful under the Marine Insurance Act, and the punishment of the assured who breached this convention should be based on the convention itself, rather than on the 1906 Act; by construing the unlawful act in a narrow way, the rigidity of section 41 will not be harmful to the interests of the assured.

9.3 Conclusion

Therefore, from the analysis above, the major proposal of this chapter is to reject the implied warranty in marine insurance and apply the common law rules when dealing with marine insurance cases.

BIBLIOGRAPHY

Articles

Dr Benjamin Andoh, "Illegality as a Defence to Negligence in English Law"
R.A. Buckley, "Implied Statutory Prohibition of Contracts" (2011) *Modern Law Review* vol 38
Malcolm Clarke, "Aggravation of risk during the insurance period" (2003) *LMCLQ* 112
Charles Debattista, "*Ex Turpi Causa* Returns to the English Law of Torts: Taking Advantage of a Wrong Way Out" (1984) 13 *Anglo-Am. L. Rev* 15
M.P. Furmston, "Illegality – the Limit of a Statute" (1961) *Modern Law Review* vol 24, no 3
M.P. Furmston, "The Analysis of Illegal Contracts" (1966) *University of Toronto Law Journal*, vol 16, no 2, pp 267–309
Walter Gellhorn, "Contracts and Public Policy" (1935) *Columbia Law Review*, vol 35, no 5, pp 679–696
F.A. Mann LL.D, "Illegality and the Conflict of Laws" (1958) *Modern Law Review*, vol 21, Issue 2, pp 130–137
Mary Coate McNeely, "Illegality as a factor in liability insurance" (1941) *Columbia Law Review* 26
John Shand, "Unblinkering the Unruly Horse: Public Policy in the Law of Contract" (1972) *Cambridge Law Journal*, vol 30, no 1(A), pp 144–167
G Williams, "Contributory Negligence and Vicarious Liability" (1954) 17 MLR 365
Percy H. Winfield, "Public Policy in the English Common law" (1928) *Harvard Law Review*, vol 42, no 1, pp 76–102
"Illegal Transaction: The Effect of Illegality on Contracts and Trusts", Law Commission Consultation Report No 154
"The Illegality Defence in Tort", Law Commission Consultation Paper No 160
"The Illegality Defence", Law Commission Consultation Report No 189
"Insurance Contract Law: The Business Insurer's Duty of Disclosure and the Law of Warranties", Law Commission Consultation Paper 204
"Summary of Responses to Third Consultation Paper the Business Insured's Duty of Disclosure and the Law of Warranties 2", The Law of Warranties
"Insurance Contract Law: Business Disclosure; Warranties; Insurers' Remedies for Fraudulent Claims; and Late Payment", Law Commission No 353
Review of the Marine Insurance Act 1909

Books

Arnould's Law of Marine Insurance and Average (18th edn)
Colinvaux's Law of Insurance (9th edn, 2010)
Clerk and Lindsell on Torts (19th edn, 2006)
Chitty on Contracts (31st edn), vol 1
Dicey's Conflict of Laws (4th edn)
Malcolm A. Clarke, *Law of Insurance Contracts* (4th edn)
MacGillivray on Insurance Law (11th edn)
R.A. Buckley, *Illegality and Public Policy* (2002)
N Enonchong, *Illegal Transactions* (1998)
Baris Soyer, *Warranties in Marine Insurance* (2nd edn)
Thomas, *The Modern Law of Marine Insurance*, vol 2
Treitel on the Law of Contract (13th edn)

INDEX

agent: illegality of performance, and 40–1
Australia 153–8; English common law factors 155; Insurance Contract 1984, section 54(2) 157–8; knowledge of assured 155–6; moral culpability 156; options for reform 156–7; section 47, Australian Marine Insurance Act 1909 153; violation of law 154–5; warranty of legality issue 55

breach of warranty: effect 50–1; Insurance Act 2015 164–6; law before 12 August 2016 24–5

Canada 160; warranty of legality issue 160
causation principle 65–8
common law illegality 53, 121–6; construction of policy 121–5; deliberate acts 121–3; insurance policies rendered illegal by public policy 125–6; wilful misconduct 121–3
common law illegality defence: warranty of legality distinguished 131–41
common law rules 129; necessary reform 129; supplementary instrument 129
Commonwealth jurisdictions 4
condition: warranty compared 47–8
consistency principle 68–9
continuing warranty 19
contract illegality: tort illegality distinguished 126–8
contract terms: classes 47
contracts rendered illegal by common law 96–113; common law 99; conduct of parties 98; corrective factors 105; consistency test 109; deterring unlawful or immoral conduct 110–11; development 96–7; different knowledge of parties 100; exceptions 107–9; general principles 97–107; innocent party, and 100; intention of parties 114;
intention to commit legal wrong 99–100; knowledge of illegal intention 103; knowledge of illegality 105; maintaining integrity of courts 111–12; minor illegality 104; origin 96–7; participation 106; participation in illegal purpose 100; profit from illegality 109–10; proportionate test 112–13; protecting purpose of law 107–9; public policy, and 96–113; punishments 112; rationale behind public policy 107–13; reliance principle 106–7; remoteness 101–2; seriousness of illegality 105–6; statutory illegality, and 98–9; statutory illegality distinguished 113–15
contracts rendered illegal by statute 91–6; aiding and abetting 95; consequences of violation 92; directory requirement 97; exceptions 93–4; innocent party 94; knowledge of illegality 95; nature of contract, and 93; obligatory requirement 97; public interest, and 93; purpose of legislation 92–3; waiver 94–5
contract law: illegality defence 91–128
contract law illegality: application in insurance 115–26
crew: sufficient or competent 36

dangerous of adventure 139–40
de minimis rule 11–12
divisibility of warranty 49–50

ex turpi causa 55–6: importance in insurance 75–6
exception: warranty, and 15
express warranty 19

foreign law illegality 4, 143–51; criticism of current marine insurance law 149–50; English legal position 143–7; marine insurance law, and 148–50; possible methods for dealing with 150–1;

INDEX

requirements for effectiveness 146–7; violation of foreign law 145–6
formation of illegal adventure 34–6

illegal adventure; formation 34–6; forms 34–5; loading operation 35–6; performance, and 37; sail without licence or convoy 35; sufficient or competent crew 36
illegal adventure by statute 33
illegal adventures because of violation of public policy and common law 34
illegal adventures by King's or Council's order 33
illegal performance of marine insurance contracts 29–51
illegality defence 2; contract law 4; investigation 3; tort law 3
illegality defence in contract law 91–128; application in insurance contracts 91–128; contracts rendered illegal by common law 96–113; contracts rendered illegal by statute 91–6
illegality defence in tort law 55–90; application of rationales in insurance 81–5; application to insurance law 74–89; benefit principle in insurance 79–81; causation principle 65–8; consistency principle 68–9; *ex turpi causa* 55–6; general principles under insurance law 77–89; illegal act conducted by claimant subjectively 57; illegality of act committed by claimant because of defendant's former tort 59–60; importance of *ex turpi causa* 75–6; intention of statute principle 74; kinds of illegality 56–60; narrow and wider rule in insurance law 77–9; "no duty of care" principle 62–4; origin 55–6; principle based on 60–74; proper way of dealing in insurance law 85–7; proportionality principle 72–4; public conscience test 60–2; public policy, and 56, 60–2; reliance principle 64–5; seriousness of illegal conduct 69–72; specifity of issue in motor insurance 87–9
illegality of performance 36–42; agent, and 40–1; control, and 37–8; formation 38–40; knowledge of assured 42; origin 36–42; scope 36–42; so far as the assured can control the matter 40–2; species 38–40; violation of common law and public policy 40; violation of King's or Council's order and licence 38–9; violation of statute 38; violation of treaties between nations 39

implied warranty 19, 31; other than warranty of legality 20–4
Insurance Act 2015 161–75; application on warranty of legality 168–73; "basis of contract" clauses 174; breach of warranty 164–6; causal link and section 11 166–8; change of circumstances, and 169; change of law, and 169; effect of remedy of breach 171; market's reaction on 173–175; P&I Club, and 174; random breach of warranty of legality 172; "risk has not been altered" 171; strict compliance with warranty 170; terms not relevant to actual loss, and 167; terms which define the risk as a whole, and 175; warranties 164–6; warranty of legality, and 161–75
intention of statute principle 74

Law Commission: reform recommendations 161–4; rejection of casual connection test 173
lawful: meaning 32–4
loading operation 35–6

marine insurance law of warranty 9–27 *see also* warranties; development 10–16; origin 10–16
motor insurance: specificity of illegality issue 87–9

New Zealand 158–9; warranty of legality issue 158–9

present warranty 19
proportionality principle 72–4
proportionate test 112–13

reform of section 41 4–5
reliance principle 64–5, 106–7
return on premium 50

sail without licence or convoy 35
seaworthiness 21–4
section 41, Marine Insurance Act 1906 42–51, 131–4; abolition of warranty of legality, proposal for 178–81; breach of warranty and loss 46–7; character and function of law, and 46; common law principles, and 179–80; exception, and 43–4; express terms, proposal for 177; insufficiencies 42–51; intention of law, and 45; intention of parties, and 44–5; nature of 131–4; post-contractual requirement 133–4; pre-contractual requirement 133–4; reform, need for 177; reform,

proposal for 177–83; specificity 138–9; technology advances, and 179; violation, statutory illegality and 132–3; warranty of legality as implied warranty 47–51
statutory illegality rules: insurance, in 116–21; intention of assured 120; unauthorised insurer 116–20
strict compliance principle 11–12, 49

tort illegality: contract illegality distinguished 126–8
tort law: illegality defence 55–90

unauthorised insurer 116–20

violation of common law and public policy 40
violation of King's or Council's order and licence 38–9
violation of treaties between nations 39

waiver of warranty 25–7
warranty of legality: chaos of issue 1–2; common law illegality defence distinguished 131–41; development 1; importance of 48; intention of parties, and 49; other warranties distinguished 49–51; section 41, Marine Insurance Act 1906, and 42–51; waiver 49
warranties: breach 13; causation 12; classifications 19–20; condition compared 47–8; construction 16–18; context 18; *de minimis* rule 11–12; definition 13–14; development 10–16; early development 10–11; exception, and 15; fundamental principles 11; Insurance Act 2015 164–6; intention of policy in commercial context 20; origin 10–16; sole description of risk 14; strict compliance principle 11–12; words of policy and 17
warranties in contract law 9–10
warranty of legality 21; current status 1–2; importance of 29–30; "lawful" 32–4; Marine Insurance Act 1906 29; origins 3, 29, 30–2
warranty of neutrality 21
warranty of seaworthiness 21–4